To Roger

With Best Wishes

4 - 4 - 06

Barley & Balloons

David Liddiard
remembers...

As told to Jennifer d'Alton

First published 1998
by Traeth Publications

ISBN 1 898368 01 5

Cover design by Richard d'Alton

British Library Cataloguing in Publication Data.
A catalogue record of this book is available in The British Library.

TRAETH PUBLICATIONS,
Pen Ffordd. Newport. Pembrokeshire. SA42 0QT.
Wales. United Kingdom
Printed by The Pembrokeshire Press, Fishguard

I dedicate this book to Jo
who has looked after our family, which has
enabled me to do all the things I've done.

This is also for
my Grandchildren and future generations.

It will be obvious to anyone who knows me and
reads this book that my grasshopper approach to life
and the telling of my stories needed a
dedicated and patient person.

I found this in Jennifer d'Alton
who translated my ramblings into a readable story.
To her husband, Richard, my grateful thanks,
also to Jennifer's Mother, Anne Lewis-Smith,
who published it.

David Liddiard

Growing Up.

The two horses were closer now, thundering towards them, getting larger and larger. He could see the riders, crouched over their straining steeds' necks, kicking and urging them forward. The impending disaster was totally out of their control!

They were so close that David could see the whites of their eyes, hear them snorting, hooves pounding, almost imagine their rasping hot breath on his neck. He wanted to block his ears from the noise, to shout, shut his eyes and run!

Both boys sat wide eyed and totally silent in the dark, every muscle tense, their hearts thumping.
David shut his mouth and gave a brief glance towards his friend whose face, in the flickering light, looked as taut as he felt.

David stared in front hunching his shoulders, twisting his cap under his knees, and digging his fingernails into it's fabric.

Suddenly, both horses swerved as one, swinging their riders towards their final goal. The ground shook, David tried to muffle a gasp as he watched the riders urge their animals' powerful muscles to take them the last few yards leaving a wake of dust and flying stones. The vast wooden gates crashed shut behind them. They were safe, the heroes had delivered the package to the fort.

Then the camera turned to the pursuing Indians, about ten of them, stripped to the waist, with bows and sheaves of arrows strapped to their backs. As they saw their quarry disappear behind the walls of the fort, they pulled their ponies up, and after circling and whooping, turned and galloped off back toward the hills.

David let out a long breath, and subsided back into his seat.

Behind him, a woman muttered something and lit a cigarette, the smoke drifted over David and filled his nostrils. His shoulders slumped down, he relaxed his grip on his cap, trying to concoct a flippant phrase which would show his companion that he had been in control, and knew what would happen, and that it hadn't worried him in the least.

But just as he turned to speak, his friend gasped *'Look, David, look, that's you!'* and pointed to the screen. There, in letters bigger than a cartwheel, right across the screen, were the words; **'Would David Liddiard report to the Manager's Office immediately.'**
He could hear a group of boys reading it out loud from the front of the cinema.
Someone shouted *'Go on Liddiard.'*

David clenched his fist around his cap, and felt his cheeks flush with embarrassment. He got up, keeping his body bent so as not to draw attention to himself, and tried to clamber over the legs and coats to the aisle.
'What yer done David?' someone shouted.

He stumbled up the steps of the aisle, tripping a couple of times in the gloom knowing that everyone was staring at him.
He fell through the red curtains and swing doors into the foyer, the comparative brightness of the dimmed lights making him blink, he stood for a second getting his bearings.
There was an open door marked Office, he knocked timidly.
'Are you David Liddiard?' the thin man said, staring at David.
'Yes Sir.'
'Well your headmaster says you're to return to school immediately.'
The man looked away, and sniffed. *'Go on then.'*

2

David turned on his heel and ran out of the cinema.

Back at Merton House School, he went straight to the Headmaster's study.

'Liddiard, your Father says you are to return home immediately. The cowman has been taken sick.

Your bag is packed, and there is a taxi outside to take you to the bus station.'

Still reeling from the events of the last thirty minutes, he was bundled into a taxi, which took him to the bus station. He put his bags onto the bus and went home to his Father.

That event, when he was fourteen, heralded the beginning of his farming life, and the end of his chequered schooling.

'I got the bus to Newbury, and then a bus home, it was about half past eight, quarter to nine by the time I got home. It was a double decker from Reading, they ran every fifteen minutes then. The Reliance coaches to Brightwalton were pretty regular then as well, I was just able to catch the last one that night.

I got off the bus, and lugging my bags, walked the half mile across the fields to home.

My Father looked up when I came in and said *'I'm glad you're home, you've got to do the milking in the morning.'*

I never questioned it, you never questioned your parents at that age.

'At five the next morning, I started in the dairy milking.

There was an Under Cowman there who was a general farmworker as well.

My job was to milk the cows, watch the herd, make sure everything was washed and cleaned down, you had to spend the day washing up the milking equipment. Nowadays it is all

3

circulatory.

Then, you had set days for set things. One day you would strip down two units, I think we had four units, maybe three, I forget. You had to light the boiler in the morning with wood and coal to get the steam up to sterilise everything. There was no electricity you see. It was all done with oil lamps and Tilley lamps. We didn't really have electricity until 1946, when we moved to Shefford .

So for electricity, we had a little Lister engine, which had a car dynamo coupled up to it to run some twelve watt bulbs, they were more like a group of tired glow worms really, there was no sealed beam or anything.

You couldn't see a lot in the mornings, the best light you got was from a Tilley lamp which worked like a Primus stove, you pumped it up and it vaporised the paraffin on a mantle.

We had storm lanterns as well, the old storm lanterns, so at least we could see the end of the shed.

So I got on with it.

'I didn't think about it, it was wartime, you couldn't get labour, and that was that!   I didn't really have much time between leaving school and starting work, definitely not a year out like nowadays, not even a day out. My Father was a hard Master, but he did let me have the morning off for my wedding day!.'

The day after he had arrived post haste from the cinema in Reading, David took on all the milking, and his Father paid him ten shillings a week. He had been helping on the farm since he was small, but now he was being paid .

After six months his Father, Bill Liddiard, called him in.
'You've done well boy, I'm giving you a rise boy. A pound a week and you can buy your own clothes. '

4

'That was the deal. Irish deal really, but at that age clothes didn't matter,' said David.

Bill Liddiard, David's father, was hard but fair, he was also quite volatile, and sometimes unexpectedly generous. He'd worked hard for everything he owned, and he expected his sons to work too.
When his cowman became ill, to Bill it was the logical step to bring in a member of the family who was capable of taking over the job until the chap was better again. None better than his eldest son even though he was only fourteen.

'As it was war time, many of the men working on the farm had enlisted, and there was a scarcity of skilled reliable labour. Of course there were the land girls, but they had only been trained to drive tractors for a couple of hours before they arrived, and taught how to dig.'

David had two older sisters, and his two half brothers were much too young to help on the farm then. David's schooling had frequently been interrupted to help with harvesting or other seasonal jobs, as most Farmers' sons had to during the war.

'In those days, everything was boiled up for the pigs, if you had a dead calf, you used to chuck it in and boil it up. '
That month, at Brightwalton, they found a dead calf, and the old Irish cowman had the job of skinning it and chucking it in the swill. But he kept the liver for his own consumption.
Now, whether he kept it too long, or whether he didn't cook it for long enough, it was never known. But he ate it, and he became very ill, dying two or three days after David had returned!

It was a bit of a culture shock going straight from school to work like that.

Fifty five years later, David sat at his kitchen table with a large mug of coffee, and began remembering his farming life which started properly over half a century ago.

'Starting at five in the morning, finishing at five, six or even later in the evening. But it was just one of those things, and you did it without questioning.

I can't remember milking my first cow, though I was probably about seven or eight. We did it by hand, not machine. My sisters probably taught me, as they milked as well. It was one of those things you saw, and you just had to get on with it.

'When we were at the farm at Brightwalton during the war, I used to help kill pigs, although I was only young.

We only used to kill a calf occasionally, but only if it was a young calf with a deformed leg or something. We'd kill them, butcher them, hang them , and then eat them.

I knew how to kill and dress a calf by the time I was fourteen years old. I don't suppose many people can do that nowadays.

We would get a licence to kill one or two pigs a year. You had to have a licence, because meat rationing was on, but you could share a licence between two farmers.

There were a few dodges though. You would kill a pig on one farm, and you were supposed to give half to the other farm, but of course two pigs got killed. They got wise to this though, and we had policemen coming up to check on what we'd done.

'I remember emptying bran out of sacks, and putting sides of bacon and hams in there and stitching them back up again. However, I think the policemen usually went away with a fairly large lump of bacon for themselves! It all helped.

'You had to give up some of your meat coupons to be able to kill a pig.

All the little cottages had a pig sty at the bottom of the garden. Every one used to grow their own vegetables, there were some lovely back gardens, but with a rich black loamy soil, nothing like the earth in the fields either side of the garden.

The reason for this was because we used to bury the 'night-soil', or 'bury the bucket' as there was no such thing as flushing toilets. The result was a really rich soil for growing.

'There was no coal for burning in those days, and there were no hedgecutters either. So hedges used to grow thick and tall.

Farm labourers used to be allowed to have a 'shoulder stick'. This is when a large stick or branch had fallen out of a hedge, and if it was small enough to carry home, they were then allowed to take it. That was their shoulder stick. They would take it home at lunch time or take it home in the evening to burn, that's how they kept their fires going, with shouldersticks.

It didn't happen every day, but if we were ploughing, and someone saw a good branch he'd say 'Ooh, there's a good shoulderstick, I'll take 'im 'ome tonight.'

'Then, all the wood ash that came out of the grates, used to be kept in a tub or bucket in the privy down the garden. When you'd done what you had to do in the privy, you used to chuck a bit of wood ash on it, to keep the smell down. Then it was all dug into the garden which is why they had such beautiful vegetables.

'I remember one tale I heard from our neighbour, old Francis Smallbone down at Streatley. He was the first farmer in the area to get a tractor

and his driver was a carter, I mean, no one was trained as tractor drivers then, you learnt as you went along.

Now we all wore flat hats in those days, caps. Very handy for pulling up a piece of barbed wire, as you didn't have gloves supplied. So if you had a piece of wire, or something hot to pick up, you used your hat.

So when this carter- turned- tractor- driver was greasing the tractor, the obvious thing was to wipe his hands on his hat!

His wife got on at him because his hat was always covered in grease. She tried to wash it, but it was no good.

'I'll bring you home something that'll help you clean it missus.' He said and so he brought her home a small bottle of petrol.

'You be careful missus. That's powerful stuff. You use it outside and don't take it in the house, it's dangerous.'

So she washed his hat in it, and it came up nice and clean. When he came home at lunchtime, the cap was hanging on the line. After his lunch, he went down the garden to the privy.

Of course the smell in there was pretty horrendous, so he always lit his old pipe up to go down there. His pipe went out, so he lit it again, and chucked the match in the privy, and then found out where she'd put the petrol!

I think he said *'It must have been something I ate.'*!

He was rather scorched.

'In those days, nothing, such as potato peelings, cabbage stalks, or leftovers, was ever thrown away. As there were no dustbin lorries coming round, all the food rubbish and leftovers used to be boiled up, they would chuck a bit of meal with it and it was fed to the pigs. They did really well on that.

Of course in those days, they never killed a pig until it was about eighteen or twenty score. Nowadays, all the pigs are killed at about five to six score.   A score is about twenty pounds in weight, about nine kilos.

'Today, people like small lean pigs with no fat on them, about four or five score. But back then, we used to kill an old large white, or a saddleback, at about twenty score, huge!

8

'You had to walk the pigs to where you were going to kill them because you couldn't carry them.

After you'd killed and bled them, you used to roll them on their backs, on some straw, with their legs in the air. Put four bricks underneath to stop them rolling over, then set fire to straw underneath and around them, to burn all the hair off.

You had to brown the skin up. If you did it too much you would split the skin. If you didn't do it enough, you wouldn't get all the hairs off.

Nowadays, they go through a big oven and a flame is blasted at them and it gets the hairs off just like that. I think perhaps they don't even do that now, they go in a very hot tub, are scalded and then go through a machine with lots of paddles which beats the hair off so that the meat is kept white.

When we did it, the outside of the meat was always brown from being burned.

'Anyway, once you'd done that, you took out the backbone, took off the head and various other bits, like the trotters, and all that was boiled and made into brawn.

Then the spleen, the liver, and the heart - we used to have stuffed heart - were used for faggots.

Then there were the chitterlings or innards, we used to wash those out. All you needed with chitterlings was dry bread, you had them fried or boiled and they were lovely cold, and cut up on bread.

'When you used to go out to work in the fields, you could have plaited chitterlings and piece of bread. You plaited the thin ones, the fatter ones you just cut up. But the little plaited ones were best.

Pigs were great big fat things then. On the streaky bacon, there was more fat than there was lean!   We used to salt the sides of bacon and ham, and they were hung up on bacon racks hanging from the ceiling to keep them dry. You still see the racks in old farm kitchens.

The excess fat was cut off and rendered down for lard. All the little bits that were left were called scruttons - scratchings they call them now, you can buy them in packets. One thing you could do with scruttons was roll them with currants and sultanas then put them in pastry, a kind of flapjack.

'The trouble is today is that nobody cooks things properly. They all want fast food, and they mix it all up, and the housewife has no idea of hygiene!

'This is where all the trouble started, not what is happening in the slaughterhouses. They are talking about E.Coli now, infection because it's contaminated with muck, but you still eat cows stomachs, and tripe.

I mean, we used to eat everything from cows or pigs stomachs.

We used to make the faggots wrapped around with the flay, the lining of the stomach. They were really tasty they were, lovely faggots.

You used to make the sausages out of the spare meat, using bread, seasoning and suchlike, home-made sausages were beautiful, they really were.

'I always remember the woman who used to help in the house, Mrs Wolford. She always used to help with this, she said. *'I loves it when you's kills a pig and makes sausages, it gets me 'ands so clean!'*

It's quite true because when working with all that lard, it cleaned her hands up beautifully. Soap's made out of fat isn't it. Anyway, we used to render the lard down, it was beautiful white lard.

10

Now you talk about modern hygiene, and then you talk about what used to happen years ago.

'There was nothing of a pig that was wasted. We used to catch the blood for black puddings, the skin was the crackling. Everything was used.

'Another thing that happened during the war was that any fire damaged food was sent out for pig food. Getting pig food was difficult, so anything that was fire damaged was put down as pig food.

'We had between five hundred to a thousand pigs up at Brightwalton, and they all had to be fed.
One day, Father was told that there was two truck loads of food coming which was fire damaged.   It turned out to be two truckloads of sultanas and currants.   The outside of the boxes were scorched, but when we opened the boxes, the insides were perfect.   The pigs didn't get many of them!
The trouble was, that the whole of the neighbourhood knew about this consignment , and they were lifted out of the shed like nobodies business!

'The story goes that Father had been out one night down to the pub, then they went back to someone's house because they had just had a ration of whisky and beer. They stopped there for a bit longer, so he didn't get home until half past one, two o'clock in the morning.
He came in the back way so Mother wouldn't hear him, and he met one of the Farm workers going out with a sack of pig-grub on his back!
He said ' Where are you going with that then Jim?'
Jim rolled his eyes and turned round.

'Back in the blimmin barn now I've seen you come!' he replied.

'Of course rabbits were on the menu at least twice a week during the war, and after. Basically we cooked them in a stew. Sometimes Jo used to like to roast them, but I think they are dry, cooked like that. I think the best recipe for rabbits is to take a half grown one, and fry it in egg and breadcrumbs. That's beautiful.

Then there is rabbit pie. Just take a rabbit, skinned, and cooked, then add rashers of bacon, and boiled eggs, and put a bit of pastry on and cook it. When the pie gets cold, there is a lovely jelly in there, obviously it is a gravy if it was hot.

We always had eggs, being on the farm, lots of eggs. But you always knew that you really had to cook a duck's egg well because of salmonella.'

Country sayings and traditions are passed down from generation to generation. Maybe you should know a bit about David's background, his family history?

Family

David William Liddiard was born on November 6th, 1929, in Ramsbury, Wiltshire.

He was the youngest child, but only son, of Beatrice *(nee Pragnell)* and William (*Bill*) Liddiard.

His Father, Bill had been the youngest of a family of ten, an average sized family in those days, five daughters and five sons.

His father, David's Grandfather, had a small farm at Upper Upham, Wiltshire.

When Bill was eleven, his father died, so his family gave up the rented smallholding and moved to the centre of a village called Aldbourne not far away.

Bill Liddiard joined the Army when he was seventeen in 1915. He was in the Wiltshire Yeomanry, and they were sent down onto Salisbury Plain to be trained on horses. Then the horses were taken away and they were sent to where all the action was, the trenches on the front.

Evidently, the last thing Bill could remember was a trench collapsing on top of him after a shell exploded He woke up in a dressing station. Somebody had dug him out.

As a result of his injuries, he got a 'Blighty' ticket, and was invalided back to England. David thinks that that was when Bill met Beatrice Pragnell, David's Mother, who was a nurse during the war.

Beatrice had received a University education, and after the war, worked as an advisor for what became the Milk Marketing Board, travelling to various districts, teaching people how to use their dairy farms, and how to make cheese and butter.

Bill came out of the army at the end of the war and started working for George Wilson, one of the big farmers in Wiltshire and Berkshire.

One day he was driving a two furrow plough pulled by three horses and Mr Wilson came out and tried to tell him how to do it.

The story goes that Bill said to Mr Wilson *'Mr Wilson, if you can do it better than me, here are the reins,'* picked up his jacket and walked away.

That was at the time when jobs weren't easy to come by, and in those days, the Wilsons farmed about twenty six thousand acres. So the possibilities of further employment on the land were somewhat limited.

Undaunted, Bill Liddiard bought himself a horse and cart and started hauling stones for the County Council to make up the roads. When he had enough money, he bought another horse and cart, loaded both the carts, hooked the carts up one behind the other and led the horses, so he was hauling two loads of stones.

This way, he built up a good little business.

Then he got the tenancy of a dairy farm at Baydon. At that time, Beatrice Pragnell was engaged to be married to one of the Singers, large landowners in that area. The wedding had been planned, and was so imminent, that the wedding cake had been made.

Unperturbed about upsetting others plans, Bill wooed her, whisked her off, and despite all her family's protestations, married her and brought her to live at Baydon. It was at Baydon where Joan was born, their first child.

Joan remembers being told that her Mother used to send her out with her father on the plough when she was about two, so that Beatrice could get various jobs done in the house. Of course Joan doesn't remember that at all.

Bill used to deliver his milk round the village, rumour has it that the round used to take longer than it should have done. One of his customers was reputed to have complained to him, *'I wish you'd deliver my milk before you pass the village pump!'*

This was because, in those days, allegedly, some milkmen used to water the milk down before they delivered it, to make it go further.

After Baydon, the family, which then included Barbara, their second child, moved to a farm at Beenham, and then on to another at West Titheley, near where Beatrice's family lived.
Eventually they moved to Manor Farm, in Ramsbury, which is where David was born, and then to Manor Farm at Compton Bassett. When David was two years old, the family moved to Manor Farm, Westridge, near Goring and Streatley.
There were some lovely old barns belonging to the farm and most of them, if not all, have now been converted into houses. You can see them from the road as you drive past.

Bill moved to a bigger farm each time, which was not difficult in those days because of the depression, they were paying you to look after them.
The County Council would build a house and some buildings, and with so many acres of land, it was the first rung on the ladder to being a farmer. You rented it to get started, and then the idea was that you then went on to a bigger farm which is precisely what he did.
There were three or four farms like that in Beenham, West Berkshire. All of them were small mixed farm units, but each had a dairy.

David said that whilst his father was farming at Compton Bassett, he got a chance to take the tenancy at Bradfords Farm ,where David ended up eventually. Bill accepted Bradfords, but the day afterwards, was offered Westridge which was better, so he took that one. 'I think they paid him ten shillings an acre to take it. That was the first year, and afterwards he had to pay ten shillings an acre rent to them, for the seven years.'

15

Bill had about seven farms in twelve years, David said that his Mother had commented to Bill, *'My dear, a rolling stone gathers no moss.'*

His reply was, *'Mother, it's not moss I'm after!'*

He was very ambitious and hardworking. *'You've got to pull your finger out and prove things, that's what it boils down to.'*

David remembers being told that when they moved to Westridge, from Compton Bassett, they came on a special train with all their goods and chattels, to Goring Station. Then they drove the cows up to the farm from the station.

If you've ever driven out of Streatley on the Hermitage road, you will know how steep that hill is.

His two sisters, Joan and Barbara, knew how steep it was because every day, they used to cycle down to the station at Streatley to catch the train to school in Wallingford, which meant though, that every evening, they had to push their bicycles back up the hill!

Westridge was over-run with rabbits, and Bill made enough money from rabbits to pay the rent every year.

'No one could imagine how many rabbits there were then, the place was over run, the whole countryside was! I remember my Father employed a Rabbit catcher and used to pay him thruppence (*three old pence*) a rabbit, and then he used to sell them to local butchers for a tanner *(six old pence.).'*

'One day, the rabbit catcher caught three hundred and thirty rabbits, and he hung them all on his bike to bring back to my Dad. The weight buckled the front wheel of his bicycle. So he asked my Father to buy him a new wheel!

My Dad said *'No, you are only on piece work, buy your own.'* I remember that.'

A new bike would cost about two pounds and ten shillings in those days, and the farmworkers wages were about thirty

16

shillings a week *(£1.50 nowadays)*.

Sadly, David's Mother, Beatrice, died in 1934 when he was four years old. She died of peritonitis, a burst appendix, and she is buried at Aldbourne.

'I remember her going off to hospital in the car, I was only four, I remember her getting in the car, and saying good bye, that was the last time we ever saw her.
The next thing I remember was when we were at my uncle's who had a County Council smallholding at Lower Beenham, next to one my Father had a few years before. One of my uncles came and told me that Mother had died.
My sisters were there, and I remember we were all crying in the middle of the road.
They are the only things I can remember about her.

'I started school not long after that and I remember saying to someone *'I wish Mummy could see me going to school'*.
When it came to aunts and uncles, David had quite a few on his Father's side.
'I remember there was Aunty Rose, who lived in Gloucester, Aunty Maud who lived in Aldbourne, and Aunty Bessy whose husband was a lay preacher in the Chapel at Aldbourne.
There was also Aunty Alice, the eldest, who never married, she also lived in Aldbourne, and Aunty May, whose husband was a grocer in Croydon they moved to Tisbury where they had a grocers shop until they moved back into this district, then he worked for Alexanders the High Class Grocers in Hungerford.
Then there were my uncles.

'During the First World War, Uncle Jim, a teacher, joined up and was one of the first to be killed from the village, I never knew him. Another brother Uncle Arthur, who was one of the Old Contemptible, joined up and was made a prisoner of war, and when he came back, started up a butchers shop in the middle of Aldbourne.

Then there was my Uncle Teddy, he used to work as a jobbing gardener, but he didn't marry until very late in life as he looked after his mother. My Uncle George worked on a farm, and then moved up to Hemel Hempstead to work on a pig farm. He actually died when he fell into a vat of boiling swill!

I was always too busy to keep in touch with all of them, shame really. I can only remember the Aunts and Uncles from my Mothers side, the Pragnells.'

David's Mother, Beatrice, was a the eldest child of Edith and Frederick Pragnell. She had two sisters, Edith and Ivy-Phyllis, and two brothers, Frederick and Albert. Albert died as a child. David says that the Pragnells were the very gentle side of the family.

Up at the Museum of Rural Life in White Knights in Reading, are hundreds of photographs of David's maternal Grandfather farming.

They were taken by David's Uncle James, who married Phyllis, and who used to be very keen on photography. He would spend a lot of time out with David's Grandfather on the farm.

'Many of his photographs were printed in the Farmers Weekly and when he died he left all his photographs to the Museum. His real initials were CS Snow, but everyone called him James. He was the headmaster of Braywood School, and Aunt Phil was a primary teacher at the school, trying to teach children to read.

'I always remember a story she told.' David said, ' She had one little boy in the class who was absolutely no good. He couldn't read a thing – and he didn't want to.

One day, she took some Farmers Weeklys in to school, so that the children could cut out the pictures of pigs, and other animals.

This little lad was fascinated, and spent hours going through the magazines.

'Oh Miss I wish I could read the price of that and how much they fetched.' he said.

So she kept bringing in Farmers Weekly, slowly going through each one with him, and taught him the basics of reading through the magazines.

He went through the rest of school, not really making his mark at all.

Then one day about fifteen years later, this bloke turns up at the school in a big car, and a sheepskin coat.

'How are you Mrs Snow, I came to thank you for teaching me to read. I've been dealing in pigs and made my fortune.'

I always remember her telling us that story.'

David has two sisters, Joan is nine years older than David, and Barbara seven years older. They didn't have much to do with him when he was young because in those days there were maids to look after him. When their Mother died, there was a housekeeper, a maid, and one of the farmworkers' wives who came in to help.

Joan remembers the housekeeper as being rather horrible and dirty. *'It's funny what you remember, but I will never forget how she used to take a dirty handkerchief from her pocket to dust.'*

After their Mother died, the children at first were sent to spend the days with various people and their housekeepers, the Burdetts at the Round House (or Manor farm) or the Walters at Bower Farm.

'Just after my Mother died, I got sent off to Aunt May and I got pneumonia. I had it pretty badly. I can remember lying in

19

bed and seeing this big tree waving about through the window, and I said to somebody,' if that tree falls down it is going to fall across the road.'

'Oh no that tree won't fall down.' I was told.

It was a very windy day, and the next thing, there was a hell of a crash and the tree fell across the road, and just missed a bus!

I must have had a premonition.'

After a time, David's Father, Bill, started courting Anne who was thirteen years his junior. She was a companion to Mrs Smallbone who lived at one of the neighbouring farms. Bill married Anne about a year after Beatrice had died and in time, they had three children.

John was born in 1936, Peter was born in 1939 and Susan was born two years later. Susan, now Lady Bradbury, lives in London, but John and Peter still live in the Lambourn Valley.

The three older Liddiard children, Joan, Barbara and David, used to enjoy hunting, they each had their own pony. Joan remembers that David had a small horse called Bright Eyes, who always had to be ahead of the field, even ahead of the Master, who always told him to get back.

One day they went out, and after they returned home, and the pack returned , there was no sign of David. No one had any idea where he was. Eventually, just as dusk was falling, Bright Eyes came trotting back into the yard, with David lolling fast asleep on his back.

Joan learned to drive while they were at Westridge. *'When the parents were out, my sister and I, and a boy who was staying on the farm, would drive the car that used to sweep the hay up.*

One day we got caught, I took it out all round the field at the top, and suddenly I could see all the parents waving at me to come back.

20

The next day, Father said that one of the lorry drivers was going to teach me to drive properly, and so I had better get up early every day. I think I was only thirteen at the time, but by the time I was seventeen, I could drive quite well. Barbara left all the driving to me. In fact it was only after she was married, and went to Hong Kong after the war, that she learned to drive. She never learned in England, she said she didn't need to if I could.'

When Joan left school, Barbara had to go to boarding school, as she would not be allowed to travel all that distance on her own. In 1943, Bill Liddiard wanted his son John to go to the Grammar School in Newbury where David was, but they wouldn't take him. Bill was livid and took David out of the Grammar School and sent him to Merton House, a boarding school in Reading, with his brother John.

As you know, David was only there a term.

Joan worked on the farm, milking. A new mechanised system was installed, and she remembers a dashing young man who came in a sports car to show them how to work it. It took at least three months to grasp how to milk by machine. When Barbara left school, she too worked in the dairy.

This was war time, and fourteen out of the twenty eight farmworkers joined the army, so both girls had to pull their weight around the farm.

They thought nothing of getting up at twenty to five every morning to milk the cows.

It was the local Postmistress who eventually declared to all and sundry that *'those Liddiard girls should be doing something for the war effort.'*

So, Barbara joined the VAD, and Joan the Mechanised Transport Corps. Joan chuckled as she recalled that she never had to work as hard again after she left the farm. She fell madly in love with James Crawford and married him. They had one son, John.

21

'Barbara married Freddie Lonsdale in 1943,' David continued '
he was a Major in the Parachute Regiment, and a glider pilot.
They had two sons, Anthony and Timothy, in fact Anthony
was born within about eight months of my youngest half
sister, Susan. So Father had a Grandson the same year as he
had his youngest daughter!
In fact, I have a feeling that Tony was born on Barbara's
wedding anniversary and Joan's birthday.'
David's first school was the Primary School at Aldworth in
Berkshire. It was in the middle of the road, opposite the Bell.
'We used to bicycle a mile to get to school, and a mile back,
Westridge to Aldworth, or we walked, we had a choice. We
went home every day for lunch, I wasn't allowed to take
sandwiches.

'There was no uniform, but all small boys wore shorts. At
Aldworth, we had two mistresses, one was Miss German, but
I can't remember the other one's name. They were both very
strict, and you had to do what you were told, or stand in the
corner if you didn't. Of course I was no different from anyone
else, in the corner quite a lot really. I remember one of the
comments in my report
*'Not only is he inattentive, but his diversionary activities upset
the rest of the form.'*
The loos were across the road. If you wanted to go, you had
to go out of the school, out of the gates, then across the road to
the 'Hole-in-the-Woods'.
I remember dancing round the Maypole, it was a big one in the
garden of the Vicarage. I think a Doctor lives there now.
We used to go to school with the Bishops, a big family, about
four or five children, I can't remember their names now, but
their Father was a butcher in Streatley, he always wore a
bowler hat.
He used to bicycle to work every day, and one day when he
was going down the long Streatley Hill to his shop, a black cat

ran out under his bike. He went over the handlebars and was killed!'

Joan remembers him too. *'He used to help us with our bicycle tyres, he always pumped them up for us.'*

David continued   'I do remember being told about one incident, we were harvesting and I must have been about four or five at the time. I evidently came across this bottle of home-made wine or home-made beer, and thought it was lemonade or something. I must have drunk a fair amount of it because they found me sitting on a sheaf, and when they said *'Come on, time to go',* I replied, 'Isn't it foggy?' -and it was a brilliant Summers day!

We had horses then, and if it was very frosty, the Farriers used to come round and put frost nails on the horses. They used to take some of the nails out and put frost nails in. They were horse nails with pointed ends to stop the horses from sliding. Like spikes on shoes.

They were important for taking the milk down to Goring Station, you had to be very careful on that hill. If you had too big a load coming back up the hill, you couldn't do it. You used to have to turn left at the bottom and take the roundabout route, I can't remember what it is called.

My Father had to take his milk by cart to put it on the train in Goring every day to get it up to London.

One frosty morning, Father and his carter were just unloading the big milk churns from his cart onto the platform to load them on to the waiting train which was hissing and steaming at the station, when the guard, blew his whistle and waved the train out.

Bill couldn't believe his eyes.

'What the bloody hell did you do that for, I have to get my milk to London?'

'I can't hold my trains up for you, you'll have to get here on time.'

With that, he tucked his flag under his arm, turned on his heel,

and swung back up into the guard's van, and disappeared .
Bill was furious.

Cursing the railways, and all who worked on them, he
reloaded the cart, swung the horses round and left.

He drove his cart straight round to Stradlings, the garage in
Goring, and bought a truck, and took the milk up to London
himself.

Then he rang around all his friends, and they joined him. That
was in 1933, by 1936 he had thirteen trucks taking milk to
London.

Stradlings were also in Northbrook Street in Newbury near
Gowrings, and they had another garage in Hungerford. They
were run by two brothers.

The engines weren't very good on the lorries though, but the
drivers used to give them to Stradlings when they got back
from London, and they would be ready with a new engine by
the time they wanted them the next morning.

I do remember that one of them turned over one frosty
morning. Up near Bucklebury. There was frozen milk all over
the road.

'I can also remember the drought in 1936, we were sending
thirteen milk lorries up to London every day, Morris
Commercials they were. The dairies would then wash out the
churns, and fill them full of water for them to bring back. The
thing was, Westridge was on top of a hill, the drought had
dried up the wells, so of course there was no mains water, and
a farm needs water for the cattle and so on.   So we relied on
London water that Summer.

Also 1936, the Milk Marketing Board opened up in Newbury,
and my Father got that contract.

'When we were at Westridge, there was a duck pond,
actually more of a slurry pit, and there was this chap used to
come down at weekends from London and stay with my

24

Father.

One day they went down to get some ducks for dinner. They shot two, and this chap threw down his gun and waded into the pond. *'I had to go and get them Bill, in case they sank!'* he said.

As if ducks would! But he stank when he got out.

The best one was when he borrowed my pony to have a ride, he always used to wear breeches, and his feet used to touch the ground. When the pony threw him off, he used to let it go. My Father told him *'Whatever you do, if you ever fall off a horse, never let it go. If you do that, they know they can get away with it.'*

So the next time he fell off, he hung on to it and he was dragged along by the reins. At that time, there were no septic tanks, the slurry was just ditched down the fields, and the pony dragged him right down this ditch. An open sewer. He was not very popular when he got home!

Oh yes, we had a bonfire one year for November 5th, it was at Westridge just before we moved to Brightwalton in 1938. Anyway, we piled all the old tyres up on the green for the bonfire, it was the best ever.

'I can remember a lot of little things, funny how they come back. I remember going up to the Downs to catch tadpoles in the dewponds.

We used to go with the Walters family, one of their cousins was my first girlfriend, and I used to get ribbed about that, but I was only 5 years old then. We used to go to their house for tea.

I can remember that the biggest treat we could have was Corona *(a fizzy drink in bottles)*. We weren't allowed it at home, but we had an Aunt who always had it. It used to get delivered to the door like milk, in crates of six.

I don't think we were very religious, although I can remember going to chapel in Aldbourne. Once a year there was one of those services where everyone stands up and reads something, an Anniversary. I am a Methodist man really, Primitive Methodist. My Mother is buried at Aldbourne but in the church not the chapel.'

David attended Aldworth village school until 1938 and the family moved to Manor Farm, Brightwalton.
'When I was eight I became a boarder at the Prep School which was for the Grammar School (*St Bartholomew's*), in Newbury. It was down Enborne Road .
We used to get up in the mornings and have cold showers because we weren't allowed to use hot water. We used to sleep in dormitories, and there was a matron in the sanatorium right up on the top floor. I was only a boarder for about two terms.
At Prep School every morning, we would walk in a crocodile to assembly and Prayers at the big school. We were always up in the balcony, and then we used to file back into the Prep School.
I was always put up in the form above my age. I can show you the reports from the school when I was a year under the average age. I was never any good at English and writing, but I was way ahead in Maths and Geography, and all the sorts of things like that.
At the Grammar School, the uniform was grey trousers, jackets, blazers in the Summer. Part of the uniform was that you had to have sports kit, rugby boots, two shirts, white shorts, then there were the cricket whites. White shirt and a pullover. Anyhow, you were charged for shoes and boots, you could get a pair of rugby boots for about seven shillings and sixpence then (*thirty seven pence*). I actually kept the invoices from the first two terms, and let the school have a look at them .

'But the trouble was, I didn't have time to do the sport. We had to catch the bus at quarter past four because we had to

26

Bill Liddiard training landgirls during the War

Thrashing at Brightwalton

Bonnie and Traveller with Tom Allder
Our last working horses at Newbury Show. 1947

Calf rearing at Brightwalton

Outdoor pigs. 1942

Cattleyard at Brightwalton

'Grandpa Pragnell'
Photograph taken by C-S Snow (Uncle James)

get home. We could never stay behind and do football practice or net practice..

The rugby matches were at weekends, and of course we had Saturday morning school in those days. But we couldn't stay.

Farmworkers worked until midday, or one o'clock on Saturdays. Weekends in those days lasted from one or two o'clock on Saturdays to Sunday nights, you know.

'I used to play rugby. I think I played for the house once or twice, but I wasn't a great rugby player. I've got a photograph of when I used to play for Newbury Rugby Club for a bit.

But then again, I was milking and couldn't get the weekends off. So I didn't do many games for them. I quite enjoyed rugby, but I thought cricket was a dangerous game. Those cricket balls are too hard!

But sports wise, I've never had any inclination. I've never been to a football match in my life. Well, seeing all those people kicking a bit of leather one way, and another group kicking it the other is counterproductive I always say!

'I've always been a participant rather than a spectator I suppose. I'm not a good spectator. Life's too full to stand around doing nothing, life is to participate in, not to watch go by.

Like sex shows, they are definitely not a spectator sport. I went to one and I was bored stiff. It's a participant sport.

'At school, each pupil was in a different school house, I was in Evers, and the rest of the family were in Evers, I even think my grand-daughter is in Evers now. Three generations there.

It was an all boy school for years, my daughter Kate got in there just as they started to take girls. Then she went up to the Girls school just as they amalgamated with the boys school.

To get to school when we lived at Brightwalton, we used to

catch the eight o'clock bus to get into the Wharf at Newbury. Then we used to walk from the Wharf up to the Grammar School . After school, we had to walk back to the Wharf to catch the four fifteen bus home, and got back to Brightwalton just after five.   So I was away from home for ten hours a day.

Then we had an hour or an hour and a half homework to do if Father hadn't got work for me on the farm.   But if it was harvest or haymaking, I was straight out in the fields helping in those days.

'Oh, when I was five I used to lead the horses. Then when I was eight, I was promoted to loading wagons. Loading sheaves on the wagons. It was very high up.

I used to wear a cap then, all the farm workers did, a flat cap, tweedy thing, you know. These caps were useful for all sorts of things, as I said earlier.   You used to turn them round backwards if you were milking, and also wear it like that if it was raining, stopped the water going down the back of your neck. They used to last ages, you bought new ones occasionally, but they weren't that expensive.

'The other thing you always had, was an Ingersoll pocket watch, tied onto your waistcoat or jacket, they were half a crown a time at Woolworths and a penknife was sixpence a go. You used to lose a lot of penknives a bit later on when you were doing the pickup baling. You used to leave them in the bale.   I used to buy two or three at a time as I always lost them.   I still carry a knife, just a little knife. No one carries a knife today.   We used to whittle with them as children, do all sorts of things with them. People have forgotten how to use penknives today. That's the problem. Nobody whittles today do they? You used to get your rabbiting stick cut with them. Things have changed so much.'

28

David pointed at his well worn pocket knife.

'This knife' he said clicking it open and shut 'this knife has helped a few times. A friend rang up one day and she had locked herself out, Kate's Mother-in-law actually. They had just put in double glazing, lovely double glazing it was.

I drove over and like an idiot, took no tools, but I was able to break in, let her in, replace the window, and was off home again in 25 minutes, and you would never know I had been there. All I used was the knife.

'Our first tractor was an International   10-20, built about 1933-34. Billy Wolford used to drive it.   I still had the original tank we used for storing the fuel in   until ten years ago, the one we used to have the diesel and paraffin in. I used it at Marsh Benham for the central heating. It was galvanised and riveted, and about three times as thick as any you can get today. It never leaked, well, I never saw it leak.

'We had horses too, right up until 1948. It's a great pity that they are not around now, they were great, horses were.   I don't know if there are any working horses left in this area?

Nowadays you have pickup trucks and Land Rovers, all four wheel drives. We did have a Morris 10 saloon, which I drove on the road at fifteen, I had a provisional licence, but no one seemed to take tests. You were supposed to be seventeen. I used it to take the thrashing gang to work.

But before we had all the vehicles, if you had a cow which had calved up in the field, it could be two miles away. You had to go up there, pick the calf up and carry it home if it couldn't walk.

It was alright with the heifer calves, but with the bull calves, the plumbing was a bit different. You used to feel that sort of warm feeling down your back, running right down!   Warm and soggy!

The other thing is that a cow is a very protective animal, you

29

should never go into a field with a dog if a cow has had a calf. They are a damn sight more dangerous than a bull because a cow keeps her eyes open when she goes for you, a bull shuts his! So if you have a dog, being a coward that it is, it will go behind you if a cow charges, so the cow will knock you out of the way to get to the dog!

People don't realise it's dangerous.

'I remember on one occasion I went into a loosebox to help a calf, In those days I always wore a Hames strap. You wouldn't believe it but I had a twenty six inch Hames strap round my waist. It was leather, it used to go around the harness, so it was very strong.

Anyway, this cow came at me. All the cows had horns in those days, you don't see them now, and the cow's curved horn hooked up under my strap, and I was hooked up and going round and round the loosebox with the cow, the strap wouldn't break. I got off eventually but it was a funny moment.

'We left the farmhouse at Brightwalton in 1941, and Father rented another farm at Littlecote. Littlecote Park Farm, up near Cakewood, we were only there a year, until 1942.

When we moved to Littlecote, we obviously didn't have cattle trucks but we did have far more heifers and cows than we needed at Brightwalton, which we were still farming.

So we drove a herd from Brightwalton to Littlecote, which is about fourteen or fifteen miles. The first two or three miles we were running all over the place, stopping them going into fields, or going the wrong way.

The last four or five miles, we had trouble to get them along. Their feet were sore, so were ours, they were tired, so were we. It took nearly all day to move them. We milked them in the morning before we left, and milked them again in the afternoon at Littlecote.

'I suppose I must have been about eleven when we moved to Littlecote. To get to school in Newbury, I used to bike from Littlecote, about three and a half miles, and when I got to Hungerford, I parked my bike up the alleyway by Ben Pratt's Father's shop, he was the butcher in Hungerford.   I then used to run up to the station and catch the 8.10am train which would take me to Newbury.

It was alright bicycling to Hungerford because it was all down hill, but it was uphill all the way home.

But I remember the Winter of 1941 which was so bloody cold, I used to be frozen after three and a half miles.

Father made me wear long trousers because of the cold, but I got into trouble at school for that, and had to wear shorts.

'One of my jobs in the mornings, was to take the cows out on my way to school. If you ask Derek Smalley, he always reminds me of the time that I went to school, and the cows had gone adrift because someone had shut the gate in the night and instead of the cows going into the field like they always did, the gate was shut so they went on into the wood!

I had to go back, open the gate, and then run around the wood trying to get them out.   There were stinging nettles everywhere, and I only had short trousers on.   Derek reckons that the gap between my shorts and my socks was just one mass of weals from the stinging nettles!

That was the Winter the rain froze on all the telephone wires and they came down.

Coming back from Newbury, we used to catch the quarter past four train, get there at quarter to five, and I still had three and a half miles to go , all up hill on a bicycle.

That was a hard year that was.   I had more illness that year than any other. I was so cold.   Twice my Father had to come and get me, hypothermia I suppose.   I was shivering all the time at school, they put me up in the sanatorium with hot water bottles to thaw me out.

There was strict discipline, you had to wear short trousers, you had to wear caps, you had to raise your cap at a master or another parent.

It was discipline as it should be, it taught manners, and manners maketh man.

Let's face it, if you are not taught discipline, you can never have self discipline.

'After a year we went back to Brightwalton, back to the buses, back to where we used to be.

Someone paid Father to leave Littlecote, the owner was having to give up his farm because they were building an airfield or something. So we gave up Littlecote, and Father bought a farm, the first farm he ever owned, Henley Farm at Shefford. He bought it for £7,500 and he sold it on for £13,000 in 1947.

'The chap he sold it to, when he gave up farming, in 1956, offered it back to Father for £26,000. Father said, *'I'm not going to give you that, I'll give you £25,000.'*

So he sold it to somebody else. Three years later, it was sold on for £70,000! That was one of the deals that Father ought to have done but didn't.

Father then bought Manor Farm at Great Shefford for £12,500 and sold it for a £1,000 more the next day. I was actually combining the day he did it, and he came up to me and said *'I've just made enough money to pay for this combine!'*

The combine cost £950.'

William Liddiard, David's Father moved to Shefford Farm in 1946. The farm was six hundred and twenty six acres, had a lovely house, and had electricity. It was up for sale at £17,500. Bill Liddiard offered £16,500 and in the end, the auctioneer had to toss a coin, and David's Father won.

32

In the Autumn of 1953, they were making hay on the long flanks of the west facing slopes from Elton Wood on the crest of the hill North of Great Shefford. The fields swept down to the Wantage Road , and on the other side of the valley were the gentler slopes of Northfield Farm, owned by Mr Whatley.

They stopped at the bottom to load up the carts again, and David's Father said *'Nip over and see if Mr Whatley will sell that farm to me Boy.'*

So David duly did what he was told and Whatley said yes!

Northfield was an extra three hundred and thirteen acres, and Bill Liddiard really wanted it.   He paid the asking price of £11,500 for it.

Whatley had married one of the Hosier girls, so after he sold Northfield, he moved onto one of the Hosier Farms.

'We used to have double Summer time in those days, we'd be out until ten o'clock at night, and then we came home, went to bed but up and out at quarter to eight in the morning to catch the school bus.

We didn't have electricity until 1946.   In fact, we didn't have electricity until we moved to Shefford. That was the first time we had come across electricity.

We didn't dare turn the wireless on unless it was news time otherwise the batteries ran out!

If the batteries weren't working when Father came in and wanted to listen to the news, you were in dead trouble!.

So I had to learn all about electricity at Shefford, and we got a few shocks in the process. I had quite a few, but the worst one I had, made me go and lie down afterwards.

I was doing a job, building a piggery, I had one hand on the rails which were concreted into the ground, and one hand on the metal drill. Pulled the drill towards me, and it shorted out. What happened was that the live wire had come off its screw, and there was no earth wire, I got the full voltage bolt straight through me. I survived it anyhow.

'I didn't feel very well after that. But I have been very lucky in my life really you know, very lucky. I was run over by the combine once and lived. I'm very lucky.

'If I'd stuck at it, stayed at school, I suppose I would have ended up as an engineering academic, but there was never any time.
I was always interested in things that might have been useful. If it wasn't useful then I wasn't interested. So when it came to things like Scripture, French or Latin, I didn't bother. Latin I thought was a waste of time, I didn't do very well with Latin.

At the Grammar school, other subjects we did which I enjoyed were Maths, Algebra, Geometry, and Geography, especially Geography.
Teaching wasn't like it is now. You see, all our top masters were off to the war.
We were getting retired teachers, teachers who hadn't made the grade, people whose real thing was scripture, they were trying to teach everything else.
'Stooge' we used to call one, he was really a retired Scripture teacher, he was a real little pipsqueak of a bloke.
I remember one of the boys at the back of the class was playing with himself.
'Boy! What are you playing with? Bring it here!'
 I used to get into trouble at school, I suppose I would have been called dyslexic today, they just labelled me disruptive instead.
As I mentioned, I was a year younger than the average age of the form. I was not an idiot, but I used to get into so much trouble, -*'we used to have serious doubts about his honesty'* - it was because when we came to doing all the algebra, adding

up sums and that, I used to do it in my head you see, never putting any working out down.

They used to think I had cribbed it off the bloke next door. Instead of written working out, I just had the answers, I used to get into trouble for that you know. -

'Where's your working out boy?'

'What do I want to write it down for?'

'You should write it down so we can see what you do.'

I was one of those people who knows, 10 x 18 is 180, easy, 11 x 18, is 180 + 18, easy, there was always an easy way of working around it. Mental arithmetic.'

'Did I tell you about the fireworks?

Someone had the bright idea of taking fireworks to school, which wasn't a good idea as we weren't allowed to take things to school like that. I could make gunpowder though, I had the opportunity to get the saltpetre. Because we used to have it when we killed the pigs. Sugar, salt and saltpetre was what you cured the bacon with.

Saltpetre, sulphur and carbon makes gunpowder, that's the recipe for it and we used to make it up.

How we never blew ourselves up, I'll never know! Anyhow, after you burned it the residue, if dropped into Sulphuric acid used to make a smell which would knock you down at ten yards! You used to take the top off this bottle, and put it on again. It was wicked. It was like everyone in the class had passed wind at the same time.'

David roared with laughter at the memory.

'I used to take Carbide to school sometimes. At Brightwalton, we had no electricity, but there was a carbide gas plant which used to make the gas to keep the lights in the house going. We had gaslights then, we made our own gas and we had a small gas cylinder.

You used to have this tray which you would slide in. You used to put a certain amount of carbide in, and then you used to drip water on it to produce the gas.

When the level of the cylinder went up it would cut the water off, and when the level went down, it would reactivate the water again to drip on the carbide.

You always had to have a spare tray so that you could slide the next one in when one ran out, and that is how we made our own gas.

Of course the joke about that was, the people who bought the farm after us, when it froze one winter, used a blowtorch to thaw it out! It never worked well after that, there wasn't much gas in there at the time thank goodness.

Anyway, I was quite a good source of carbide for them, and in those days, we never had a formroom of our own, we would go from room to room. There were so many classes 1a, 1b, 1c , 2a, 2b, 2c.

We were getting a great many evacuees, and refugees, the German Jews, the Austrian Jews, the French Jews were coming across. People like Greenbaum, he changed his name to Green and I think he made the papers for taking the Foreign Office for the most amount of money, and losing the most amount of money - millions when he went bankrupt. He was in the same form as me.

I can't remember many names, but there was David Gerschowitt who is now Dr Ryde in London, and I think he is the Doctor for the British Table Tennis team. Anyhow there were all these people coming in from abroad and the classes were big. As you left one formroom to move to the next, you would drop a small lump of carbide in the inkwell and it used to bubble up and come out all over the desk!

'Going back to the fireworks, well - we were rotten sods, we really were. When you were in the laboratories, if you took the Bunsen burner off the end of the gas pipe, put the gas pipe in your mouth, turn the tap on and blow, then turn the tap off,

turn the tap on and blow again, you could actually blow the gas back down the pipes. So when the master came to light the Bunsen burner, it would just blow the match out.
We overdid it once, and blew all the Bunsen burners out in the lab above! Our Master was confused - a chap we called Crusty Connor, but the Master in the lab above, knew exactly what had happened and he came and gave poor old Crusty a hell of a dressing down on how he couldn't control the children in his class.

'Then someone else took the burner off the pipe and attached it to a water pipe and put water down the gas pipe, and when Crusty turned the burner on all he got was a fountain of water!

'I can remember a few of my friends from then, there was Steven Mildenhall, Steven Cogger and Charles Eady, then of course there was Reg Piper, Titch Taylor, Jimmy Gore, was another one who used to come on the bus with us, Robin Wilson, and Alan Vince who was the prefect on the bus, used to try and keep the order. Great friends with them still. Tubby Lewis - he's died now, Ben Pratt, Juicy Norman.'

'Juicy Norman did well, he captained oil tankers he was right at the top of his profession. Oh yes, then there was the time that David Hopson, of Camp Hopson, nearly blew the lab up! I don't know quite what he did, but he was messing around and I think he lost his eyebrows, but it didn't do any permanent damage but I remember it.

'Then the firework.
Somebody brought a firework to school. It was only a penny banger.
But once you've lit the blue paper, there was about an inch

and a half of tightly rolled paper, it started to burn, then it started fizzing and you had to get rid of it quickly then. You couldn't hold it then or it would blow your fingers off! You weren't supposed to hold it at all. We weren't supposed to take any fireworks to school either. Somebody brought some in, and we thought we would go into the bogs, and let them off.

Somebody lit one, and suddenly realised it was going to make a hell of a noise, chucked it in the loo and flushed the loo! But it had started fizzing, and going into water didn't put it out!

It just got round the bend when it exploded. It demolished the loo at ground level, and also, there must have been a bit of marsh gas or something down there, because all the other little sods who were sitting on the other loos came rushing out covered in water- and everything else!

Yes, it was quite an explosive situation.

Then there was the other time with the carbide, we had a treacle tin for the carbide, and we only had a few bits left, so we put some water in the treacle tin from the tap by the old pavilion, and put the lid on. We waited and the lid would come off, 'boing' and it would go to different heights depending on how hard you had put the lid on. We were just coming to the end when a prefect came in.

'What's in that tin Liddiard?' He shouted.

'Carbide Sir'.

'Give it to me' he bellowed

We didn't tell him there was water with it as well. He grabbed the tin with one hand, grabbed me by the ear, we were walking back to school and lid came off, all over him, and his black jacket was covered in white substance from the carbide.

That was the only time I got a report card and got the slipper.

Prefects were allowed to give you the slipper, and he did. I don't blame him, it ruined his jacket. I did a get a report card from one of the Masters, I forget what it was for, and you had to get it signed in every form to say you had been good for a week. Then go down and see the headmaster at the end, and if you had too many black marks on it, you got the cane.

'The other thing, at Assembly in the morning he would frequently say 'Would the boys from the Brightwalton bus report to my study after break.'
or 'Would the boys from the Lambourn train please report...'
One occasion he said 'Would the boys from the Hungerford train please report.'

'What had happened was that somebody had broken a window in the Hungerford train going to school. They had swept all the glass up and chucked it out the window, so there was no glass inside, just an empty window frame. But they glanced out and there was glass on the running board. So the silly fool opened the door of the train and brushed the glass off with his hat just as they were passing a signal box, and he was seen. It was nothing to do with me.
Then there was another occasion when one boy had a brass paperclip in his mouth, someone patted him on the back and he swallowed it, nearly killed him, there was a hell of a row about that. They got it out, and he was alright, actually, he is a parson now, John Pattison.
What else, oh yes, there were the two who were caught on the train doing what they shouldn't have been doing. One of the High School girls and one of the boys. He was so upset and frightened after he was caught, that he went down and put his head on the railway line and was killed!

'They also had a Cadet Force, but Father wouldn't let me go into that. So while all the others had the fun of going off with the Cadet Force, I ended up with extra lessons, while the others were playing soldiers.

'He didn't let me join, he just wouldn't. He'd been in the Army. The other thing was that at the end of the war I wanted to get away from farming and I volunteered for the Fleet Air Arm, for a year I would go in as a trainee, an apprentice. I really wanted to fly. But Father wrote to them and said that I was in an exempt occupation, and he wouldn't allow me to go. So I had to stay at home.

'I got to fly eventually, though not so fast as I might have done in the Fleet Air Arm. But I always fancied myself as a Fleet Air Arm Pilot. But there you are, I ended up a hot air balloon pilot..

'I can show you some of my School reports, *'Farming is not on the School Curriculum', he arrives at school tired and falls asleep during class.'*
During the war you could legitimately be kept off school, so sometimes I didn't go to school. Potato picking, harvesting or haymaking.

'During the war you couldn't get new buses and the old buses were a bit cramped. I remember one Market Day, Thursday morning, when it seemed everyone went into Newbury shopping, we had seventy six on a twenty six seater bus! I think there were four of us standing on the bottom step, and one sitting on the mudguard outside. The hill from Winterbourne up to Snelsmore Common, on many occasions, used to be too much, and the children had to get out and walk up it. We definitely walked that day!
'The market was in the same place as it is now in Newbury - outside the Corn Exchange, and the cattle market was on the same day as well. There weren't so many cars around then and everyone went in by bus.
Hedges used to run a carrier service, taking orders for the shops. On one occasion, he had to pick up a new bicycle for

someone, and he strapped it on the top of the carrier wagon, and when he got back to Brightwalton, it wasn't there! They drove back into Newbury and came across it hanging from a tree over the road! I don't know how damaged it was.

That was the time when Harry Chandler, a neighbouring farmer, was just coming back from market and the trailer came off! He was going round a corner, it came off and went straight on luckily, it didn't hit anything.'

Jo, David's wife, said that David had a very hard childhood, she added that he had all the material things, but missed his natural Mother. David's stepmother naturally favoured her own sons over David, and so he always had to prove himself. His Father was always strict, but more so with David than his stepbrothers. Bill Liddiard was hard but fair, he'd worked his way up and he expected his sons to work hard too, but he could also be stubborn and pigheaded at times..

Jo added *'The only thing I can say is that he had a very hard childhood, a very hard Father, self made man, and they usually are, do you know what I mean? Seriously they are, because they have had to rough it themselves to make money, and so he was very hard on David.'*

David interrupted,

'Someone asked me once *'What's your best asset? Why do you do it?'*

I said I think I suffer from an inferiority complex, which makes me have to do better to be equal.'

'It makes you boastful too' added Jo seriously *'it does, because you have always got to be ahead of everybody.'*

'Yeah yeah, but the other thing which is why I've got on so well, is because I have an ability to turn my set-backs to my advantage. If something goes wrong, I think well what can I salvage out of this?'

'The opportunity of a lifetime is just the lifetime of an

41

opportunity.' was his answer.

David has a wealth of old sayings which he adapts, and can always bring into conversations to lighten a subject. He credits old Mrs Wolford with some of the sayings.

'The grass over the fence is always greener, but it takes just as much cutting.'
'Still waters run deep, but they all stink if you stir them up.'
'All these old sayings, it was one of the ways they had of getting a message across, or teaching country logic. Country logic unfortunately is gone today
Another thing was that I never connected these teachings with ballooning until I got a bit of a down draught flying one day. They always said that your crops would get a down draught eight times the height of the tree at the side into the field.

'If you have a tree at the side of a field which is one hundred foot high, then eight hundred feet into the field is where you will find the wind damaged crop, the curl-over you see.
It's the same effect when ballooning, and you come over a hill say – five hundred foot high - then in four thousand feet you're going to hit the ground, so you had better do something about it!

'Did I tell you about the accident I had when I was about fifteen years old?

'I was repairing the elevator with a mechanic and I was standing by it and it had this old horse gear on it. We'd converted it to run with an old Lister engine. I didn't realise I was standing astride the spindle. It took me trousers off!
It nearly took all me wedding tackle with it too. I had to go to the doctors for about ten days having 'it' bandaged up. Of course when he examined it and bandaged it, it needed two

42

yards, by the time I got home I only needed half a yard!'
David chuckles now, but I bet he didn't then.

'That was when I was about fifteen years old, I thought the
end of the world had come!
Oh the other thing that happened that year- you can see my
nose is not straight? - Well, I was trying to start a Fordson
Tractor. You hold the starting handle with your thumb tucked
so that if it kicks, the starting handle doesn't break your
thumb.
That's all right unless you are pushing down at the time and it
kicks back and hits you in the face!   That's happened to me
twice.
Once it kicked and hit me in the face and broke my nose, and
the other time it got me on the shoulder and threw me back.

Our first tractor was a Fordson, and the other was a Case LA,
a much bigger tractor.   It was the Case LA that chucked me
about five yards and I landed flat on my back!
I remember lying there, blood pouring out of my head, my
shirt ripped, and the tractor driver coming over and looking
down at me.
After a second he says 'Is yers dead you?'
I might have been. God it hurt!'

David remembered that the best place to go to get a decent
meal in 1943 and 1944, was to the American camps, and he
also remembers going up to Welford and lying in the back of
a DC3 and getting a flight.
There were a lot of Waco Gliders, they were sent over to the
UK, to Welford in vast boxes and made up over here.
The boxes were then used as living accommodation for the
troops, most of the woods around Lambourn had these boxes
in.   At the end of the war, the locals squabbled between
themselves such a lot about who owned them, that the

43

Commander built a big bonfire and burned the lot!

In fact the barn at Bradfords Farm (*Marsh Benham*), the wall at the back of the loft part was made from salvaged Waco Boxes.

He remembers watching the aerial rehearsals for the VE Day celebrations, all the planes practising their flypast for Churchill & Eisenhower.

'On VE Day, I was the only one left on the farm working, I had to milk the cows, Shorthorns then.

Everyone was celebrating, and the pubs were open all the time. I was only about fifteen years old. I was the only one who couldn't dodge out of work 'cos I lived on site!

'I know that one Christmas morning, I had to get Father out of bed at half past eight, but I'd been working since five, I'd done all the milking myself. The cowman hadn't turned up. He'd got drunk the night before and never turned up for work on Christmas morning. I needed some help at half past eight to finish up.

'The animals rely on you. You're more or less tied to a cows tail when you're a cowman.

I think it was AG Street who made a comment about a cow that it was a dirty mistake, you pour grass in one end and it comes out the other -then you have to shovel it all up!

In those days it was really hard work. You used to have to shovel it all up with shovels, no machines, no tractors. Oh you used to have to pick every bit up, wash the yard, sweep it down.

'You had to know a lot about their welfare as well.

You had to feed them, drench them, cut their toes, do all sorts of things.

Some of these cows, their hooves, toenails used to grow and

used to turn up. If you didn't do anything about it, it would be really bad. It could have crippled them.

The vet used to come in and do it, and it was a hell of a job. They used to go through hacksaw blades like they were going out of fashion. Of course nowadays they have special equipment to restrict the cow's movements.

One day the vets were in, and I was watching, and I had an idea.

I said *'I can do a better job than that!'*

They said *'How?'*

I went into the workshop, I got a bit of a hay rake tine heated it up, and made a sort of a sharp knife out of it. I put a bit of rubber hosepipe on the end so it didn't jar your hand.

They used to get the cows to stand on a big plank of wood.

I used to put the knife where you wanted to cut it, went pow, with a big hammer, cut it off, then ran away before the cow kicked!

The vets liked the idea so much, I had to make them one each. They thought it was a wonderful idea for chopping cows toenails with!

That was going back a few years.

In those days our vets were Carter and Curtis. They used to have a practice in Hungerford. Then Curtis died, and Carter carried on, on his own.

Then Carter was coming into Stockcross one day, he was going out for a drink, someone drove across the road in front, and he hit them sideways on, and I think they both had broken necks. Him and his wife, killed just like that. So we went to another vet. Crawshaw and Galbraith, from Newbury.

The cows had to be all tuberculin tested, every one had to be injected twice, and then got in two days later to see if they had showed any reaction.

I remember we were doing it at Northfield one day, just after we had got married. Jo had made a cold lunch for me and the vets, and everybody stopped.

We had just got a little nine inch black and white television, it was Father's old one, he'd bought a new one. Blimmin' great set, with a little screen on it.

Anyway, we came in for lunch, and the vets said *'What's the cricket score?'*

So we turned it on, and it was the day that Evans went in and hit about - oh I don't know how many, but it was a real slog, and he scored runs like it was going out of fashion.

The vet turned to me and said *'I'm not going out until Evans is out, they can wait for me!'*

I think I can safely say that that was the only time that television came before farming!

'As I said, until we came to Shefford in 1946, we never had electricity on the farm. Only little Lister engines for working the vacuum pump.

We had the boiler, and we had to light the boiler, throw all the wood on to get it up to steam for sterilising. We had to do that every morning.

Miss Matthews, then later, Miss Beck, used to come around, test the milk equipment, take swabs and take them back, and if your cell count was too high, they'd be down on you like a ton of bricks.

We cleaned and sterilised once a day. There weren't the chemicals in those days, everything had to be stripped down and cleaned once a week.

All the teat cups had to be pulled to pieces, scrubbed, and the rubber used to stretch so you used to have to cut strips of rubber off so that you got the same tension on them. The milk pumps had to be pulled down, cleaned. The cooler had to be taken down and washed.

'There were long brushes to go through the tubes, a steriliser, you had to get the hot water, clean everything, sterilise it with steam. You had to let the steam go through it to kill all the bugs.

Nowadays, they just circulate the steam with chemicals and they only strip it down once a year.

The advances are so much. You used to milk eighty or ninety cows and if you got a hundred and forty gallons of milk a day, you were lucky.

Nowadays, I mean, my son is milking double that amount and producing a thousand gallons a day. It's down to breeding as well.

In those days, we started off with buckets, carried the milk out, and tipped it through the cooler. Then we had a pipeline put in, the milk went through straight into the cooler. That was marvellous.

After that, nowadays, it goes straight through into a bulk tank. When we used to do it, it went through over an open cooler, with water running through it to cool the milk. When the churn was full, you rolled it out and chucked it up onto the milk stand.

Nowadays, it goes straight through a filter into a big tank, is chilled down and is picked up every other day. It then goes straight into the tanker when it comes round, you don't need a team of men any more.

'All the milk that we got when I was a boy, had to be chucked up onto a stand a few feet high so that they could throw them up onto the lorries when they arrived. I was fifteen then, and I could chuck a twelve gallon churn up onto the milk stand. I was quite strong.

'I was used to carrying a hundred weight and a quarter of cake from the granary, across to the dairy, up three steps and then tipping it in the top of the hopper to feed the cows with at milking time.

They were light hessian sacks, and I always remember the

47

dust used to go down the back of your neck, most uncomfortable. So what you would do, was get an old flour sack, invert on your head like a hood, to stop the dust going down your neck.

'Then there was loading the corn, that came in sacks of two hundredweight, or two and a quarter hundredweight. If you were short of sacks, which you sometimes were, you used to fill the wheat sacks up as high as you could. That used to make your knees bend when you had two and a half hundredweight on your back.

'They tried to get me one day. They started to run the sacks onto the elevator as fast as they could. I thought there were only two of them, but Bert told me there were three of them doing it.

My job was to take them off the top and stack them. On that occasion, I stacked six tons in twenty minutes, which was sixty sacks. That was three two hundredweight sacks a minute that I was taking off the elevator. That was lifting, stacking, and being there to pick the next one off the elevator. Twenty seconds a sack, I'll tell you what, it was hot work, but they never beat me!

'Corn, until quite recently, always used to go off the farm in sacks. There was no bulk handling of corn. I suppose bulk handling, as far as we were concerned, didn't come in until, Ooh - I don't know, we didn't have it at Marsh Benham, I think we had it when we took on Ashmansworth, that must have been about 1970. That was the first time we had bulk handling on the farm. Everything else was in sacks until then.

'In 1967 on my thirty-eighth birthday, I was lifting a two hundredweight sack of Barley when the floor of the trailer,

which had recently been replaced, gave way and I fell through the floor .
The boards had been replaced with elm which is a very short grain. They shouldn't have used elm, it should have been oak.

'I seriously damaged my back and had to have a Spinal Fusion operation on the bottom four vertebrae on my birthday.   In actual fact I had three operations in three weeks.
The first being the Spinal Fusion at the Nuffield Hospital, the second one for appendicitis, then a third when the stitches went.
Despite all the warnings, I was walking after seven weeks and back on the farm in thirteen weeks.   During that period I learned how to run a thousand acre farm by telephone. Quite a birthday present wasn't it?
The following Tuesday after I'd had my back done, my leg went dead, that was thrombosis, and the following Sunday I had a stomach ache. The worst place to see a Doctor is in a hospital.   You know, they don't bother.

'By the time I saw the Doctor it was Monday evening, and they suddenly realised I had acute appendicitis.
I was coming round, and I was on a plaster bed. They were examining me you see, and one of them stuck his finger up my 'you know'!
He said *'Coo! That made you go red!'*
I said 'I was a blimmin' virgin until you did that!'
Anyway they got the knives out to do a cut, and then they got the notes down and said *'Oh, we can't!'*
'Why not?'
'You're on Warfarin! We daren't cut you, you'll bleed to death!
A slight complication.
'When did you have your last Warfarin?'
'About two hours ago I suppose.'
'Well we'll have to give you an injection to thicken your blood

up.'
'What's in that then? '
'Well it's snake venom actually!'

'So they gave me rat poison and snake venom, and they didn't kill me!'

'I always remember the next day, they came along, and said they were taking me down to the Churchill hospital, from the Nuffield.
I was in this special bed, that they had made, a bit like a Mummy case, that had been made especially for my back operation.
My ankles stuck out one end, and my head the other, and they only put the top on when they wanted to move me.

'They wheeled the bed down the corridor, out of the door and there was a bloody great furniture van! They wheeled me up into the furniture van. The bed was roped in, and there were two nurses, and four hospital porters.
They took me down to the Churchill, wheeled me into the operating theatre in my special bed.

'I remember that when they had done my back, I could remember that I had been conscious that I'd stopped breathing. First they gave me an injection to anaesthetise me and then they gave me an injection of Scrolene to paralyse all the muscles. Scrolene is the stuff the Kiara Indians use in poison arrows.

'They gave me an injection, and I can remember thinking *'I can't breathe! I can't breathe!*
I was still conscious of the fact that **'I can't breathe, I can't move, I can't open my mouth! How can I tell them I've**

stopped breathing! It was a frightening experience you know! So when they came to do my appendix, I said I didn't want to be put out, and told them what the problem was.

'Do it on a local!'

They wouldn't do it on a local. When I came round, the nurse said to me,

*'You **were** worried when they gave you the injection. It took two hospital porters to get your fingers off my hand. You broke my hand where you gripped it so tight!'*

She said *'You are strong aren't you?'*

Anyhow I had the operation, and went back to the ward.

'The next day the nurse came in. *'Here's your lunch.'*

It was baked beans and sausages. I said 'Are you sure I can eat this? I've just had my appendix out.'

'Oh it'll be perfectly alright.'

So I ate it, cos I always do what I am told. – well, alright, I ate it because I was hungry. God, did I have constipation! Ooh I had it like nobody's business. So they had to give me suppositories! Of course I was in this plaster bed, so the nurse had difficulty, I felt sorry for her actually, and she said *'tell me when it's in the right place, and I'll push it in!'*

I said *'I've heard that before, but it's the first time a girl has ever said that to me!'*

'I had the operation on the Tuesday, and the stitches came out the following Tuesday. That evening, someone came in to see me, and I coughed.

I said *'For Christ's sake get the nurse, my stomachs fallen out!* There was blood every where, and remember I was still in this bed, and they got me a 'many tailed bandage'.

'To cut a long story short, it was the night of the staff party, so there were not too many happy chappies with me, because they had to open the operating theatre up for an emergency

51

operation. By the time they had finished and washed up, it was about half past one in the morning, so quite a few of them missed the staff party.

'But I've always been glad that I've been a blood donor since I was eighteen. I had 14 pints of blood during those three weeks. Its rather nice, I must have given a few gallons in my life, and this time I needed it as well. You know you're helping someone who needs it.

'I actually 'walked ' out of the hospital seven weeks after the operation.. It was supposed to have been sixteen weeks. I suppose it was quick because I was fit from farming. I remember walking down the road, they were shooting on the farm .This is when I got home. I went and watched from the field where I first flew from, not right down at the bottom, but the field we used to use as a car park. I watched the shooting for a time, but I had a hell of a job to make it back up the road. I really had overdone it. I hadn't been home more than two or three days. Anyhow, I went back to work thirteen weeks after that operation.

'Brightwalton was a mixed farm, pigs, cattle and arable. In those days you needed a lot of workers to run a farm. I remembers the last harvest, we had seventy six ricks and there were thirty six people working. But I don't know, things have changed, all the camaraderie has gone out of farming. Not so many people working on farms now. You are on your own in a big tractor. Everything is specialised. It really has changed. We used to work as a team.

'Geoffrey Wallis, a farmer, said to me the other day, after I'd got him to stand for local election, *I'm going to quite enjoy it, farms have got very lonely places nowadays. You never meet anybody, it's nice to get out and start talking to people.* '

He's right, farms are very lonely places today.

'At Brightwalton, we used to have a lot of outdoor pigs, the heavy hogs, all about eight score, which went to factories for pork pies and lard. There were not the numbers that you see today, no electric fences that you see today. All the pigs were tethered, and we used to have pig arcs that you put out in the field. The sow used to wear a harness, and a long chain. You used to see these great big circles where they would go around and eat the grass. You would fix it so that she could just get into the hut but not behind the hut. In those days it was Wessex Saddlebacks, and we used to cross them with a Large White boar. We used to fatten the pigs in the Danish piggery, then take them down to Calne in Wiltshire, or Trowbridge to sell. We used to have an old army lorry which we converted to take them, and I used to drive that down.

'Then we got Land Rovers, and we got two trailers. My brother Peter used to take the two wheeler trailer and I used to take the four wheeler.
When I look back, I had about two and a half ton on that Land Rover. When you used to drive that far, down to Calne or Trowbridge, the first thing you wanted to do was to pull in and have a rest.

'When I think about it, how we never killed ourselves with all that weight going down Marlborough Hill, I'll never know.
Peter had a Collie, a white border Collie, funny dog. As a matter of fact he had a go at my son Richard once who had to have four stitches under his eye. He used to go everywhere, and if you were taking a load of bales, he would sit on top of the load, and as you went under trees, he used to bite them, and snap at the branches. One day he bit at this branch, held on too long, and we looked round and there was this dog hanging off a branch over the road!

53

'Another time, John was driving Peter, and they were driving through Weston, the village next to Shefford, and they came up behind a guy with no indicators. This bloke slowed down and put his hand out to wave them on and indicate he was slowing, and as they went past, the dog bit his hand!

'Another time, they were going down through Marlborough, just the other side, and Peter was in front, I was behind. This old chap was biking along quietly on the road minding his own business. As Peter went by the dog leaned out and barked suddenly. He didn't actually bite him, but it was right by his ear, and this poor bloke went straight in the ditch, bike and all! You can laugh now.

Another time, brother John and I were going all the way to Trowbridge. He took his Grandfather with him. We dropped the pigs off and we were on the way back and got to Devizes. We stopped there to have a beer. We drove in, stopped and John came over and said *'Where's Gramps then?'*

'Well he came down with you!' I said.

'Oh he got out of my vehicle and was going to come back with you!' John exclaimed.

We'd left him in Trowbridge!. So we unhitched the trailers, and went back to find him. He was walking up the road towards us. It was a laugh.

'I used to hate buying pigs. My brother John was the animals man, I was never an animal man. I was a machinery one, I could mend anything.

'One day Father bought some pigs in Newbury Market, and we were loading them up and one escaped. It ran all up Market Street, towards the railway station, into the Goods yard. Round the Goods yard, over the railway line, back up Market Street! I couldn't cut it off. Round to Bartholomew

54

Lunch during hay making

Farming in the 1950's

Turning the 'emps'

Street, and I just caught it in the foyer of the Regal Cinema. If the doors had been open it would have been down under the seats and you can imagine what mayhem that would have caused! I threw myself on top of this pig, and I was lying on top of it, and we were actually both exhausted.

Someone came up and said *'You're cruel to that pig!'*

I looked round and said *'Cruel? Here you are. You take it back!'*

'Another time a heifer got away, and I got in the truck and chased after it, got ahead of it up by the Rokeby Arms. I stood in front of it to stop it. Of course, that was a stupid thing to do. A bull is one thing, but this was mad heifer, and she came straight at me! I put my hands out and grabbed it by the horns. As it went by I twisted it round because I had hold of her horns, and I put my feet out in front, and I was being dragged along!

'The hobnails on my boots were getting hotter and hotter. I managed to twist her horns and head around and stopped it and we tied it to a telegraph pole. Then someone came along and untied it! I had to catch it again. It came straight at me again, but I had picked up a large stick, and hit it over the head. That stopped it! It was going to be it or me at that point! We got it back in the trailer, it had quietened down by then.

'It is a shame that Newbury Cattle Market is gone. When you went there, you did a deal, and shook hands on it and that was more binding than one of these solicitors things. In those days, on Market day, the pubs were open all day. The Dolphin, The New Market Inn, - that's not there any more, it used to be where the little car park is on the corner of the Kennet Centre near Beatties. There was a cafe just near there, where you could go and have meat and two veg. Beyond there, where Oakes Bros used to be, there was a big building which used to be Walls Ice Cream. Of course during the war when there wasn't any Walls Ice Cream, Dreweatts took it over as a Sale Room. That was where Dreweatts used to hold their furniture sales. It's been pulled down now.

'I have a book, 'Record of an Aeronaut' about Bacon, the balloonist who lived in Cold Ash, and there is an aerial photograph of Newbury taken in 1900, and where the Cattle Market was , was still a field then. Another photograph in the book is when he took off from the gasworks and it shows that area there, and was completely different.

'Going back to the Market, the pubs were open all day, but you never saw anyone really drunk. They had the Spring Sales, people were taking cattle in which had been in all the Winter, and as they were going out again on the grass. There were two auctioneers, Dreweatts, and Neates, two separate firms then. They would have their Sales on alternate weeks. Then there would be the Pig Market, the Calf Market and the Cattle Market. There were three separate auctions. Thursday was 'Pig & Paper Day', when the Newbury Weekly News came out, and when the market was held. On a Spring Sale day, there would be people going round the market with bakers' baskets, big square baskets filled with lovely crusty bread and big lumps of cheese.
It was the staple diet anyway, years ago. The farmworkers used to take out bread and cheese to work.
They would take an old Cottage loaf, pull it to pieces, cut a bit off with a knife if they wanted, no butter of course, Their meal was bread, cheese, and cold tea. If they wanted a hot meal, they would take a raw onion, or a pickled onion. That's where the 'Ploughman's Lunch' comes from that you eat in pubs now.
But the pickled onions you get in the pub today, are not like the pickled onions that my Grandmother used to make. She always put a lot of brown sugar in with them. They were

56

sweet and really brown. You went into a cottage garden in the old days and there would be rows of shallots. That's what they pickled, shallots, not onions.

'I've had some shitty times - literally. There used be at Northfield, a big tank in one of the old farm buildings to catch all the waste from the stables before it went into the soakaway.
We put the cows in this building and of course cows drop a lot more than horses and it sealed all the joints up. It was about two foot deep at the bottom of this tank, and we had to get it out. We dipped out what we could with buckets. Then I was sent down to get the hard stuff out, and shovel it into the buckets! There was only a little square hole at the top for me to get down into it. It was about eight foot deep and about eight foot round. So I was shovelling into buckets, and the other chaps were pulling it up and wheeling it away in wheelbarrows. When they pulled it up, it used to dribble down on top of me.

'Now one day, Miss Beck, who was the Milk Marketing Board person who came round and took all the swabs, and checked you were keeping everything clean, came round to see the cowman.
'Is Mr Liddiard around?'
'Yes, he's here!'
'Where?'
'Down the hole Miss!'
She left it that day, came back another. It was a mucky job, it really was. Farming always will be.'

Farming

'It's a lonely place on a farm now. There is no camaraderie like there used to be. There are no teams needed. That's progress.

Farming is lonely, if there wasn't the two way radio, farmers wouldn't talk to anybody.

In the forties and fifties, there used to be two or three of you ploughing, now, when you stop for lunch, there's only you! No longer do you all gather round toasting sandwiches on the exhaust manifold of the tractor, and heating your bottle of tea up in the radiator.

Nowadays, you've got rubber tyres on the tractors, you can jack up the plough and go home, I mean the speed they go nowadays is amazing! We never went home for meals, it was too far, and there were no pick-up trucks. No means of getting there other than walking. All the tractors had steel wheels or steel tracks on them. There were a few tractors with rubber tyres, but not many.

When you were ploughing, you always had your steel wheels on, and the rubber tyres went on in the Summer if you had them.

'When we used to stop for lunch, we used to roll the radiator blind up, get it really hot, take the radiator cap off, which was the size of a tea plate, and stand the bottle of tea in there. We used to have the old lemonade bottles with the screw tops. We obviously had to unscrew the top first, then when you got to the end of the field, you had hot tea!

The tractor was really hot, and you could stand four half sandwiches on the manifold. So you had hot tea and toasted sandwiches for lunch!

'I used to drive an Allis M Crawler with a five furrow trailer plough on it. There were no hedgecutters in those days, and the hedges were pretty scraggy. I reckoned I could light a fire using stuff in the hedge. You started it with dried cow parsley

58

or stinging nettles or something like that, then the dead twigs and any dead wood. I would stop, and if you didn't have any matches, you had a bit of paper in your pocket, dip it in the petrol tank, take a plug lead off and spark across to get a light, to light a fire.

'I could start a fire, and have it ready to toast in fifteen minutes, I used to cut a stick off a nut tree for toasting fork.

'I never really wanted to be a farmer. I wanted to do engineering, something mechanical, be a pilot, fly planes. But, having had the die cast, I had no choice. I was a farmer, and what ever you decide to do, you have to do it properly or leave it alone.

'Because there are not so many farms nowadays, there are not so many Farm Sales, sales of stock.
We always used to go along to farm sales, see if we could get a bargain or something you wanted.
I've only had one farm sale, that was when we left Ashmansworth. Everyone comes hoping to get a bargain. There is a rule of thumb that you never bought stuff that had been recently painted and done up, you always bought stuff that you had been to see working.
They have two sales a year up at the Newbury Showground, they held them at the racecourse at one point.
They are sort of collective sales now, where people just put stuff in because they don't want it anymore. Sometimes you get a bargain, sometimes you get something home and find it doesn't work!
They sell everything, from the small handtools up to the combines.
Oh yes. When I came out of Ashmansworth, what I sold at the sale came to £76,000. Well, there were two combines, I was a bit disappointed actually, I only got about £17,000 each. That

was half the sale.

'Some of the big boys now have them on lease for a year. A combine now is more than £250,000. They're all electronic and everything, but a lot can go wrong with them.
I remember our first Combine Harvester when we were at Shefford, it came by train in two big boxes. I helped to hand-wind the crane to get it off. There were two gears, one to swing the crane, and one to make it go up and down.
The Fitter came from Bakers of Compton. The machine was a Massey 21, came with a complete set of tools for construction, two sets of belts, all the nuts and bolts and spares to keep you going for a couple of years.
When we ordered it was only £750. But it turned out to be £950 delivered. To put it in perspective, in those days you could buy an acre of land for £50!   I reckon we were probably the third or fourth farm in the area to have a combine.
It definitely cut down labour costs, compared to when I was sixteen and up at Brightwalton Farm .
You had to apply to the government to get a permit for a combine or any other big tractor because all machinery was in short supply.

'The greatest advances in farming, I think, were between 1945 and 1985. They are a lot more advanced now. I'm very glad I was farming when I was.
I mean, in 1945 if you got twenty five hundredweight to the acre, it was a good crop! You didn't have the sprays, you didn't have the hybrid varieties with higher yields.
In those days, we had a coke fired dryer for the grain. it was a Kennedy & Kemp Dryer. It caught fire occasionally, I remember being caught one time when I was trying to move some burning dust, someone opened the hatch and poured water all over me!

60

The modern fertilisers were just coming in, combine drills were just coming in, which really made the downlands.

Then they had better ways of putting fertilisers on, phosphates and potash were going down the spout with the corn so you weren't wasting any.

'Then from the combine drills, it went on to the close spacing drills.

Close spacing drills are where they used to drill with nine inch spacing, then it was cut down to four and a half inch spaces. The seed, where it used to be dribbled out, was brought out more precisely and more evenly spaced.

Then of course they started tramlining, which was leaving two spouts shut off, the width of a tractor's wheels apart, so that you had a specific place to drive your tractor. The distance between your rows of tramlines would be set up to the width of your sprayers and fertiliser spreaders.

'So once you'd ploughed the field, worked and drilled it, the tractor just went up the tramlines so you didn't compact the ground. I suppose, having done that, the fertiliser spreaders got wider, so your tramlines got further apart there was less ground run on. This had a knock on effect, because your ground was not compacted, so when you ploughed it, it crumbled better because it was in better condition.

'Going back to ploughing. In the nineteen forties, there were no hydraulic ploughs so you had to leave a big headland, and you ploughed all through the year- well - all through the Winter rather, to get it ready to plant corn in the Spring. Consequently, it was wet when you were ploughing.

'Then the ploughs got bigger, they had hydraulics so that you could lift them up. You could get two way ploughs which could go up and down the field, and whereas in the olden days you had a furrow press which pressed four furrows and they

61

looked so nice. The ploughing matches were all judged on standing furrows up and all the rest of it.

'Today, your ploughs are so designed that they break the ground as they plough it, and a furrow press is not something that makes each furrow look nice, it crumbles the whole lot up so that you can actually drill straight on top of your ploughed ground.
'There are no furrows to go through, no dips in the ground like there used to be with the old emps, where you used to plough both ways and have a sort of channel down the field. Now you plough one way so your fields are smooth, you can go across them whichever way you like.
Basically, the soil structure is so much better today because of that.

'Then of course another advance was that you used to have to bale all the straw behind the combine, then they stopped you burning straw if you didn't want it.   So manufacturers brought in these straw choppers which were built into the combine, so you can plough straight onto the spread straw.
The whole thing is getting faster and faster, and better and better.

'When I was learning to plough, if you had a five furrow plough, it was a big one.   Now you get eight, ten furrow ploughs, high speed ploughs on big rubber wheeled tractors. Chaps sit in air-conditioned cabs now, we used to be out in the cold. There were no cabs , never heard of a cab on a tractor.
If it was wet, you sat there in the rain. You had a 'West o' England' sack tied round your shoulders and one across your lap, they were big thick hessian sacks, and they kept the rain off.
If you had to repair anything, or change a shear, you had to get off in the mud to do it and we used to work right through

the Winter weather in those days.

'For that kind of weather we wore rubber boots and if it was cold, your feet were very cold.
I remember one day, we had stopped to have our mid-morning break. It was a very cold day and there were four of us ploughing.
I was driving the Crawler, and another chap was driving the 10-20. Bert, who still works for me now, was standing by the 10-20, holding his boot over the exhaust which used to come out at about belly button height. He was holding his boot there to warm it up.
Now the 10-20 had an advance/retard ignition on it. If you advanced it-retarded it and then advanced it, it would backfire. One of the chaps went and advance-retard-advanced the ignition, the tractor backfired and Bert's boot flew across the field about 15 yards!
When he went to pick it up, it was split from top to bottom! He had to get his knife out, get some string and lace his boot up the back to keep it on.

'The 10-20 was the best tractor, it would start up on an egg cup of petrol.
I remember, and I was only about thirteen at the time, during the war, I was sent off to fetch this tractor which was about two miles away. When I got there, there was no petrol in the tank, which meant I would have to walk back home two miles, and back again.
The petrol was in a round tank, about five inches round and fifteen inches tall. Fuel in those days was not always clean, so the pipe inside used to stand about three inches up from the bottom of the petrol tank, so that if any dirt or water got in there, it didn't go down the petrol pipe.

'I looked in and there was a little petrol in there but below the outlet. As the only water I had was what I was carrying myself, I peed in it just enough to raise the petrol and get it into the carburettor. I started it up, changed it straight over to the TVO *(Tractor Vaporising Oil)* and drove it back to the farm. So it was 'My P' not 'BP' that started it!

The radiator cap on the 10-20s was big, and you were always pouring water in to them. Nowadays you don't think about pouring water into tractors, but then it was always leaking it or boiling it away. You had a radiator blind on the front so that you could keep the tractor warm so it vaporised the TVO.

'The fuel had to be taken up to the field. I remember building a trailer for the fuel. I made it from three fifty gallon barrels and the front axle of a car, welded them up myself, got a pump which came off a Wellington bomber, a manual hydraulic pump, it lasted ages.

'I got the pump because they were breaking the bombers up after the war near Little Rissington and I saw one of the chaps who was breaking them up. He gave me the pump which I fitted it on the front of my tanker trailer so we could pump the fuel into the tractors. It's a different story nowadays.

We used to build the ricks in those days, so I learned to thatch corn ricks. Nowadays, I could build a rick if I had to, but I wouldn't be that good at it because we stopped building them when I was about sixteen.

That was when we had a Morris 8 Tourer which I used to drive around to pick up the chaps who were in the thrashing gang. I was the head of the thrashing gang.

Our Case LA tractor drove the thrasher by means of a great big long flat belt. You put all the sheaves up in the ricks, then you chucked them down onto the thrasher, I fed it in by hand.

'Bit different nowadays. I mean, you used to have a gang of people working all day, and you would probably get ten ton of grain. That would be with two on the rick, one on the thrasher, one on chaff and cavings. Then one or two taking the straw away, one taking the grain away. Seven minimum in a thrashing gang working all day for ten ton of grain.

Nowadays, they will go out on a combine, which does all that in about half an hour. Three quarters on an hour at the outside to fill a ten ton trailer, depending on the crop of course. In the old days, they would be wheeling two hundredweight sacks across rough ground in a field to where the lorry would come and pick them up, then chucking everything up on the lorry by hand.

When you look back at the work we did in those days, it was amazing.

The dust was unbelievable sometimes, barley was itchy, but wheat had dust.

'The last year we were up at Brightwalton, we put up seventy six ricks. Then for the rest of the year (1946), after we left Brightwalton, we spent the whole Winter thrashing corn ricks. You used to get through about one a day. We had our own thrashing machine, and we used to do about four ricks a week.

We got about a 110 to a 130 sacks of corn off each rick.

My job, as I said, was to feed the thrasher, I used to stand at the top near the thrashing drum which was a big revolving cylinder which you chucked the sheaves into, and the straw came out one way and the corn came out the other way.

Some of the straw was baled, and some went up the elevator into a big rick.

'You could make corn ricks square or round. We used to make them square.

You put the outer layer round with the butts outwards like a bottom layer of bricks. The next layer went round a bit farther in, with the butts inwards to even it up. Then you built up the four walls and then fill the middle in.

When you got to putting the roof on, you built the middle up and you put the inside sheaves in first so that the outside ones were leaning outwards, so that any water would run off. There was an art to it, the old guys did it really well.

'I was loading sheaves onto the trailers when I was eight.

You had to load the sheaves onto the trailer so that they didn't fall off on the way to the rick. If they fell off on the way, you were in trouble!

So I suppose I'd learned how to build low ricks on the trailers, the sheaves had to stay on there crossing all the roads till they got to where the rick was being built.

There were various sorts of trailers   Some flatbeds, some Berkshire wagons, some Wiltshire wagons - they're the ones with the big arches in and you built the middle up. Every one was different, I can't remember them all.

'We got filthy.   You used to come in at night absolutely black, and I was allergic to dust.   Not fresh dust, but thrashing, I used to sneeze and sneeze and sneeze.   So with having had pneumonia when I was young, I developed a touch of 'Farmer's Lung' as they call it.

'Barley is very itchy, and -funny this- if you were building a rick and putting barley into a stack, it had to be dry when it went in. You could actually put wheat into ricks when it was wet. But barley would go mouldy.

We've built wheat ricks during thunderstorms.   But when you took them out, the dust was unbelievable.

Barley wouldn't dry out like wheat, barley straw was softer, wheat was very course, very hard. It used to prickle and stab you, and all the thistles were amongst it too because there were no sprays in those days to kill them.

66

'Before combines, you used to have to go round chocking up, or stooking, whatever you like to call it, to start it drying. I started doing that when I was about eight as well.

I remember there were three wheat ricks down the bottom of Long Ground. It was the year we left the farm, and we had to go back up to the farm after we had handed it over to Edward Whedbourne.

The dust that came off them was unbelievable, I'll never forget those ricks. You could stand on the thrasher and look down, and you couldn't see anyone on the ground below, eight foot down, it was that thick. When you coughed at night when you got home, it was all black.

It's no wonder that so many farmers have bad chests.

'My Father said the Brightwalton was the best wheat farm he had, the ground was really good for wheat.

Barley was grown basically for pig feed or for malting, and wheat was basically for bread, flour and bran.

I mean there's another advance that has gone on. When I was farming, the last thing you fed to a cow was wheat, you never fed any wheat to a cow. If you ground it up, it formed a paste in their stomachs and they couldn't digest it. If you gave it to them whole, it would swell up and kill them. You'd also really get into trouble if you ever let a horse eat any grain off a shock of wheat because it would swell up inside them. Now, you use whole wheat, treated with Caustic Soda, left for two days, mixed with silage and feed it to milking cows.

'Horses were very important, they were the early tractors really. When you stopped for your tea, or your lunch, you would never eat your lunch until you'd fed the horse.

You used to take the nosebag out there for the horses, and put it on the horse before you sat down to have your own food.

You used to have these big bags, which were full of straw, oats, bran, hay, all chopped up. You used to have a straw

67

chopper which chopped it up for them which was a big set of knives on a wheel going round. You used to push it through and it used to chop it up.

You used to make sure they had a drink as well. The water was taken down to the fields in old churns for them.

You can still see all these old wagons, and the horse nosebags and buckets up at White Knights Park, the Museum of Rural Life (Reading).

When we had horses, you had to lead them to make sure the drills were straight. Sometimes you would get a horse that would go straight, but more often you would lead them.

'Another crop we grew then were mangolds, mangel-wurzels. A mangold is like a big juicy swede, orange with a pinky sort of flesh. More water than goodness, but the cows and horses used to like them, chopped up of course.

They differed from turnips and swedes because a turnip is white fleshed, a swede is orangey pink, and a mangold is orangey on the outside and pinky white on the inside.

The drills were about eighteen inches apart for mangolds. The trouble with mangold seeds was that there were four or five mangold seeds in each husk, so when they had grown, you had to hoe them out, there were no sprays, you had to hoe them. The fields were eight to ten acres, and people were paid piece work to do it.

You used to have the teams of Irish Dids, or Irish tinkers, that came around. You would pay them so much for a rod, pole or perch, you know.

'The guard would have a stick and he would measure it, marking out the rows, and you would pay them by the rows measured. They went through them once just to single them, and then probably once or twice more to keep the weeds down.

When it came to mangold pulling time, you used to get gangs

out there with an old rip hook, pulling them up, and cutting the leaves off to stop them going slimy in the heap.
They were sharp those rip hooks.'

David showed the white scar on one of his fingers,
'I was about thirteen when I did that.
With mangolds, you used to go along, cut the tops off and chuck them into heaps. Then someone would come along with the old Scotch carts or dungcarts, and take them back They would put them in clamps, covered them with straw, then you dug a trench down each side and chucked the dirt from the trenches on top, and that would keep the frost out. You would use them in the Winter for the cows.
The last year but one at Brightwalton, we had a mangold clamp about a hundred and twenty yards long! A huge heap, lovely mangolds they were that year.
There were competitions at the Newbury Show for mangolds, the ones with the best roots were the winners.

'Mangolds were put into a chopper which would cut them up because you couldn't give the cows anything too big otherwise it would choke them.
You used to chop up straw, and put a layer of chopped mangolds, a layer of straw, and a bit of fishmeal to make it palatable, maybe some groundnuts, rolled oats or linseed cake. You would make a great big pile, layers and layers, so it was all mixed when you took it out. You just took what was needed and you knew what was in it.
We fed that to beef cattle, but today you can buy sacks of cowcake. But for dairy herds you needed to give them protein, so they were given pellets which used to be delivered in one and a quarter hundredweight sacks, one hundred and forty pounds a sack. That would be delivered in the granary, because that was out of the way of the rats!
When I was fourteen, I would carry those, from the granary

to the dairy, then climb three steps to pour them into a hopper. The sacks weighed more than I did then!

'Nowadays, you can't get anything in hundredweight sacks, people aren't supposed to lift them. So it is all half hundred weight, (*twenty five kilos*). I used to lift two and a half hundred weight a go. You had to, you didn't think about it, you just did it in those days. You didn't think *'What a clever chap I am with two hundredweight on my shoulders!* 'you just got rid of it as fast as possible.

'We grew oats for the horses and cows. You could get twenty five to twenty seven hundredweight of oats to an acre. The trouble was, it was a hell of a job to cut them. There are not many oats grown today, but there are not many horses to feed them to anymore.

There are so many advances, thanks to the plant people at Aberwystyth and Cambridge, and advances in plant breeding. Little Joss (wheat) and all that sort of thing, there are so many hybrids now in wheat, and if you don't get three ton of wheat to the acre now, you've got a bad crop.

'Last year we were hearing of over four tons to the acre. Basically, it is a better quality seed, a hybrid seed, the right sort of fertiliser, put in at the right spacing, and the right sprays.

I mean the average farmer does not know everything about sprays and soils, they employ an agronomist. They go around and advise which sprays for which weeds, how to make up soil deficiencies. It is a science today.

There are some farms which have gone back to organic farming. Fine, if they want to go back to organic farming, but the crops won't yield so much. They shouldn't go back completely, there is a level which will suit everybody. Some people go too far by putting too many sprays on, and some

70

people don't.

'You couldn't afford the rents today that people are asking for land if you went organic. It's fine for Prince Charles to say you can do it, but he has an income from elsewhere!
I mean, there is this place over at Hamstead Marshall, the Old Farm Trust, they couldn't make a living at it. When you see how many weeds they are growing, it is amazing
I can remember when I was four or five, we were paid one penny a hundred to pull up docks. They take a bit of getting out of the ground. Then there was thistle cutting, there was a special little tool which we used to go thistle cutting.

'Talking of special little tools, we used to take the horns off the cows, I suppose it was about forty years ago we started sawing them off. We did it because you always had boss cows. They would go around and terrorise the others with their horns.
So we took the horns off, it meant you could put more cows safely in the yard without them being terrorised. otherwise you always had to watch. I mean, it's animal nature, you put too many pigs in a pen, they will eat one another.

'Anyway, to remove the horns, you used to inject them with an anaesthetic just around the horns, and then tie a piece of binder twine or string around it to cut off the blood supply. Some people used a big pair of croppers which wasn't any good, some used saws, which also wasn't easy, you could break a saw blade if the cow moved its' head which made things difficult.

'They came out with a German invention which was a cutting wire like a cheesecutter. You sawed very quickly with it and the heat built up with the friction and sealed the blood vessels as it happened.

71

If you got a cow with a really good blood supply to the horns, it would shoot all over the place and you'd get covered in blood, and you would have a job to stop it. They used to cauterise that with hot metal. A bit of hot iron.

'Nowadays, you just take the growing bud out at birth, or within a week or two, with something a bit like an electric soldering iron. You just inject the area with anaesthetic, and you put this soldering iron to the growing bud and it destroys the blood vessels. So now you get cows with no horns.

'I could have been a vet, I mean in those days, I could give injections and all sorts. If you had a cow with milk fever, you used to inject them with magnesium or calcium. Milk fever is a lack of calcium in the blood and it affects the brain. It was the same symptoms as BSE really. BSE has probably been around for years but no one had ever really analysed it because they've never cut their brains out before.
Cows used to go down with the staggers, we used to call it 'grass staggers'. It is very similar to BSE.
There are many things today which are labelled, which were about years ago. I mean AIDS, has probably been around for years, and cancer, but you died of consumption, or TB, then. Now, they've got so clever that they can tell you what you've got after you are dead.
Whilst farming, we've had beef cattle, dairy cattle, and pigs, in fact, the only animals I have not had much to do with, is sheep.

'I am one of the few people left around who used to harness horses to work on the farm. I used to ride horses a lot, I learnt to ride when I was four. My Father used to take me round the farm sitting in the saddle in front of him, or I would stand behind him, and hang around his neck. My Dad's horse was 'Brown Jack', and I learned to ride on a little strawberry roan called 'Bright Eyes'. There was a little loop on the front of the saddle I used to hold on to so I didn't fall off. I remember the saddle slipping right round once, I was hanging on for what seemed like ages, and it was agony until I was rescued!

'We still had a lot of people working for us during the war. When Bert Cannings, who still works for me now, joined us, he said *'I ain't married you know, I got an 'ousekeeper.'*
'That's alright.'
'Er's married, 'er 'usband's in the Merchant Navy. Comes 'ome occasionally and stops with us.'
'That's alright Bert, the house is down to you.'

'One day, I was working my thrashing gang, and this chap came up the road with two suitcases.
Now we all stopped mid-afternoon for a cup of tea and a smoke. No one was allowed to smoke near the straw when they were thrashing. We were all sitting there away from the straw, and up came this chap with his blue suit and suitcases.
One of the chaps said *'Oo be that then?'*
The old carter, who was about seventy odd, and on chaff and caving, said *'Aagh, that be Bert's wife's husband.'*

'Bert's wife's husband eventually divorced her and Bert lived with her then until his Mother-in-law came to live with them. Whereas in those days you could claim for a Common Law wife, you couldn't claim for a Common Law Mother-in-law!
So somebody advised him to get married. He did it just right, just before April, and he got this great big rebate! '
'Gawd!!' he said *'Look at the money I got back! I wished I'd got married years ago!'*

'Bert was one of these people who were so untidy, wasn't he Jo? Nothing was mended. He had this girlfriend and he was

73

taking her home one day in his car, and they were going around the Clock Tower in Newbury and the door fell open and she fell out! He went round again and picked her up! He was a gentleman then!

'Evidently one day, he'd been at the Blue Boar at Chieveley. Someone said to his wife during the next week 'Oh I saw Bert up at the Blue Boar.'

'So she said to him when he came in, 'You never told me you'd been to the Blue Boar last Sunday!'

'He said' You never asked me! - and if you had of done I wouldn't have told you!'
Bert's eighty seven now, and still works for me up here, drives a Massey 135 that is 35 years old. He is getting on a bit though. I was talking to our policeman the other day and he said 'I think you'll have to stop your man driving very soon.'
'Why's that?' I asked.
'While I was on point duty at the top of the hill coming out of Shefford with that broken down lorry, I put my hand up to stop Bert, he waved back and went straight on!'

'The best one was one couple who lived next door to the family where she had married one of the brothers.
Saw her one day and said 'Oh I hear you're expecting again?'
'Yes' she said 'Jack always wanted one of his own.'
I have a feeling she was shared by the other brothers.

We had another chap working for us. He lived with this woman, had a daughter of sixteen/seventeen, and then he went and married her.
'You got married then? ' I said
'Yeah' he said 'I thought we'd better give Maureen a proper name.'

74

'Three years later, they were divorced. Amazing really, when they weren't married, they lived happily with each other for years. The minute they got married they seemed to fall out all the time.

'Then there were the Landgirls. They came in, in about 1940. They were supposed to be able to drive a tractor. One of ours tipped a tractor on top of herself one day, luckily she wasn't hurt. Another one, took her foot off the clutch and went straight through the side of the barn. They only had about two hours on tractors before they came to us, they didn't have a clue.
We had two good Landgirls during the war. One was a Scottish girl, and the other was a local girl, she is still around actually, Tilly. She lives in Shefford now, married a local lad, Vernon. When this house, College Farm, was a cowshed, he used to deliver cake here when he was working for Doultons.

'Tilly used to live at Chaddleworth, her Father was a woodman for the next estate, they lived in the woods near us. When she first came, she was only about fourteen, and she was employed to look after John, my little brother who was a baby then. She wouldn't stay with us when we moved to Littlecote because she said the house was haunted. But after we moved back to Brightwalton, she came and worked on the farm.
She said that she used to keep in touch with the Scottish landgirl and then all of a sudden it stopped. Tilly had sent her an invitation to her wedding, she had written back and said she was coming, but she never came, and Tilly hasn't heard a thing from her since. But she used to work in a big rubber factory up in Scotland, and there had been a big explosion and fire, and Tilly thinks she might have been killed in that.

'When I was talking to Tilly, she was saying about how she remembered how my Father used to knock me around a bit.

75

She remembered one time when she heard a lot of shouting, and she saw one of my boots come flying out of the door and into the greenhouse, breaking the glass, and then she saw me flying through the air to land in the same place! She certainly witnessed my Father's temper.

'After the war, many of the Landgirls went off to do other jobs, but many married the farmers. For a lot of the farmers, it was a marriage bureau. There are quite a lot of people round who married land girls. John's still got photographs of Tilly on the thrasher with Father telling her what to do and how to hold a prong.

Of course the Americans were all round us during the war. 'David Rabbitts, a farming friend of David Liddiard, remembered the Americans during the war, *'They had all those gliders, Wacos. They used to do their route marches through my farm. Amusing it was, they had two or three lorries following picking them up as they fell out! This was 1941-42. 'They were all training to be dropped by glider into France, but it never happened. We used to get the boxes from the gliders, good wood that was.'*

David Liddiard continued, 'We saw the airfields being built. They nearly built one across our farm at Brightwalton, they surveyed it but they built the one at Welford so they didn't bother with ours. When you go up the hill to Brightwalton from Woolley, at the top of the hill you look right and left, it was flat, it would have been a hell of a long runway, but it wasn't quite in the right direction.
Between Beedon and Peasemore, they had a dummy airfield with red lights and things that they used to switch on at night so that if the Germans came over, they would drop the bombs there instead of Harwell.

'The airfield at Harwell was built before the war, but they built Aldermaston, Greenham, Welford, Membury, Ramsbury, and Hampstead Norreys. Hampstead Norreys was a bomber station, that was a British one, I think Aldermaston was too. The others were American, 101st Airborne. They had DC3s, and Waco Gliders.

'Another thing they did, well, the local blacksmiths did, in case of invasion, was to get concrete drums, put a big steel spindle in, a cart spindle, and they were then concreted into the side of the road. They would then fix a big old tree trunk to it, and so they were able to swing the trunk across the road like a barrier, and block the roads. They would have another concrete post the other side, and you could lock them. OK, so a tank would have gone straight through it, but it made people feel better. They also used to go around and pick up all the old fertiliser and grain sacks, fill them with sand and make gun emplacements near these concrete drums. There was one on the way up to Brightwalton from Woolley, near the war memorial.

'We used to go up to Welford Airbase when I was about thirteen and get special food like ice cream, and peanut butter. They'd look after the kids so that they could get to know their elder sisters. They used to come up to the village dances and such like which was great for the local girls.
Nowadays, young folk say life is boring, there's nothing to do. In those days, we didn't have television and the like, we used to make our own entertainment. Although we had radios, they were the old ones and the batteries used to go flat. There were no youth leaders, no money spent on youth entertainment. We had a little gang, and used to make our own fun.

'The dances were held in the village hall at Brightwalton, sometimes we would bicycle out to Leckhampstead or

77

Chaddleworth to a dance. I was only about fourteen then so we used to sit and watch. It was usually a gramophone, but sometimes the Americans would bring one of their bands along, or we had small village bands, nothing big. They would be three or four piece bands, and all the village halls had a piano, out of tune of course. Gramophones were quite rare because there weren't many records around during the war.

We didn't wear suits, I used to wear a sports jacket. Clothes were all bought through coupons then. Coupons for shoes, coupons for everything. You even needed a permit to get a thermos flask in those days.

'During harvest time, you could apply for extra tea, sugar, butter and jam, to take sandwiches out to the men in the field when they were working late. You were supposed to use them to make up the sandwiches, but when we used to get the coupons, we used to share them out amongst the men to take home and they supplied their own tea.

The men always used to take cold tea to the field, no milk, and maybe sugar, and it was really thirst quenching. Tea was on ration, everything was on ration. The only thing we got plenty of was milk because we used to produce it.

There were always eggs as well. Every farm had chickens in those days, you had ducks if you had a duck pond, but you never ate a duck's egg unless it was hardboiled or cooked properly.

'We used to go out and collect wastepaper for the war effort. They recycled it so we used to collect anything paper, books, magazines, papers. Some of the stuff that must have been thrown out must have been criminal, all those books. I remember we were given a whole load of books one day, and one of them was full of old stamps. Some of those would have been worth a fortune today. We were like a small scout group except we weren't scouts.

I learnt how to build my own radio, a crystal set, but I had a job tuning that in. We had no batteries. I had a pair of old earphones that the Yanks had given me that had been taken out of an old glider. I used to get these little crystals, cats whiskers, and a coil from the radio shop. I built my radio in a cigar box, one of those wooden ones.'

The Mill, which was sold for over two thirds of a million pounds in 1996, was derelict in those days. David used to keep chickens and pigs in it to make a bit of extra money.
'When I first went to Shefford, I didn't have a car. If I wanted to go to the cinema in Newbury, I caught a train. On the way back after an evening out, if the train was going slowly enough, I used to jump off as it went past the farm, otherwise I had to walk back to the farm along the railway line from Shefford Halt.
I eventually got an old Ford 8. It had terribly bad lights, like glow-worms, I couldn't see a thing. '

They had started at that time to break some of the US Forces vehicles up, and David went and bought two army six volts sealed beam lights off one of the lorries, which were the same shape as the lights on the Ford.
'I sprayed them black and replaced the old Ford ones with my new acquisitions, and they were great. I remember driving back from Newbury one night and all the traffic was pulling over to let me pass, and the next day, a farming friend said to me
'What the bloody hell have you got on your car, search lights?'
'Why?'
'I pulled over when I saw the lights, I thought it was at least a Bentley coming!'
Fantastic lights. '

Whenever he and Jo wanted to go out, off he would drive in

the Ford, wind the windscreen up, and drive around the fields shooting rabbits with his Winchester 22, and sell them the next day to the butchers to pay for a night out. Jo cooked rabbits and pheasants quite a lot. During combining, David would be coming home with between seven or eight rabbits a day. He used to stun them with the combine's starting handle, he admitted he got quite a dab hand at it. They had a little terrier that used to catch them too.

'We never really had any sheep. Father had sheep once, but he said you can inject them with this, and you can inject them with that, you can do this, you can do that and the buggers will still die! So he didn't bother with them any more. He reckoned they would die for the want of something better to do!

'Animals don't mind being cold, but they do object to being wet and cold. If you are cold you can cope, but being wet and cold you can be really miserable. They say that when you take on a new carter, you always asked if he had two overcoats. If you got one wet, and you couldn't get it dry by the next morning, you needed a dry one. In those days we used to work out in the wet, and those army greatcoats, if they got wet, they were blimmin' heavy!

'All the field boundaries used to be hedges. Hedgerows were planted by the farmers originally as a means of keeping the stock in. They were in the gap between the field and the farm. There have been a lot of hedgerows taken out in this part of the world, but you can go to other places and there have been no hedgerows taken out at all, Devon or Cornwall, they follow contours of the land as well. Sometimes we would take down hedges and it was two separate fields, and although the hedge has been completely removed, you knew that they'd planted a hedge there, because one part was workable, and one part wasn't. Here, where we are on a rolling downland countryside, the Chiltern hills and suchlike, hedges are not part of the scene. But farmers cultivated them to keep stock in until barbed wire came in about a hundred years ago. Until then the thorns kept them in.

'But for the wildlife, it isn't just that the hedges have gone, you ploughed through the winter in those days, so as you were always turning the soil, there was always a fresh supply of food. You didn't have the combines, so you put your corn up in ricks, and there was always a ready supply for the rats and mice which meant there were always rats and mice around for the owls. Now we've got rid of the rats and mice with poison, and there is no food for the poor owls.

'Now, we are planting hedges again. There have been more hedges planted in the last couple of years than I've seen planted in my whole lifetime! Hedges have a job to do, and let's face it, the countryside has been created by farming, it isn't going to stop being shaped by farming. It isn't going to stand still. If you stop things they don't go anywhere. If you have a car and leave it, it rusts out. You either drive it or you don't. But if you leave it on one side, it rots away.

'People forget, the countryside is not a museum. The countryside is a living breathing place of work. It is a factory. Take footpaths. If you look at them, you will see that they were created going from one village to another, to a church or to a pub, it was a means of getting to work on the farm. Now the Ramblers have taken them over and they are theirs by right! They will not bend and co-operate. A lot of farmers also make the mistake of not bending and co-operating. If we in the farming community do not go out to meet the general public and teach them our ways, then it's our bloody fault if they walk all over us.

81

If a farmer doesn't make a profit, then he can't look after his farm properly, if he can't look after his farm properly, the whole countryside suffers.

'This is one reason I am on the West Berkshire Council. Hardly anybody on the council, knows or understands the ways of the countryside and farming, they need someone like me. They call themselves town and country planners, they are town planners and urban planners, but they know so little about the countryside, and they plan it so badly, that the villages are dying. It is a known fact that there are forty percent less people in the villages today, but a five hundred percent increase in houses. There are diminishing families in the villages, no more big families, attitudes have changed, there are no more extended families in the villages, they have been replaced by outsiders. People do not understand the countryside, and we've got the do-gooders coming down who are trying to tell us how to run our lives. They don't want the smells, they don't want the cock crowing, in some places they don't want the village bells being rung, or cricket balls being hit into their gardens. They have got to come down and accept what they find. If it's not what they want, they should stop in the towns.

'Don't come into the country and try and change it, that's the answer. The countryside is not a museum, it is a living working factory.'

Bradfords
'I had always wanted a farm of my own, and we tried for a couple and didn't get them, but we got Bradfords from Mr Langley. There was a story with it which goes back to 1932. My Father actually took the farm in 1932, he was offered it, but then he was offered a bigger and better farm and he let Bill Langley have Bradfords, on condition that if he ever left it

he would give Father first refusal, before letting anyone else have it. He did.

'We took over Bradfords on 28th September 1956, Father bought some cows on 29th September, I took them back to Bradfords, tied them up in an old cow shed.   We had no milking machine so I had to hand milk these five or six cows that night and the following morning. I had to do that because I had to have milk on the stand on the 30th September and arrange for it to be picked up.

'As long as you had voluntarily been tubercular tested by the 1st October, you got an extra penny a gallon for five years. It really was against the clock.
We were having a milking machine put in, and builders then are like builders today, they dragged their feet, and we were handmilking twenty six cows at the end of November to the beginning of December. The milking machine didn't look as if it was going to be ready for two or three months, so we went to a farm sale where they had an old bucket plant. This is where you milked into buckets and then carried it and tipped it into the churn.
It was in the auction, and I bought it for £25, on condition, as I had seen the owner before, that if I bought these four buckets and machines, I could have the vacuum pipe that went with it. He said yes.
Next day I went back and took all the pipe down, and put it through the building that we had the cows tied up in and I had a bucket plant working in twenty four hours, and did all the work myself.

'£25 was a lot of money in those days. We used it until the new machine was put in, well, not a new machine, a second hand machine which I bought for a £150.   We bought it off 'Skylark' who had a farm at Appleshaw, it was advertised in the paper. He was the King of the gypsies, and his word was his bond.

When he sold us this machine and there were no teat cups with it, so he said

'Aagh, my sons have got those, using them. When you're ready, let me know and I'll get them for you.'

I rang him up when we were ready for them.

'I'm sorry my boy, my son does not want to get rid of them, but go into the local merchant, get yourself sixteen stainless steel cups, tell them to send me the bill.'

I said 'Are you sure'

He said 'Yes'.

'A gypsies word is their bond. Gordon Passey is the same, his word is his bond.

Anyway, these stainless steel cups came to about £110 and that came to nearly as much as I paid for the milking machine.

He kept his word and he paid the bill.

'When we bought it off him, it was all concreted in to this building where he had done the milking, and we had permission to dig it out. We borrowed a compressor, I went down with that and my brother came down with our corn trailer and two men. We dug it out, pulled it to pieces, marked it and had it back home in eight hours.

'I also remember on the way down, I was running over the pheasants and my brother was picking them up, we both got a brace that day.'

Talking of pheasants, when I was driving down to do the milking at Northfield from Shefford at five in the morning, you couldn't avoid them, they ran everywhere, I could have had a brace a day! We got fed up with eating pheasant.'

'We moved into Bradfords farmhouse on October 3rd 1956 after harvest.

Young Farmers Clubs
(David Liddiard front row kneeling far right)

Newbury Rugby Football Club. 1950 - 51
David Liddiard centre back row.

East Shefford Farm. 1950
(notice David's 'hames' belt)

David and Jo at the Glebe. 1952

Jo on their wedding day - May 17th 1952

The Liddiard family

James Liddiard

Edward Robinson   Kate Robinson   Richard Liddiard

Fiona Liddiard   Anthony Robinson   Sara Liddiard

Benjamin Liddiard   Georgina Robinson   Henry Liddiard   George Liddiard

Emma Liddiard

Elizabeth Liddiard

Rebecca Liddiard   Laura Liddiard

David and Jo on their wedding day. May 17th 1952

(left to right - back)   David, Jo and best man, Ben Pratt
(front)   Sister Susan, James Bracey, Elizabeth Bracey

*Jo on their honeymoon.
Torquay 1952*

Jo at Paignton. 1966

Ivor and Hilda Gores' wedding. Oct 1952
(left to right)
David Liddiard, John Bowden, Jack Williams, Tubby Lewis, Pat Harris, Bob Harris, Tony Teal and Derek Smalley

As a proud dad, David made many toys for his sons Richard and James. 1958

'James was only nine months old then, and I remember Jo putting a car blanket down on the drive and sitting him on it whilst we moved in.

'I suppose my building, and redoing things started at Bradfords. The kitchen Jo inherited was very, very small, a poky horrible little place, with no kitchen equipment at all in it apart from an old copper in the corner.
We didn't have builders in to do it, just a friend who helped me. There was an outside porch, and a horrible outside loo and a coal shed. Just a waste of space.
So we took all that out, took the kitchen wall out, and rebuilt it making a larger kitchen breakfast room with the sun coming in from the East, with a window which I found somewhere and put in. It made a terrific difference. I then went to a surplus place and bought a glass fibre sink and a draining board. Not stainless steel, but glass fibre, it was a colour Jo liked and we could afford it. Then I made her a kitchen unit, it made quite a difference.

'Then there was a garden shed across the backyard with a stone floor and brick shelves, so we put the outside loo in that, and joined it to the house with a roof across. This meant I could come in, drop my gum boots off and wash my hands, before going indoors.

'One day I went into Passey's and there were two deep freezers in there, the Americans were just moving out of Greenham and there was a whole load of stuff. I saw these two deep freezers, chucked on the scrap heap and gave them a good looking over. Despite the Americans putting a pickaxe into them, they hadn't hit a pipe, so I got the two deep freezers for £15. I took them home, took the dents out, pop riveted some patches over the pickaxe holes, and then got them working. I put them in the brick shed by the back door

'One of them I couldn't work out, it would freeze like the clappers, and then thaw out. Then, two o'clock in the morning, lying in bed half asleep, going over things in my mind, as you do, I worked out what it was. I leaped out of bed, went downstairs, ran out to the workshop in my pyjamas and my gum boots, and altered one of the thermostats. One was the temperature to go down to, and one was the variation when it was switched back on, and I had them set at about fifteen degrees apart instead of two! It worked well after that. Anyway, I asked Jo which she wanted, she said the smaller one, and I sold the other for £30, that gave me money to buy some meat to put in ours. Nick Spence, who bought it off me, had it for thirty years before it packed up.

'Another time I went to see Gordon, there was a great big American cooker in there, four big rings on it. I took that home and cleaned it up, we had that all the time we were at Bradfords. The oven was huge. At first Jo didn't want the deep freeze, she wouldn't be without one now. She didn't want the big cooker at first, too big. The only complaint when we moved to the Mill was that she didn't have an oven as big as she had at Bradfords.

'Another little acquisition up on the scrap heap was the tumbler dryer. I took that home and got that working. *'I don't want a tumbler dryer!'* she said.
Now ask her about being without a tumbler dryer.
'There were a lot of transformers chucked away as well, so I had them. I had them in the workshop, and I also had a rectifier which brought the voltage down from 110AC to 110DC, so I picked up quite a lot of American tools, drills, grinders and things and was able to use them.

'I had my own welder, and I been on a fortnight's welding

86

course when I was seventeen up at Pressed Steel in Oxford. Pressed Steel was one side of the road and Morris Cars the other. I had a really old welder, and I took it with me when I left Bradfords and do you know, I've still got it.   It's oil cooled, and I used to do all my own welding. I had a very comprehensive workshop at Bradfords, I could tackle almost anything.   I had an insight into the way things worked or didn't work. One night, I had a break-in to my workshop, and all my tools were stolen, but they wouldn't have been any use to anybody because they were all 110DC not AC!

'I would never have been any good as a scrap man because I would never want to throw anything away.   When other people went off to play football, I used to go down to Gordon Passey's as relaxation.   I used to go there on Saturdays, and come back with all sorts of things, fridges, cookers, useful things.   The funniest thing was when I found this electric petrol pump.   I knew Father wouldn't let me put one of those in, but it was only £15.
I thought 'Well, I'd like to buy it, I really ought not to, but it would be nice to have one.'

'I was in the workshop shortly afterwards, and Jo was filling her car up with the hand pump, and suddenly I heard an enormous crash.   I ran out, and there was the petrol pump going up the road behind the car!   Jo had forgotten to unhook it after filling up.   She broke it clean off the top of tank, and she hadn't noticed.
Well, we couldn't get any fuel out of the tank then, so I went down to Gordon's and bought this electric petrol pump.   I had it working within twenty four hours. We had an electric pump after that.   I had to get it rewired eventually.

'I actually stopped having petrol on the farm in the end, it was too pilferable. People seemed to think that because it came out of the ground, it didn't cost anything.   So we packed up keeping petrol on the farm.

'I don't mind giving people things, but I hate it when people take things, or assume. All the farmers used to keep oil in a fifty gallon tank. I used to think that was silly, because your oil jug stood there and collected all the dust that flew around there, and it buggered up the tractor engine eventually.   Also you never knew you wanted more oil until it was empty.

'I did a deal with the oil company, and bought gallon cans for the same price. You always knew how many there were left then. You stack a row of cans on a shelf and the men knew exactly how much they were using.
It was also pilferable, but less pilferable in that you can keep a better quantity control on it. Let's face it, you know that certain things are going to be nicked, you know that they would probably put it in their cars. I did warn them that the oil we were using would probably mess up the engines in the cars. The diesel detergent oil we were using would probably be too much for the old petrol car engines.

'It was exactly the same effect as using helicopter petrol in the vehicle. We had a helicopter crash-landing on the farm one day. It was up at Ashmansworth, an emergency landing. A lorry and crane came and took it away, but before they did, they started emptying the petrol onto the ground.
I said' *You can't put petrol on the ground like that ruin the soil. Let me go and get some cans'.*
So I went and got all the five gallon cans I could and we had all this aviation fuel. I used to put it in the Landrover, it went like Hell! But it burned all the valves out.
I remember my neighbour had a Wellington bomber come down in his farm on one wheel, and petrol was running out where there were bullet holes. They put some fifty gallon

88

drums underneath it and caught it, so they were alright for petrol for a bit. But in those days they mixed it with a drop of paraffin, we always mixed a bit of paraffin with petrol to make it go further.

'When we were at Brightwalton, we were in the airspace of Welford, and we had quite a few gliders come down, Wacos. They would come along, take the wings off, put the back up on the jeep and tow them away. That was the first time I had ever seen one winched up. They used to put the glider one end of the field, put the tow rope on two poles, and they would come in with the tow rope with a hook on the end trailing from a DC3 and snatch the glider up . Perfect for places they couldn't get in or out of. I believe they had a big drum in the back of the plane with a slipped brake on it, so when they snatched it, it didn't grab, it was gently done. I never got a chance to go in a glider.

'We had a Tiger Moth land in our fields when we were at Littlecote, a chap going cross country got lost. I think it was John, who must have been about four or five then, who the pilot put in the seat whilst he swung the propeller, and because he hadn't got any chocks, the plane started to move, the pilot had to run after it and jump in and turn the engine off. I never saw any dead bodies or nasty crashes though.

'About two years after my back operation, my Father died. It was   on 23rd April 1969 (St George's Day) about eleven months after Annie, his wife, had died with cancer. Jo had the job of trying to find a nurse for Bill after Annie died.
'He could be a very awkward individual, but he could be jolly nice too.' She remembered 'There I was, scampering across the countryside, trying to find someone to look after him, and they would walk in, but never stay. He was an absolute nightmare! However, we got through it all.

It was no good me falling out constantly with them, we relied on them, and we didn't want too many upsets, you know what I mean?'

David is very like his Father which is why they didn't get on.

I got on well with his step-Mother, though they thought that David should marry a farmer's daughter, Gina Bucknell or Freda Chown.'

'Oh she was never in the running'

'I think she was! I used to get fed up hearing about her! That was the first time I was jealous. You had been out with her just before me.'

'My brother John moved into Shefford the minute Father died. We couldn't have moved in because we had a rented farm, and one of the rules was that we had to live at Bradfords. The terms of the lease stipulated that we had to live in the house to retain the farm. There was the Mill, but that was let.

When they came for a rent review one day, we were arguing, and they wanted £1,000 more than I was prepared to give them. I said 'Tell you what, I will agree to give you what you want, if you will delete in the agreement that I have to live in the farmhouse.'

It cost me £1,000 a year not to live in the farmhouse. They took it back, and then they let it out for £500 a month or whatever, so they were on a winner. From the agents point of view, he had a very good deal.'

Jo came in then *'Well, I was the culprit there really. I wanted to go to the Mill. I had watched all David's brothers going into nicer houses, Peter to Manor Farm, John to Shefford, and I was living in what was really a glorified council house. I was upset.'*

'Yes the house was thrown up at the start of the war, about 1940.

'Anyway, we were given a year to get out, and the Mill was let to Mr Odhams of Odhams Press at that time, and we had to give them notice. '

David Rabbitts remembered that before David and Jo had the Mill, Barbara (David's sister) and her husband had it, and they were doing it up, and they had a builder in, Lewis. Bill Liddiard owned it, and apparently Bill had to come and interfere, and he would tell the builders to do a bit more here, and do a bit more there, and the final bill came in, loads more than expected, and the son-in-law split it and said *'That bit is Bill Liddiard's bill. Give it to him.'* Of course Bill wouldn't pay it. There was trouble then.

'Anyway, the Odhams moved out in the middle of May. Now we had planning permission to build two more bedrooms, a kitchen, a utility room, and a garage.
So, I was ballooning, running two farms, and building at the Mill. I found every bit of timber, every brick. I found a burned out cottage on the estate and got permission to pull that down and use the bricks from that. They wanted a building pulled down on Nalder Hill, I offered to pull them down for nothing as long as I could have all the salvage. I got all the tiles and all the bricks to build the house and the garage. All the timbers came from the old buildings.

'I got the brickie I wanted, Rex Vellender, a good brickie. I didn't know the carpenter but he was alright as long as you kept with him. For instance, I had two pieces of timber which when they were bolted together in the barn, were 42 feet long. I only wanted 41 foot 6 inches. So I told him to saw 6 inches off the end. He sawed 18 inches off!
'I had the rule round the wrong way.' he said.
I made them the right length by plating an old zed purloin over the joint.

'I used to make trailers, and they were made of old zed purloins. They were what you used to put up on these twenty foot span roofs. They were a piece shaped like a 'Z'. I had got a whole lot of them where they had been run over on a site and two foot of them squashed, so I bought them.

I made a few trailers for ballooning. I cut the purloins up to the lengths I wanted them for. I had a few left lying around, 6 and 8 foot lengths. I used to weld them up, put a few boards in, put a pair of Mini wheels on, some suspension, and there you had a balloon trailer. I made 4 or 5 of them, I think I sold a couple at £100 a piece. Dante's original 'DL' trailer is still going strong 27 years later. Of course I had built all the trailers on the farm as well.

'During this time, whilst I was still at Ashmansworth, I started my own workshop up. Well, where the old dryer came out at Bradfords, the old grain pit was turned into a pit for servicing cars. There used to be a grid where you used to drive the grain trailers over and tip the grain in, we cut a opening in it, concreted the rest so that we had a sort of underground room. I fitted it out, you know, with a bench, and tools, and we had two blokes down there doing car repairs and such like. It wasn't one of my best ideas, but it saved me lot of money.

'Now the Mill, I got someone to draw up my plans to get it through the planning. Then when that was done, they went in the drawer. There used to be a water wheel there, until after the war, but it was so out of kilter it was shaking the house to pieces. We did the whole of that building, all the renovations and building for about £22,000. Not bad eh? It was all salvaged stuff, there was a lovely beam in the kitchen. I pulled a barn down at Hoe Benham to get the beams. I got my chaps to help me with pulling it down and don't know what happened, but something caught fire. They were burning some straw, and it caught the roof of the barn. Evidently they had the foreman running up and down the ladder onto the roof with a bucket of water. But the bucket had holes in it, so he only ever had half a bucket full when he got up there! It was quite hilarious. Anyway, we put it out.

'I organised and did all the building myself like I normally do. I was running two farms, ballooning like mad, sourcing the countryside for all the timbers and bricks to match the Mill, and building it. We were twenty days late in the end. There was a lot to do, a brand new kitchen and bedrooms. We moved in October. That was the nearest I ever came to collapsing. I was overdoing it.

'It came up to the Newbury Show, which was at Siege Cross that year, and I was stewarding. I got up at six in the morning as I normally do, but I couldn't read the signs on the road, my eyes went all funny, I almost flagged out when I got to the Show!
David Harbottle said to me 'You don't look too well.'
'I don't feel too good, and I can't read these signs, my eyes have gone all funny!' I replied.
'Come on, get in the car and I'll take you home.'
So he took me back home. That was the only Newbury Show I've really missed, I spent the day in bed. It was only a one day show then.
I never missed a show ever. I mean, because of the show, I've turned down trips to China, trips to all over the world. I don't want to miss the show. It means too much to me.

'Anyway, the Mill was lovely, and we went on working on the outside for years after that. I moved the drive, and used to put 4 or 5 sacks of daffodils in down the side of it every year. It's lovely now.

93

Now in the bog ground of the garden, I had another idea which nobody else had thought of, I used throw the daffodil bulbs in, they used to sink down between the dandelions and nettles, and then in the Autumn, when the leaves came down they got well covered in and they have been beautiful. You didn't have to do anything.

'The avenue of trees, going up the drive I grew from nothing you know. I took cuttings, found odd little saplings, oh yes, I grew them all. There are only two trees which I didn't grow and my son-in-law Anthony bought me two more for a Christmas present.

'I also had redone the river, we did all the river bank up. Before we were there, there were no hatches. In 1976, that dry time, there was hardly any water in the river. It was just a muddy little trickle coming down. So I got some bent crash barriers, cut them up into lengths, drove them in vertically on the river's banks and then filled the gap up with dirt so that you couldn't see the crash barriers, and you had a nice edge to the river. Then we re-did the dam, put hatches in which we made in the workshop. I had some big bits of steel, stuff that came from Colthrop, the paper mill, all had brass collars and steel. We did the dam out of old sections of a concrete silo. We put those in, we made the river bypass the area while we were doing it, because we didn't want concrete in the water, and then let it run back to it's course when it was set. It is still there. The little footbridge going across the dam is two crash barriers bolted end to end, and then filled with concrete.

'Gordon Passey, the scrapman, was so helpful, he used to ring up when he got something that he thought might be a help. He was marvellous, but then he knew I would do something with them. He came up to see some of the things I did, like the cattle troughs.

'At Bradfords, we had calves, and the water troughs needed putting in, and I made them out of old army urinals! It worked very well.

'I used to win prizes at Newbury Show for farm improvements and such like. I always like to leave things better than I found them. This is why I get so cross over planning things. I'm the sort of person who likes to do things properly, and some of them have no idea at all. They can't see things, I can see things, how they might be, in my head. Transferring it from my head to someone else, is difficult, so when a thing is being done, you have to be there all the time. With the farm at one point, I had 14 farm cottages to look after. I had to maintain them and keep them decorated. The thing is, that all the farmworkers had a free house so that was 14 houses that I had to look after, with no income to look after them. So we used to have to do them up ourselves, that's where I learned all the building from.

'When I work it out now, what those cottages are yielding. I mean, those cottages now are yielding £100 a week in rent. Whereas, a farmworker never had to pay rent for them. I've got 7 houses left, and that's my sort of pension. We used to move farmworkers in and out of their houses. It was very much a rolling thing.

'Towards the end, it got much more sophisticated. They weren't just farm labourers or general farm workers, you had Ned the tractor driver and Bill the Cowman, you didn't change so much then. In the old times you used to change quite a lot and the usual farm had quite a high turnover of workers. I don't know the statistics.

'What was rather nice about it, I've got one chap now whose been working for me for fifty years, but of all the men I employed personally, after Father died, there is probably only one who wouldn't want to see me again. I gave him notice. Well, he'd hit me with a tractor once, he was not safe on the road. The second time, he wrote a vehicle off and I was sitting in it! He was driving a big tractor, and I was driving a Mini Pickup. That was unfair competition in my eyes! Anyway, he was using the tractor to go to the pub to get some cigarettes. The tractor wasn't licensed or insured for that. I had warned him about it twice before. I was so cross, he nearly killed me, and it wrote the pickup off.

'That's the joke of it, every time I'm involved in an accident, no one says *'Well are you alright?'*, they always say *'Was the vehicle very badly damaged?'*
'Yes, it's bloody written off!'
I walked out of it that time with just a cut on my head. If you are alright, you get back to work. It's a bit like flying a balloon, any landing you walk away from is a good one.

'I had had this ambition to farm 1,000 acres before I was 40, and I signed the papers for the farm at Ashmansworth 4 days before my fortieth birthday.'

Jo.

'I learned my public speaking with the Young Farmers, I joined them in 1946 and eventually became the treasurer, Vice Chairman and then Chairman, Cecil Brown in Newbury knows all the history of the Young Farmers Club. I think it was started in 1945. Although the real Young Farmers didn't start until then, I joined the newly formed Calf Club in Newbury in 1938, I was only eight then, the youngest member, and I was only in it because my sisters went.

'What the club did was to borrow money from the bank to buy all the members a calf each. They had to rear them, and teach them to lead, and then show them at the Spring Show at the Newbury Cattle market, where they were sold.

That was the start of the Young Farmers Club. I had this calf, it was a Shorthorn, I reared it and in the end, I came third I think, but mine fetched the highest price when it was sold. So I have been one of Dreweatt's customers for 60years!

'My sister, Barbara, became the first secretary of the Calf Club, Herbert Cottrell was the first Chairman, I remember that, and we used to hold meetings around different people's farms, we were all children then. Then the war came along and it all stopped.

Other people in the Calf Club were Charles Moore, the three Goddard boys, Peter, John and Michael, Jim Brown, Francis Wallis, and loads of others. But there again, there were so many young farmers in those days. Now, you would have a lot of trouble to find enough to make a club.

'At one point I belonged to three Young Farmers Clubs , Shefford, Reading and Newbury. The reason I joined Reading was, you could get petrol coupons to go to young Farmers Club and Reading was quite a way. So you got extra coupons if you had to go to Reading.

'As a matter of fact, my brother-in-law was a barrister, and he filled out my petrol coupon claim forms in proper jargon. When petrol rationing finished, I had so many petrol coupons left over, it was unbelievable. By filling it out in Civil Servant language, they gave me everything I asked for.

He said *'Oh we had better fill in a supplementary one as well, because you might want a bit more!'*

The other thing was that we had an old Ford Prefect, and when petrol rationing was on, if I put in four gallons of petrol, I used to put a gallon of TVO in with it.

'My car used to smoke a bit, and possibly didn't start as well, but it used to stretch the petrol out. Father used to get some in for the farm and we used to do the same there, 200 gallons of petrol, and 50 gallons of TVO in it. The old cars smoked a bit, but they went alright. You could run a car on kerosene.   I knew someone who took the petrol pipe up, coiled it around the manifold and then into the carburettor, so as the kerosene went round the manifold and into the carburettor it had heated up and would vaporise.

'I was living at home, and we had a student living with us, Dave Gardner, and for a while Edward Geary was also sharing our room. Edward Geary's father had bought him a farm, and the house had to be completely rebuilt, and he was living with us until it was done. My Father had met old man Geary before the war, and they had been friends ever since.

Anyway, one night, the three of us came back from the Young Farmers, and my Father was having a bit of a supper party, lots of cars in the drive.   The Horwoods were there in their car, and all the Young Farmers who were with us got together, lifted the back of the car up, and I put bricks under the back axles, and then we lowered it down again, and the wheels were two inches in the air. Of course they came out and thought that the car had gone wrong, it wouldn't go!

'They found out eventually, and came up and tipped us all out of our beds.

Another time, and I suppose this was naughty of me, we were all sitting in bed, and I said to Edward, 'Do you want some chocolate?'

'*Yes please,*' he said, and I chucked him a slab of Ex-Lax, you know, the laxative, just one slab. He ate it, so I said 'Do you want some more?'

'*Ooh yes please.*'

So I chucked him the rest. He ate two slabs! He didn't do much work the next day, but he went through the motions!

'We had a lot of fun in the Young Farmers, but without malice, all good clean fun. You always expected your car to be got at if you got married. We put live chickens in the car, put kippers on the manifold. There were only two occasions when I think people went too far. One was when they put molasses on someone's car to stick the confetti to and it was a hot day, and it set, it never came off. The other time was when someone wrote in lipstick on the back of the bride's going-away coat. That was awful.

Anyway, that was the Young Farmers' Club, and then at seventeen I was put on the Newbury Show Committee and I have been on there ever since. Fifty years in 1997.

'It was George Wallis who put me on the Committee. I was helping with the first show after the war, helping to steward the Heavy Horses. Father was looking after the Heavy Horse section. George thought that I ought to be got away from Father and given a job on my own, so he put me on the committee, the Cattle Committee, and then in 1947, I was elected onto the Newbury Show Committee.

'George looked after me, he was very good. I remember in 1948 or 1949, we had a very, very wet harvest. Now George

99

had two combines and they were trailed combines, you had a tractor to pull them along. They were MMG8s, Minneapolis Molines. They were always breaking down, they were awful. We had a Massey Harris 21 with special lifting fingers on it and a pick up reel. There was a lot of flat corn that year, and we had got all our harvest done and George asked Father if I could go along and cut some for him as he couldn't harvest his.

'We actually cut the last field in November, that's how late we were that year. But George had one field there that was so wet that the drive chains were always breaking. When he was getting stuck, the stones would fly up with the mud and snap them. Anyway, this one field, he had tried to cut it with his combine, he had tried with a binder, and even tried with a grass mower, but it was too flat. It was oats and vetches, they were growing it for cattle feed.

'There was a beautiful hot sunny day in November and George said, *'Do you think you could have a go at that, my boy?'*
I said, 'Yeah.'
I went up against the lay, one way only, and in the end I cut that field, it took nearly two days to do 20 acres, but I did it. I brushed it the right way, cut it, and when I'd finished, George Wallis came up to me and said *'That's a good job you've done there, my boy.'* And he gave me £5. A fiver in those days was more than a weeks wages to me!

'He was a good man in many ways was George Wallis. He was the one at the Parish Council meeting, where they were discussing the churchyard, and getting the grass cut. Somebody said *'Well can't we find somebody with a scythe? Get some of the old men in the village go in there and cut it.'*
George said *'Madam, all the old men in the village who can use a scythe are already in the churchyard!'*
The Wallises were, and still are, well known farmers in the

area and I reckon George was the best of them.

'Frank Wallis was the father, a renowned figure round here. He was very astute, he bought all the land up around Thatcham, all the gravel land. Then the Wallises ended up with a bit of a dilemma, whether to sell it for houses or gravel! He had a number of children, there was Bernard, he was a butcher, then became a farmer and went out to Kenya and made his fortune. Then there was George, Francis (who had a farm at Boxford), Dick (who had a farm at Kintbury), and Rupert who was in the Army, he was the gentleman of the family and became an Officer. Then there was Edward who emigrated to Canada, and there was one daughter who married a Canadian serviceman. Francis had five children, one daughter was killed in a farming accident, it was tragic, she was only little.

'In a way, it was through the Young Farmers that I met Jo. It was at a Young Farmers dance at Marlborough Town Hall. I was 18 years old and I had gone with a group of chums to chat up some 'fillies'. First time I had been there, and the last. It was just one of those things you know, you look across the room, and it suddenly, well - you know- it is just one of those things .

'Funny, remembering back all those years. Nearly fifty years ago that is', he said, examining his biscuit carefully.

'I met her when she was 14 and she's 63 now. Funny old world.' Jo had come to the dance with her older sister, Stella, and she was wearing a dark brown dress with a big white collar.
I was wearing yellow shoes as well', Jo remembers.

David had no idea how old she was, but he went over the hall and asked her to dance. He then discovered that she was only 14years old. But he knew she was the one, he didn't pursue it further that night, but he knew and he waited. He had known from the first that he wanted to make her his wife.

David told all his friends and they still remember.

Stan Lewingdon from Kintbury was one, he was then running Oakes, the local agricultural firm in Hungerford. They became the leading dealer in the area because they would always stay open in the evening for people to pick up spares.

A year or so after the dance, David went to pick up some spare parts for the combine one evening and as he stood talking to Stan at the gates, Jo and a couple of friends walked past in their tennis gear and David said to Stan *'There's the girl I'm going to marry.'*,

Stan asked how long he had been taking her out?

'I haven't taken her out yet!' David retorted.

She was 16 years old then.

David remembers going to a dance and telling someone else, John Pegler.

'I told him I was going to marry Jo', he said.

Jo remembers telling her school friends from St Gabriels about David. One of them was Shirley Povey whose parents were farmers, and they all knew each other.

It was shortly after that that David managed to spend a little time talking to Jo.

'It was the fair', Jo remembered.

The fair in Hungerford, the Michaelmas Fair, is held on the Wednesday before 11th October, and the Wednesday after 11th. It is a watered down version of the old Hiring fairs. Marlborough call theirs the Mop fair and it is still running, the whole of the main street is closed for the event. It was at the fair when Jo and David first really talked together. But the first time a date was arranged was late in the Summer of 1950 when Jo attended Ben Lloyd's wedding.   Ben is now the Monumental Mason in Bedwyn, a pretty village in Wiltshire.

'A lot of young people went to the wedding, and after the wedding, Norman Allen persuaded Jo to come with him and go out with the rest of us. We always went out on a Saturday night, a whole crowd of us, all Young Farmers. We all went off to the Lambourn Social Club, and then we went up to White Horse hill.

We were always doing mad things, we grabbed packets of crisps and things and went up there to look at the stars or something.   That night we decided to walk over the White Horse, and whilst we were up there, I managed to seize a chance to talk to her when Norman was elsewhere.   Norman was trying to covet her.'

It was then David discovered that she had left school.

He said to her, 'What are you doing tomorrow?'

'Oh, I'm going to the seaside with Mummy and Daddy.'

'What a pity, I've got tomorrow off, I'm not milking, I could have taken you out.'

'I think I can put it off' she said.' *Ring me in the morning.'*

I rang her in the morning, Mummy and Daddy had gone to the seaside, and Jo had stopped at home!   She asked me round for tea, and it started from there.'

Jo was the younger daughter of George and Elsie Neale of Hungerford. George ran a Master Painters and Decorators, JE Neale & Son. as had his Father, and his father before him, at premises near the Police Station. David Howard has a pet shop there now.

She should have been a boy which is why she was called Jo, it should have been Joseph. She has one older sister, Stella, and so there was no one to carry on the business really after that.

Jo used to catch the milk train to school as well, but later, she started at St Gabriels when she was 11yrs old.

'I used to catch the ten to eight, or the ten past eight, I forget' she said,

'I can remember running down from Northview, running down the steps. When I first started at St Gabriels, it was where the Newbury College is on the Oxford Road, (St Gabriels moved down from Mill Hill, London, during the war.)

I used to walk from the Station up to the Oxford Road. Near the end of my schooling they did get a mini-bus, although sometimes I got a lift from Glenna and her Father.

Sometimes people did give me a lift because it was such a long way. You couldn't take a lift now, but you didn't think about it at the time, especially in those days, you just did it.' Jo laughed.

'I courted Jo for two harvests. We were living at East Shefford then, and I used to come in off the combine, go through the bath, (when I say through the bath, that was basically it!) change, and be in Hungerford within 15 – 20 minutes! Well, a horse always goes faster to the manger than when it goes away from it! Haven't you heard that one? The other one is that 'it will draw you from farther than gunpowder can blow you'.

'One night, Dave Gardner, the student who was living with us at the time, and myself wanted to go out. We were just going to get ready and we were told that we had to go and help kill a calf. Now we both wanted to catch the bus, so we tossed a coin to see who would get ready first while the other one went to help kill the calf. Of course the short straw was the one who got ready first as he would get bloody again, but at least we would have been shaved and so on.

'I won the toss, and then Father found that I was inside ready to go out, and Dave was outside killing the calf. That was it.

He didn't listen or wait for explanations. He lost his temper, picked up a stick and chased me out of the house, round the garden, and back into the house. I ran upstairs, into the bedroom and locked the door, and he put his shoulder hard into the door twice, broke the door open. I jumped out of the window, went down the drainpipe. He was cursing and bellowing, and I ran up the garden to get away from him, and lay down in the potato halmes. He couldn't see me, but he went on rushing around yelling for me. I stayed there and waited. When I couldn't hear anything, I got up, crept into the house, packed some things and left home.

'I went and spent the first couple of nights with my sister, and then I got a job in Ramsbury. I also managed to find myself some lodgings there with a Mrs Collins. Jo was working for Barclays in Marlborough then, she used to go to work on a train, but came home on a bus which stopped in Ramsbury which was handy. We were courting by then.
During that time, she had to go to Potters Bar to do training for Barclays Bank, and that was the only time I ever wrote any letters, five of them. I have a mental block against writing, I can't spell either. They would call me dyslexic nowadays.

'I got a job with 'Boy' Chamberlain who knew I could do fencing, and so he put me on fencing for him. He farmed around Ramsbury, and had buildings and land all around Ramsbury airfield. Chickens were kept up there, and all the corn was stored in these buildings. The Chamberlains were friends of my Father's and Mrs Chamberlain had been a Wimbledon champion, they were very keen on tennis, they had their own hard courts. I remember putting up the first fence for him, and his wife came up and she couldn't get through it or over it because it was too tight, so I had to make a stile for her further up.

I fenced better than they had ever seen in their lives because I had been taught to do it properly.

'One day, Mrs Chamberlain asked me to get some concrete slabs for her. While I was moving them, one of them slipped and badly crushed two fingers. It was agony, I thought it was the worst pain I'd ever had. I couldn't sleep, I couldn't do anything.

I went and stopped at Jo's parents for the night, but by then I was nearly fainting with the pain. In the morning, I went to see the Doctor, and he sent me down to Savernake Hospital. I shall never forget it, it was a cold morning, I drove myself down there, and when I got there, they X-rayed it . Then the Doctor came in, with his overcoat on, he looked at the plates, and said *'Humph, nothing broken, '*

Then he looked at my finger, and said, *' Oh dear nurse, what a mess, I shall want a long thin sharp knife.'*

He came up to me, grabbed my hand, and put it under his arm so I was standing behind him, and proceeded to put a knife down under each finger nail. Blood everywhere!

'Right nurse, dry dressings.'

It was the only time I ever fainted and the nurse just caught me.

So, ever since then, if I have ever crushed a finger, and I've done it once or twice, I get a needle in a pair of pliers, hold it over the gas, and then pierce the finger nail with a red hot needle. Makes people pass out, but you don't feel it, there's no pain. Relieves the pressure you see. I can do it to myself, and I can do it to other people.

'I remember my daughter Kate did it once, she was going around the village hall packing up tables, and got her finger caught. She came home crying with pain, so I said 'Let me do it.'

'No no no no, you can't do that Father! No.'

106

Then at about two o'clock in the morning, she was racked with pain, came in crying her eyes out.

I said,' I told you I can take the pain away, let me do it.'

'Anything Dad, anything.'

She came downstairs, I had the pliers and the needle and the gas turned on. I said 'Put your hand on the work top and look the other way.'

'You've done it haven't you!' She said.

'Yeah.'

'Oh, the pain went just like that, I never felt a thing!'

The blood had spurted out and relieved the pressure just like that!

'Anyway, after I had had it done to me at Savernake, I went back to work, perfectly alright and I worked for 'Boy' for about five months in all. During that time, Jo's Mother was exceptionally kind and looked after me very well, she looked after me like a son. It was rather nice in the end to be able to offer her a home, to live with us. But I was rude to her sometimes wasn't I, Jo?'

'You were very good really David. If you remember, for twenty five years she used to come here every single week. Regardless of whether we were speaking or not, she was there. She could walk in and tell exactly what the atmosphere was.' Jo said.

'Anyway, back to 1951, Father wanted me back home, I think he missed me. But what probably brought it to a head was that George Wallis's brother was in South Africa, or Rhodesia at that time, and George was trying to get me to go out and join him, but Father didn't want me to go abroad, and so he asked me to go back home again.

'I left home in the Autumn of 1950, and spent my twenty first birthday away from home, and then returned home in January or February of the next year.

'I asked Mr Neale if I could marry Jo, and he said yes, he'd be very pleased if I did. So we bought the ring, but they said that they didn't want her to get married until the next year, because we were too young, and so they kept the ring . Then they wanted us to wait two years before we started a family.
Jo's Mother was dying for us to get engaged and she gave it to me and we took it out with us on the Thursday night, and I put it on her finger. Maundy Thursday, 22nd March 1951.
We went to the Swan at Shefford and had a drink to celebrate, which was unusual for us to go there.

'I did blot my copybook one night with Jo's parents. There was one time when I was supposed to be taking her out to a dance. I said to my Step-mother, I want to lie down and have a rest before I go because I'm tired, wake me up at such 'n such a time. They didn't! That caused a bit of a ruckus. Jo was all dressed up ready to go out, and I wasn't there, her parents weren't too impressed either. It wasn't my fault though!'

On May 17th, 1952, David William Liddiard married Josephine Neale at St Lawrence's Church in Hungerford. He was 22 and she was 18. Their best man was Ben Pratt, a school friend of David's from the Littlecote days. David had been to a school with Ben when they lived at Littlecote House farm and they had stayed friends ever since. In fact Ben's sister, June, married David Rabbitts who was one of the three in the Monte Carlo Rally in 1954.

'Of course, on our wedding day, I knew all the tricks that they might get up to with our car so I hid it!' remembered David. 'I had asked Jimmy to drive us off in his Citroen which was parked up the drive, but they decorated it and blocked it in so it couldn't move. We came out of the house, said good bye to everybody. We then ran back in through the back door, out of the front door, and Father's Humber Sceptre was parked in the drive. So we piled into that, and they noticed. Now there was a pair of gates to the drive, and they rushed down and slammed one of the gates shut, but my Best Man held the other one open, and the gap was about one inch wider than the car! I got through, and everyone was amazed.

Anyway, they all started to chase us, and I threw off everyone else except Michael Goddard who was in his sports car. I drove up to the station at Shefford, which was a no-through-road, spun round in the station yard, went down and stopped in the middle of the road. I got out, went up to Michael Goddard, leaned into his car, and said, 'You rotten sod.' Then I grabbed the key to his car, and just as I was getting it out, he grabbed my hand, and in the ensuing struggle, his key got completely bent! So we left him to sort that out.

'Anyway, we went back to the farm where our car had been hidden. It had been in a barn, and they had been looking for it, but the Farm Manager saw them about to go into the barn and yelled, *'Get off the bloody farm.'* And they all scarpered, and they never found it. The only one who actually got to us was Jo's sister Stella, she filled Jo's suitcase with confetti.

'We were told, you can't drive too far on your first night you will be too tired, book somewhere close. But we didn't book anywhere, we couldn't afford to. We stopped the first night in a hotel in Bath, and that is when we discovered all the confetti. It went everywhere, so we swept it all up, put it all on a piece of newspaper, and I shook it all out of the window. We watched it cascade down, and then the wind took it and blew all of it back into the front door of the hotel. The next day we drove down to Torquay which is where we spent our honeymoon.'

Jo said that she had some shocks in store for her when she became Mrs Liddiard. For instance getting up at 6am! *'I must admit though, it has never been a boring life, never!'* Jo said with a big smile.

After they were married, Bill Liddiard gave them Glebe Cottage to live in, at the end of the drive in East Shefford. The cottage was just by the gates of the long drive up to Shefford Farm, which was, and still is a most impressive farm house.
David was earning £6 pounds a week then. They had their dockets for their 'Utility' furniture. You could not just go and buy furniture in those days, but the Utility furniture was a range designed and sold for post war newly weds, all the pieces had a distinctive trade mark like two 'C's on it. In fact David and Jo still have two tub chairs, they have been re-covered a few times, but if you turn them up, there is the sign. 'It wasn't special, but it was sturdy and basic.'

Glebe Cottage was freezing. Jo and David both reckoned it was the coldest house in the world. In the morning, you could tell it was frosty, not by the frost patterns on the glass but by the glistening of the frozen damp plaster between the beams of their bedroom ceiling!
When Jo and David married, Jo was working as a bank clerk at Barclays . It seemed only natural that with her head for figures, she should take on the wages at the farm. Jo ended up doing the books and the wages for Liddiard Farms for forty years. Never really moving more than six miles from where she was born.
'We haven't moved far, but we've seen the world.' said David 'So many farmers stand on the outside of their farm and look in to see what they've got. I stand on the inside and look out at the world.'

After eighteen months of gazing at frozen plaster on the ceilings, Jo and David moved into Northfield Farmhouse, bigger and a bit warmer. Despite the long hours of farming,

110

the young Liddiards had an active social life, pubs, clubs and parties. Two couples they got on with really well were David and June Rabbitts, and Jackie and Auriol Bolton.

Monte Carlo Rally 1954

In the Summer of 1953, David Rabbitts, who farmed at Maidencourt Farm, and Jackie Bolton, who had the garage at Shefford, decided that they would like to take part in the Monte Carlo Rally. First they had to have the right car. David and Jackie scraped up £500 between them, and they went down to the Southampton Car Auctions, which were held in a Nissen hut in those days.

Unfortunately, all the cars were too expensive, but at the end, there was a Singer which had not sold. They put in an offer, which was basically all their money, and bought it for £500.

The car was then stored in a thatched barn at Maidencourt for three or four months until they could do something about it.

On top of the cost of the car was the entry fee. That was £100, a lot of money in those days. But they also needed a third man. David Liddiard was the obvious choice, and he jumped at the chance. Jackie asked David, and David said it would give him a chance to get away from the old man. David was working on his Father's farm next to David Rabbitts' farm.

David remembers it well.

'My neighbour David Rabbitts had bought a second hand car in the Auctions in Southampton, and he thought it would be a good rally car. It was a Singer SM1500, forerunner of the Singer Hunter.'

David remembered how himself and Jackie used to spend long evenings tidying it up. David Rabbitts ran his own farm and left the car overhauling to David and Jackie.

David recalled long evenings polishing up all the inlet valves of the head with a little grinder. They got so much speed out of it

111

that they broke two speedometers because they were not designed to go that far round, they only recorded up to 75mph.

'Someone in a Jag once said, 'What the hell have you got under the bonnet?' He reckoned we were going 90 in that! We were lucky we didn't kill ourselves, but we came 76th out of 290 in the actual Rally.'

They worked long into the nights, retuning and cleaning it. Jo spent those evenings with Jacky's wife, Auriol. Jo said that the three of them all had the same thing in mind - they were all adventurers, and had to get it out of their systems. June Rabbitts agreed. It did not bother her that her David was driving off to the South of France, but it worried her parents because June and David's third child was on the way. They were not sure when it was due, but it might have been January, when the Rally took place (As it was, Jeffrey Rabbitts was not born until March!).

David Liddiard also remembered how their little dog, a Jack Russell mongrel, called Titch interrupted them one evening. Titch was devoted to David, went everywhere with him, even on the Combine. But in the evenings, whilst David was at Jackies, and Jo was with Auriol, the dog was shut in the house. Anyway, one evening he turned up at the garage yapping. David thought this was strange because he had left him shut in the house, Jo was at Jacky's house as usual. David followed him home and discovered a log had rolled out of the fire and was smouldering on the carpet. The dog had chewed through the wood of the back door and come and got David.

The little dog had his nose put out of joint when the first baby arrived, and Jo found him up on the Moses basket that was used for the children, and so they packed his spotted hankie and he went and lived with David's brother, John.

112

The finish of the Monte Carlo Rally. 1954
Jackie Bolton, David Liddiard and David Rabbitts

Lunchbreak at Northfield Farm 'Titch', David and Richard

David after winning first prize for a crop of wheat.
Newbury Show 1960

Root competition, Newbury Show. 1963
Examining mangolds are:
(left - right)
Henry Billington, David Liddiard, David Rabbitts, James and Richard Liddiard, Jonathan Rabbitts and Bert Fiddler

Newbury Market. June 1969
(left to right) David Liddiard, George Baylis, Alfred Baylis and Bill Carter

Prize winning stand at Newbury Show when David was Chairman. 1966

When John had two children, the little dog walked under a car and was killed.

At last, the three chaps finished the car, had got everything together and were ready to drive in 'The XXIV Monte Carlo Rally.'

'We had no idea what rallying was all about, never done one before. We left home at 7am on a Sunday morning in January and drove to Glasgow. We got up there at about 4.00pm, it was quite exciting, great atmosphere. The next day, we left Glasgow at about 11.30am. We were doing really well until about Carlisle and suddenly all the electrics packed up! '

The electrics were overloaded, too many lights had been added.
'We went into a Lucas garage and said we wanted a voltage control.
He said, 'I only do exchange ones, give me the old one first.'
'How much would it cost if it was new?'
'Oh, about £5', or whatever it was.'
So David put a £5 note down on the counter, snatched the control, ran out, and they drove off.
The trouble was that it was dark by then, and although Jackie knew how to replace it, he didn't have a workshop or any light.

'We drove down to the next garage - remember we were running to time - we drove into the garage, and said, 'Quick - we've got to get a voltage control changed', and the owner of the garage happened to be there in his car.
'Oh you can't get it done here', he said.
'Go down the road, second left, in there, second right, and there's a garage there who'll do it for you.'
'When we got there, three blokes came running out with a tool box. The guy had rung up, it was another one of his garages, and he had told them that they had to do it as quick as possible

113

and not charge us. (We did have the Monte Carlo rally sign on the front.) They got it done in about fifteen minutes, and we made our time up to Llandidrod Wells, or wherever it was, with no penalty points!'

David did the night driving, so he took over at Llandidrod Wells, and they drove down and got to the road at Oxford. He drove around one roundabout twice to find the right road out, but from there it was down to London and then on to Dover.
'We drove through one place where there was a crowd of people who were running after us, and we didn't realise until afterwards that it was the Singer Owner Drivers Club and they had brought a whole load of sandwiches to give us!
The Club were quite annoyed that we hadn't stopped, we were the only Singer in the Rally, and they had soup and all sorts of food to give us, and we drove straight through them. We didn't realise. Anyhow we arrived in Dover in time to get a complete service and oil change, and then got on the ferry, and it gave us time to have a bit of sleep. Ferries were a bit slower in those days.'

Then they reached Calais - France at last. David continued.
'I always remember giving a talk to the Round Table once, and Jackie Bolton was with me (I was always giving talks, I've done it many times) and I was saying that I was glad I didn't have to drive out of Calais, as I'd had too much to drink, and Jackie said, 'Well I'm glad I didn't either, I was too tired.' I said, 'But you did drive, you silly bugger!''

He remembers that they did get lost and went round and came back through the control point again which confused everyone! He remembers driving into Paris, and still wonders how they didn't kill themselves.
'We got lost quite a few times, and occasionally you would follow another Rally car, but they were probably lost too.

114

Rotterdam, Amsterdam and then back to Paris, Fontainbleu.
I remember driving through snow that was so high that the organisers had cut a road through and we drove between two big walls of snow possibly seven or eight foot high. We thought it was amazing, but the French and Germans thought nothing of it, they were used to snow.'

They drove through three nights, David Liddiard doing all the night driving. He remembers coming down into Monte Carlo, driving down with the sunshine on the mountains. They felt an incredible sense of achievement as they entered the small Principality. The elation was somewhat squashed by the French drivers saying that it was a lovely afternoon's drive!
They were exhausted, but Shell and some of the other organisations asked them to a big reception, so they went back to the hotel to get ready.
'A maid ran the bath water for us, and we all had a bath, and we didn't wake up until ten the next morning! Missed the reception completely.
It was really expensive in Monte Carlo, and somebody said, *'Go to Italy. It's cheaper.'*
'
He gave us directions to get to this nightclub, wrote them down. The three of us got in the car, and with David Rabbitts driving, headed off on the road to Italy.
David Rabbitts always was a fast driver. I was sitting next to him and as we pulled up at the Customs, I said, 'It's Italian customs here, don't they have any French customs?'

'We were sitting there waiting to go through and this bloke comes up and puts a rifle through the window at me! Evidently we had gone through the French Customs post at 60mph on the wrong side of the road. They had us out, and stripped us off. Went through my wallet, found my passport, and inside my passport was a piece of paper with the address of the nightclub and instructions on how to find it. When he saw that, he showed it to his mate, they all had a bloody good laugh and said, *'Go, go, go! We know why you're in a hurry!'* It was an interesting evening.

'Oh God, the last night, the celebration night in Monaco, we were in a bar and Jackie Bolton was playing the piano, he was banging away on the piano pissed as a fart. Everyone was singing and dancing. David and I were tired out, and we went back to the hotel.
The next day, we were all packed up and ready to go , sitting on the hotel steps waiting for Jackie. Eventually he rolled up, all dishevelled, in his dinner jacket. We didn't wait for him to change, we just bundled him into the car because we hadn't got enough money to stay another night, and drove back over the Alps. Monte Carlo to Boulogne, twenty two hours, through the snow and ice, with no money.'

David Rabbitts remembers that they had to sell one wheel for the night out in Monaco.
'We had to sell our other spare tyre to get enough petrol to get home, we were really broke.'
'We got to the ferry with ten minutes to spare!'

David said that if you finish the Monte Carlo Rally within a certain time, you get a badge, and however many times you do it again and finish in time, you will never get another one. It is a 'Once in a lifetime achievement'.

'Of course nowadays you can get sponsorship, and people get backing to do the rally, from manufacturers etc. But in those days, you paid for yourself.'

David Rabbitts was also amazed at the French loos, holes in the ground for women and men. *'I'd never seen anything like*

116

them! The buildings were just a lot of ruins as well because it was just after the war,'

When asked if any of them spoke French, David wondered why anyone would want to speak French. 'The French had to speak English otherwise we wouldn't understand what they were saying!'

The whole rally took less than a week. They left on a Sunday, and came back the following Saturday. 'Couldn't take more time off than that.'

When they got back, David Rabbitts kept the car as his, and ran it for years, never had any trouble with it, and drove his family everywhere.

David Liddiard remembers his team-mates.

'Jackie Bolton was a great friend. He was just a few years older than me, but he used to smoke like a chimney and drink like a fish. He gave up the garage, and bought into a pub called the 'Nut & Bolt' at Burnt Ash, Yattenden.

He married again to a journalist, and they emigrated to Spain where they had a wine bar. We heard that he was not very well and had cancer of the lung, and cirrhosis of the liver.

We heard nothing for some time, and then we heard he was dead, and it wasn't until about a year afterwards that we heard that he had been murdered. Someone came in to try and rob him, he tried to stop them, and they hit him over the head and killed him.'

'I mean, it just goes to show you, it wasn't the cancer or the cirrhosis of the liver that got him in the end. But as an adventurer, and living the lifestyle he did, he would have preferred to die in an exciting way', Jo said.

'Oh yes.'

David's other team mate, David Rabbitts, was older than David, he had bought Maidencourt Farm from his Uncle in 1950 for £29,000, and was farming land that was adjacent to

Bill Liddiard's farm in Shefford.
David Rabbitts married June Pratt from Hungerford, and her brother Ben, was David Liddiard's good friend and best man.
'I think when I came back from the Monte Carlo Rally, I thought I ought to settle down.

'In 1965 or 1966, I took on the Chairmanship of the Newbury NFU, and it was really on the ground. There was no dinner, there was no dance. Alan Bayliss was the Chairman before me, and I said, 'We'll have a dance, Alan.'

'I helped to organise it. We couldn't afford to have the Corn Exchange, so we had to have the Plaza which was the north side of the Corn Exchange, where Dreweatts are now. There was an arcade with a cafe, shops, hairdressers in there then. There was a hall behind where they used to do all the blood donor stuff. Our dance was held just after Christmas, and we really worked hard for this one.

'I went up to Suttons and picked up all the Christmas trees that they hadn't sold for Christmas. We had a trellis and all these Christmas trees, and we used netting to hang it all up. Today, a fire officer would have a fit! We got someone different in to do the food, the Greens, two brothers who had the cafe in the arcade. It was a superb meal, and from the success of that dance, the next year we could afford the Corn Exchange.

'Anyway, it was the most beautiful decoration, people could not believe it was the Plaza, it was such a grotty run-down hall. The Postmen were having their dance after ours, and they said, *'Could you leave the decorations?'*
'Of course we can!' I said. 'On the condition that you take it all down and clean up.'
That saved us a lot of time.

'It was really good, and I was on the dance committee helping for 10 or 15 years. Then I said to Jo, 'I've had enough.'
We came off the committee, and down it went. The NFU is still in Newbury but there is no dance. It's a lot of work when you do these things, and I've always said that if I'm going to do something, then I will do it to the best of my ability.'

The year after the Monte Carlo Rally, Jo became pregnant.
Jo's Mother knew she was pregnant before Jo knew, as she had been watching her like a hawk waiting for a grandchild. Then she went round and told all her relations.

'We were living at Shefford then, and I was working hard, and really didn't have an awful lot of time to spend with her. Richard was born on the fourth of January 1955. It was snowing, my sister Joan was staying with her little boy, aged two and a half. Joan's husband was in the air force and was away a lot on different postings. Joan was on her own a lot of the time, so she came and stayed with us a lot.'
Jo remembered that it was foul night. *'I was twenty one then. I went for all my ante-natals at Hungerford, and my Doctor was Doctor Wallis. So that is why we went to Savernake.'*
David continued.
'Middle of the night, she woke me up and I had to take her down to the Savernake hospital. A very lovely old fashioned hospital then.
It was about one o'clock in the morning when I rang up and said we were bringing her in. The matron, Aldridge, met us at the door, took the case out of my hand said, *'Thank you, I'll look after her now'*, and slammed the door in my face. That was it, as far as she was concerned I'd done my bit!'
David roared with laughter.
'Richard was born at about three o'clock.'
David had to ring up to find out if she had had the baby, and what it was. Jo stayed in for fourteen days, not because

119

anything was wrong, but that was how they did it in those days.

Jo remembered the time well, *'It wasn't a very happy experience for me at Savernake. I couldn't feed Richard, didn't want to either, which was probably part of the reason. This wretched Sister Aldridge, I hated her, and she hated me. She kept coming in with a breast pump. 'You WILL feed this baby', she kept on saying.*

Dr Wallis was my saviour, he said 'If you don't want to, and you haven't got any milk either, then you needn't!' So I didn't!'

'Richard was quite a lad'. David takes up the story. 'He was walking at 11 months. He was very adventurous, when he was about 13 months old, Jo left the door open at Northfield. Richard went out of the front door, down the drive, climbed a five bar gate and fell in a pile of cow muck! Another time we had a French fire guard in front of an open fire and a poker with a hook on the end. Richard stuck the poker in the fire, got it hot, pulled it out, burned through the arm of a leather chair, the seat cushions, and then slid his hand over the hot bit, and burned it so much, his hand was just one big blister. It was awful. There was a gel they put on it, yellow stuff, like Vaseline which was on a gauze.

'James was due almost to the day of Richard's birthday two years later, but the little so an' so was early. We had decided to have a Christmas party, we like parties, so we had a party up at Northfield. Jackie Bolton and all the usual gang were there, and this went on until about twelve o'clock.

Jo was sitting on the floor, and she said to me, *'Get rid of them, my waters have broken!'*

So I said 'Come on you lot, Jo's got to have some rest.'

By the time they left, it was about half past twelve, quarter to one, and I drove her down to a nursing home near Swindon and she had James. I was told to go back home.

The next morning was Christmas Day, I was going to work, and I knocked on the door at a friend's house to tell them that I had another son.

She opened the window and said, 'What do you want?'

I said, 'Jo's got another son.'

'What! We were only there a few hours ago!', she said, and came dashing down in her nightdress - very see-through!'

Jo remembered that the bill for the private Nursing home was £25, and she was there for ten days.

'Whilst I was in, my sister Stella came and looked after Richard and David for a few days. Mummy wasn't really free because Daddy was ill.'

So James was born on Christmas Eve 1956. Just less than 2 years later than Richard. James who was christened at Welford Church, has never forgiven them, he says, as he only ever gets one present a year, not two. Kate was born in 1962 just after Jo's Father died, and Jo's Mother was a great help then.

'I think Kate took my Father's place in Mummy's eyes, and she spoiled Kate dreadfully', Jo remembered. 'But children grow out of it, they don't want to be spoiled all the time. Kate didn't, she made her own stand. I remember David telling me 'Your Mother is ruining that girl.' But she wasn't. Kate was christened at Hoe Benham Church, the last child to be christened there.'

'Jo was the first Mother to have disposable nappies for the children. I had this idea, so I used to take her boxes of milk filters in from the dairy, which she used to put in the terry towelling nappies before she put them on the children. When they were small we used the 10 inch, and when they got bigger, we went up to the 12-14 inch ones. A milk filter was a gauze and cotton wool for filtering the milk, well, it filtered the children as well! I should have patented it. I look back and think what a bloody fool I was, I didn't patent it.   It made things easier for Jo, and I never thought I might be able to profit from it. They were busy times then, busy times. Not even a lot of time for home.

Jo said, *'The right sort of childhood is for the father to take part.'*
'I admit I was naughty there, Jo takes the credit for bringing the children up. I was too busy earning a living to spend as much time as I'd have liked to with the children', David said forlornly.
'Yes, you were, honestly', Jo added sadly. *'The dos and hoo-hahs when the kids wanted to go and play football on a Sunday morning. There were more arguments when the kids were small, because you wanted them on the farm, and I felt they should have some recreation as well. You know.*
I couldn't cope with it all again'. Jo roared with laughter at the thought of it. *'It's so easy now!'*

'They're quite well adjusted children. I think it is simply because we always sat down and ate our meals together. It's very important. This is where so much goes wrong, good plain cooking and a kitchen table is most important.   James does it now, they've got a lovely old kitchen table round there now. During the Icicle Meet (*which is a famous ballooning meet held now at James's farm*)   Fiona cooks breakfast for the whole Dante Group (*the organisers*)   and their wives and hangers-on. There must be thirty or forty people through for breakfast.

'We've always had a policy of having an open door as a family.   Like in my election address, they asked if I was going to have regular clinics?   I said I wouldn't have 'regular' clinics, but I was only a phone call away. I think that's more important than having a regular clinic where you might sit

122

there and nobody turns up, or 5 people all turn up at the same time! But I will always answer the phone, I will always give people the benefit of my advice, everyone's entitled to my advice. Whether they take it is a different matter!

'We always say that about someone we know. Everyone is entitled to her advice - at least she thinks they are!
You know, I've always had my views, but I've never held my views as being the be all and end all. I would fight for my ideas and my views. But if people don't hold with my views, I don't hold it against them.
Well, I'll tell you what. My daughter had to marry a handyman to get anybody like me! The boys are absolutely useless! Compared with me, they're useless.'
'They are', Jo agreed.
They both went to college.
'Yes, but when it comes to putting a nail in, or turning a screw, they are useless. I mean, to change a light bulb, they'd put the bulb in and turn the house!' David added jovially.
'Well not quite that bad, but you know what I mean. Well, all this is compared with me. But I am a bit of a perfectionist I suppose.
I mean, look what we've done to this house in a year. But with James, nothing has got that urgency about it.'
Jo came in remembering, *'They had no heating down there for three or four days, during the time when it couldn't have been colder, just before Christmas.'*
'That's right, and I went down there at about half past five, half past six? I got it working that night.'
'It was a fairly new boiler, though, wasn't it?'
'That's right, and he hadn't got the right grade of diesel and it was freezing. I took some heaters down. Sorted the whole thing out and finally got it working. That pipe is still across there, he hasn't put it back where it should be.'
'It was so cold, but they did have open fires.' Jo chuckled at

123

the memory of the whole affair.

'David continued, 'If anything goes wrong, it is, 'Father, can you help us?'

'*They should have rung us earlier, shouldn't they?*', Jo said.

'Richard's just the same. Hasn't got a clue.'

'*Yes*', sighed Jo.

'Some of the things they do are absolutely horrendous. I mean this is the trouble with half the world today. They're so highly educated, that they've lost their intelligence. The world is becoming more full of educated people, and less full of intelligent people. This is the way I look at it.

'I mean, I know I'm dyslexic, I can read, but I can't spell. I don't like writing, I never write anything because I can't spell! I kept up my logbook from ballooning in a manner of speaking but if you looked at it, you wouldn't understand it, I mean there is probably lots that is not in there.

I would say that at least twenty percent of my flights never got into the logbook I just didn't put them in! You know, I did the flying, enjoyed the flying, but never put them in! I never realised in those days how handy they would be later. When I thought that I had lost the logbooks in America, I felt devastated actually. But there cannot be many people who have had their dirty washing and logbooks sent back on Concorde!'

This related to a trip taken just at the beginning of the research for this book, when David's luggage had been misdirected, with his logbooks in the cases!

Jo chuckled again, '*I remember stuffing all the laundry into the case, and I said, 'Shall I take the logbooks out?' and he said, 'No, leave them where they are'.'*

'Never mind, it all turned out alright in the end.

'Back to the children - they have never let me down. I mean James is doing a good job farming, Richard is doing a good job where he is, Kate is a wonderful Mother, what more could you wish for? Nothing. Now we've got all these wonderful grandchildren around.

'It worries me sometimes that I've had such a bloody marvellous life that something will go wrong.   We have always had a good social life, hectic, fitting things in where we could.   When we were first married, we used to go to the Henwick Club a lot.   There was a whole gang of us.   The Henwick Club was a Country Club with tennis courts, bars, a dance floor etc.   It was in an old barn on the site where the Regency Hotel in Thatcham is now.   The Club got burned down eventually.

'I remember one New Years Eve, we were all up there having a good time, and we all had to wear paper hats, and Wally Allen's had a tassel on it. I couldn't resist it, I got my lighter and set fire to it. *'What's happening, what's the matter?'* he was saying with smoke coming off his head!   Everyone was laughing their heads off.

'We were at another party, and there was this young lady, who was quite 'well endowed', and she knew that one of my favourite tricks was to go up behind young ladies, and unhook their bras without them knowing and everything would fall out. Anyway, I went up and tried it on her, and she said *'Aha, you won't be able to do that this time, this one does up at the front!'*
I just happened to lean back, and put my hand on the sideboard, and happened to put my hand on a pair of scissors. Talk about luck or fate. Well, I thought, this is too good to be true, so I pulled the back of her dress back quickly snipped the back of her bra, and put the scissors back quickly and

125

stepped away. David Wallis just happened to be walking past at the time, she turned around, clouted poor old David and shrieked, *'You! You can buy me a new bra in Camp Hopson's tomorrow!'*

Poor old David Wallis didn't know what was going on!

We've had some good times. I've worked hard and played hard and there hasn't been a lot of time in-between.

My friend John Goddard is going to celebrate fifty years of farming next week, maybe I should celebrate too, not worry!

'I reckon that farming between 1939 and 1989 were the best years. Take combining, they get 20 foot tables, we couldn't have done it in our day, the fields were too uneven. We had to do it with a two way plough, you had a big furrow about every forty yards, or a high spot every forty yards and ploughed into it.

Nowadays, you plough one way and you've got level fields. It makes so much difference. You haven't run over the fields and rutted them, you've just got the ruts where the tramlines are. So when you go to plough the fields next time, it turned over easily, things are so different today.

'They are having a ploughing match this year, but the difference in ploughing then and ploughing now, you had to stand everything up and everything had to be right, straight. But nowadays they don't have to worry, they can plough the fields like a dog's hind leg.

Some days I was doing two flights a day and farming.

If you want a job done, you give it to a busy man. If you give it to a man who has nothing to do, he'll always think, *'Oh, I can do that tomorrow.'*

Give it to a busy man, and he says, *'Well I'll do it when I've got 5 minutes'*, and he does it straight away!

'For three years running, when we were at Bradfords, we

hosted the Young Farmers' show. One year, I arranged for some parachutists to fly in. The main ring was in the field the Hungerford side of Bradfords, by the A4, and the parachutists were supposed to land there. They flew over in an old de Havilland Rapide, then all bailed out and were free-falling, and all their chutes opened except one, and he kept dropping with no chute, it didn't open, didn't open and eventually he landed behind the trees on the other side of the road. Although his parachute did eventually open it was not completely deployed as he disappeared behind the trees. He was alright, not hurt at all. He was treated for shock and laundry and that was all!

He actually landed in the field where the Rapide was landing. After the plane landed, the pilot offered to give us a ride, and this is where the Liddiard dynasty nearly came to an end, Kate, James, myself and two others got into the plane. There were no seats in it, and no door either. Anyway, he taxied to the end of the field, but the grass was a bit too long, and he had a hell of a job to get the speed up, he only just got it up by the end of the field, and only just cleared the wires at the end, he nearly went under the wires at the end rather than over them. Very scary.

'We had four thousand pigs up at my other farm in Ashmansworth. I had had a chance to buy an old chicken farm that went bankrupt, and I turned it into a piggery. My brother Peter was going to look after it. We converted the old chicken houses into pig sties. I never liked it. It was the modern way of doing it, all the sows were tethered so they wouldn't lie on the piglets. It was a high tech unit. We dug these big channels along the back of each shed and put slatted floors in the back.

'A pig is a very clean animal. Given the chance, a pig will lie on a clean area, so we made a bedding area which was insulated, they didn't need any straw which would have clogged up the slats at the back of the piggery.

They had a feed pipeline down the centre of the shed which was computerised, so you just plonked the feed and water into a container, and the machine mixed, measured and fed to order. You had to go down occasionally to dust down and that. There were proper ventilation fans in there, all insulated and high tech.

We had to pump the slurry out of the channels with a big vacuum tanker, and I remember when we had a new one delivered which would hold about 2000 gallons. On the first day, the foreman said he would try it out and check it was working. So he came in, sucked up 2000 gallons, and then went into the field next to the piggery and started spreading it. It was working beautifully until it had pumped out about a quarter of it, and then it stopped.

'We all watched as he got down and went around to the back of the tanker and looked down the spout. Then he walked over to the side of the field, picked up a fence post, came back and rammed it up the outlet spout, there was a brick wedged across the opening. What he had forgotten to do, was to depressurise the tank. The brick and the pole shot out, hit his ankles which knocked him over, and they were followed by about 1500 gallons of pig slurry! Every time he tried to get up, he slipped back down into it again!

Word got back to his wife before he did, and when he got home, he found the doors locked and his wife hanging out of a window yelling at him to hose himself down thoroughly before he even thought about coming in! That was one of the only problems with working with pigs really.

'We used to castrate all the pigs and calves ourselves, techniques passed down through the generations. There's only one thing I would give way to and that's a sow. I would never stand ground to a pig, never.

I remember we were castrating litters of pigs in a field and we had the sows shut in and one got loose and my brother and I were up on the roof of this pig sty, and the old sow was chomping the boards off underneath us! It was frightening. I suppose I was in my twenties then.

Of course the sweetbreads were beautiful to eat, but I never brought any in when Jo was at home.

'I remember we used to have a student living with us at Bradfords, Ivor Denton, and he was helping me castrate. Jo had gone off out for the day, so we kept all the sweetbreads, took them in, washed them all off in salt water and fried them for lunch. We never castrated more than two or three litters at a time. I had a little terrier that always went around with me, and after we castrated the piglets, I would chuck the sweetbreads over to the terrier, and he would grab them and eat them. He would never eat them if they touched the ground, he always had to catch them in the air and swallow them whole.

'One day we did about seventy piglets, and after about forty, the old dog wouldn't eat any more. He went off and slept for a couple of days. He was really 'ballsed up!'

I used to have to stitch up animals, I've seen piglets with their heads nearly falling off where the old sow's lain on top of them on the edge of the tin shelter. I stitched one up which had a cut from the top to the bottom of his neck where you could almost see his windpipe! I took him indoors, got the needle and thread, and stitched him up. Two days later, if it hadn't been for the fact I had used black cotton, I would not have known which one it was. It healed so fast.

'On the other hand, if you got bitten by a pig, it didn't heal very well. They've got sharp little teeth, and if they nipped you while you were trying to castrate them or something, it took ages to get better.

I also try to take advantage of opportunities. One day I read

129

that a company who made these big silos had gone bankrupt. On trust I bought all the stuff they had. I was buying it in at about £18 a ring- there were about eight sheets a ring. We had enough to put up six 200 ton silos, and we had enough sheets of stuff for the roof at £1 each, to do about seven roofs, and we decided to do about eight silos. After that, each sheet was costing me £18 and it ended up costing me £200 to finish the last one. But in the end, I had storage for 1,600 tons of grain up there at Ashmansworth for a very good price. I bought a steel shed from Greenham Common when the Americans left, from Gordon Passey. We put it up ourselves and installed the dryer and processor in there.

'One year, we had nearly finished combining, and we only had a small four or five acre field to do. I know it sounds silly to send three combines along to do one small field, but if I'd only sent one, it would be bound to break down, and we had nearly finished the entire harvest, so we went along with three combines and a couple of trailers for the corn. I led the convoy down the narrow roads to make sure the traffic didn't run into them. When we got to the field, someone had parked a car right in the gateway.

'Well, with three combines, two trailers and my vehicle, we were blocking the road, so the chaps got down and went up to this little Triumph Herald. The four of them lifted this car clean up took it over the other side of the road and put it in a ditch. I opened the gates and we drove in. The first combine, driven by the foreman, had only gone about seventy five yards when it stopped. There were no cabs on those combines, and he stood up, and beckoned to the others to come and have a look. All the crews ran over, followed by me, and there in front of the combine was a young couple trying to get dressed as fast as possible!'

Cash and Crash.

'In 1974, we moved to Shefford, but I still ballooned and farmed Bradfords. I still ran that one, and another farm at Ashmansworth, which was another eight miles on after you've driven to Bradfords. To get to work, I had sixteen miles to drive, all cross country.

Do you know, the whole twenty years I was driving that 16 miles to work and back I only had three crashes. Two of them, I wrote the vehicles off, but on both those occasions, I walked out of the vehicles!

'I gave up Ashmansworth, three months before I gave up Bradfords. Fate had a hand in it.

I am a great believer in Fate.

'We went on holiday to the Caribbean. Now I like to read a newspaper, and there were no newspapers coming in. But someone brought the Financial Times in. Well, I never read the Financial Times and I don't think I've ever read it since, but that was all there was to read.

'I read that BAT, British American Tobacco, had spent a £100M on buying something in America, GUS Stores or something, and they were looking to sell off their non-profit making odds and ends.

Well I knew my farm was worth £1million at least and BAT were getting about £27,000 a year in rent for it. Which wasn't a very good return on capital. So when I got home, I rang up the agent, and offered them £1million for the farm.

I hadn't got a million pounds, but I knew I could sell it for about £1.3-£1.4million, and I thought it would be a quick turnover.

'Unfortunately, just after I made the bid for that, I had my first bout of pancreatitis, which everybody thought was a heart attack. I ended up in hospital and the deal went cold.

I went down to Southampton and had an 'Angiogram'. They make an incision in an artery in your groin, and push a tube with a camera, right up inside and examine the heart. You lie there conscious, and you can watch it on the television screen.
They said, *'What do you feel now?'*
'Ooh', I said. 'My ears have gone hot.'
The surgeon said that was fine, then asked, *'What do you feel now?'*
'My thumbs have gone hot!'
'What do you feel now?'
'My toes have gone hot!'
That was fine. All I kept saying was, 'My nose itches, I must scratch my nose.'
'You mustn't move.'
So the nurse kept scratching my nose whilst I was just lying there. I don't know what they give you. Anyhow, I was taken back into the ward, and the Doctor came in that evening.
'You're the only good news I can give this week, I can find nothing wrong with you.'

'So that was good news, I got my pilot's licence back, that was February 1986. Anyhow, in May, the agents rang me up.
'Mr Liddiard, we'd like to come and look around your farm with a view of a rent review.'
'Fine, when would you like to come around?'
'As soon as is convenient for you.'
'Right.'
'How about next Tuesday? We'll meet you up there at 9.00am.'
Talk about a game of poker. First thing I did was borrow a Range Rover.
I always used to think about Range Rovers that those people who need them can't afford them, and those people who can afford them don't need them.

'Anyway, I borrowed this Range Rover, they arrived, and I

132

said I'd take them around the farm. It was a beautiful May day. The crops were looking absolutely wonderful.

If I had been showing them around for a rent review to keep the rent down, I should have shown them all the poor bits of the farm, but I took them around every bit that was good.

I showed it off as if it was a wonderful farm.

When we got back to the buildings at about 12 o'clock, they said, *'Well Mr Liddiard, the farm looks wonderful. Now you did offer to buy the farm, and we said we wouldn't sell it to you. But we would pay you to give up the tenancy.'*

'Oh yes? How much?'

'Well, how much would you want?'

I said, 'That's a quick question for me, how about £500 an acre?'

So they left the boy talking to me, and the three of them went off into their car for a huddle and had a talk. They came back and said, *'Mr Liddiard, I think we are able to come to an agreement, when can we talk more about it?'*

'Well', I said. 'It's lunch time now, I think we should have some lunch.. I'll treat you, we'll go down to the Chequers.'

If you're going to talk business, do it over a decent meal.

So I went indoors and rang my son Richard, who works for Dreweatt & Neates.

'Richard, whatever you are doing, cancel it, come to the Chequers and have lunch with us. I think we've got a deal here.'

So Richard met us. We sat and had a nice lunch, talked about farms and various things. Then they said,

'Well Mr Liddiard, I think we should get together and hammer this deal out. I think we are within part agreement. When would suit you?'

Richard got his diary out and said, *'What about next Wednesday?'*

'That's fine with me, Richard, but what about you, Mr

Liddiard?'
Richard said, 'We don't want Father there do we?'
They all looked at me and I said, 'Let the boy deal with it! It's no good raising children if you can't let them get on with it.'
So it was all done like that!

'The chap said - two or three times actually - 'You're a pleasure to do business with. You say what you mean, and you mean what you say and you stand by your word. That's a lot more than you can say for some people today.'
I think the deal was settled at £300,000 for 56 acres of land, the farmyard and the house.
This was where I had the pigs with my brother. It worked very well until Peter decided he didn't want to do it any more. I then went into partnership with someone else until they decided to give up. I sold it eventually, not as a going concern, but with planning permission to put two houses on it, when I came out of Ashmansworth I didn't want it anymore.

'By the time I'd sold the farmyard, house and land, it was a fair bit.
Anyway, when my other landlord heard about it, he said, 'But we didn't know you'd give up for money.'
I said, 'Yes, of course I will!'
'How much do you want?'
I said, 'Well, you're too late now because James wants a farm and he's got a tenancy here, and the tenancies run for my lifetime and his lifetime.
If I sell this tenancy, what's he going to do?'
'Well, how much do you want?'
'At least £700 an acre.'
'Who are you going to get to deal for it?'
'John Pallett'. He got £390,000 for giving up 450 acres.

'We had to leave all the crop and all the machinery behind

134

though. We didn't do that at Ashmansworth - we sold it all separately. When the pig unit closed down, no one wanted it anymore. The person who bought the farm did not want that part of it, so I sold that and 50 odd acres of land.

'The best bit was, and I didn't know it at the time because I was retiring on health grounds (I'd had another dose of Pancreatitis by then), that I could take the equivalent of six years rent, tax free!
£225,000 tax free. It takes an awful long time to save a quarter of a million pounds! The only stipulation was that I didn't want to hang about, I wanted the deal to be done immediately.

'We agreed the deal in June and walked out of the farm at Ashmansworth in September. It was sold to a neighbouring farm for about £1.6million.
But the crops were mine to sell, the beef cattle as well, all the machinery, also there was a standing crop of maize, when that was ready I sold that too. There were pigs there on about 5 acres and I was in partnership with someone, but we sold that for a good sum and sold the land with planning permission for two houses on it.

'The other one, it was about October by the time the insurance and the trustees had finished and all that. We walked out of there on the 1st January. So from having no savings, and never invested in anything, I had this money. This is where Fate came in again.

'Jo and I were driving along the A4, off to babysit, and there was a car broken down on the side of the road, and I stopped to see if I could help. To cut a long story short, he had a bit of pipe broken. I took the pipe, went back to farm, came back, mended it for him, and sent him on his way.

135

He said, '*What do I owe you?*'

I said, 'Don't be stupid, someone will do the same for me one day.'

'*Let me take your address so I can write and thank you.*'

So I gave him our address, one of my cards. Never thought any more about it.

'A fortnight later, I had a dozen bottles of Claret delivered, a very nice letter thanking us, and a note saying would I get in touch with his secretary, and arrange a mutually agreeable date when I could go and have lunch in his office in London.

So we did. We went up there after we'd given up Ashmansworth.

After we'd had our lunch, I asked, 'What do you do for a living, Andrew?'

'*I invest peoples money for them.*'

I said, 'It's funny you know, I've never had a penny in my life before to invest. Someone must have put you here for me. Would you invest some of mine?'

That's how I found my stockbroker. He's had my money for ten years now, and after what I've taken out for airships, weddings, holidays and the rest, the money up there is double what I put there!

'It's Fate. You know, I trust everybody - once. If they do you, and you trust them again, it's your own bloody fault. I've had a wonderful life.

We were talking about coincidence and fate this morning. I've got some units, and some good people who rent them from me. I went down one day and Gordon and Alan had cut a grid for a window, that was their business venture. Off they went to fit it. About three hours later they were back. I asked them what was the matter. They looked a bit bashful.

We got the measurements wrong.'

They didn't tell me where it was.

136

Anyway, the next day, Jo and I were going down to Bournemouth driving down a road I don't very often go along, through Collingbourne Ducis and that way. As we drove past this petrol station, there were these two blokes getting out of a van and carrying a grid and putting it up on the window!

I said, 'That's Gordon and Alan!'
So we turned round at the next opportunity and went back.
'We've just come back to see if it fits or not!'
'Oh no, trust you to drive past!'
I'm a great believer in luck.

'I mean, James rang me up one day. He said, *'I've got to get a fire escape, Dad. I've got to get it in a hurry, because my units aren't legal unless I've got a fire escape. I've got people moving in in ten days! I've been quoted £2,500 - £3,000, and anyway they can't do it on time.'*
'Don't worry, I'll go and see Gordon Passey.'

'But Gordon said, *'No, haven't had one in for years.'*
So I sat there talking with Gordon. We always have a bit of a chinwag. A lorry pulled up outside and I glanced out at it.
'Christ, Gordon, there's a bloody fire escape on it!'
'Don't buy it here', said Gordon. *'They're going in next door.'*
So I went outside and saw the bloke.
He said, *'We've got to take it in for scrap.'*
I said, 'I'll buy it off you.'
Gordon said, *'Take it back round home, and he'll follow you round.'* So I did. I saw the boss man, and said, 'What are you hoping to get for that fire escape?'
'£40.'
I put my hand in my pocket, gave him £40 and said, 'Take it to Shefford.'
'Oh, I shall want more than that.'
'Here's another £20, take it out there.'

137

So they did. James, Alan and Gordon couldn't believe their eyes. I'd only been gone an hour and a quarter!   I'd come back, with a fire escape which had only been cut in the one place that they would have had to cut it to make it turn the corner!   Do you know, it fitted absolutely to the tee!
They said, *'No bugger but you could do that!'*

'James has got units at Savernake and I have some at Shefford now. The reason we got the units at Savernake was when we gave up the farm, James was out of business, he had no farm to farm. Nothing to do, he wanted to go into Northfield Farm.
I said, 'No you won't James. That's mine and all under control. We'll find a farm for you.'
Within six months, he had moved from the Home Farm of Suttons, to the Home Farm of Aylesbury's.   When we looked around the farm, I saw these buildings, and I said 'Cor James, this wants turning into this, and that wants turning in that!' We could see the potential the minute we looked around.

'James was offered the tenancy even though it was a dairy farm, and although James has never been a dairy man, he got it. I think it was probably because we were local, the name probably helped, and we were given very good references from our last landlords saying that we had always helped, always given them access to do what they wanted to do, how we had always helped with everything. So James got the tenancy.

'Wonderful landlords. Complete new dairy, and things, mind you we've probably spent a few hundred thousand on farm buildings and the same on the industrial buildings. That was our money, but the Landlord benefits from it anyway. Better land, better quota.

'James has got about 12,000 square feet of units up there. He
138

has renovated and converted all of them now, and they are all let. I didn't do the conversion but I started the ball rolling, James did all of it himself. The art of rearing children is to let them get on with it! You know, the churchyard is full of indispensable people.

'Everybody likes to think they are indispensable, but they are not. It is a galling factor. You think nothing can happen unless you are there. But when I had my back fixed, I found I could run a farm from a telephone.
But you've got to work at it.
Someone once said to me, *'Coo, you are lucky!'*
I said, 'No, the harder I work, the luckier I get.'

'Luck is being at the right place at the right time. Recognising the opportunity and then have the guts enough to take it. All through life, I've never had anything unless I could pay for it, never had an overdraft, personal. I ran one with the company, at one point we were £400,000 in the red. It was quite a business though. Quite a big farm. All my calculations were done in my head, mentally. I was lucky, some people can't do it without a computer.
James said to me one day, *'Father you can't go on running a business like this. You're not making any profit!'*
I said, 'My Father told me that any fool can make money but hanging onto it was the answer.'
The way I do it, we don't pay a lot of tax, because I re-invest it.

'At the peak, before we started to split the company up amongst the children, when I gave up farming at Ashmansworth, and Marsh Benham, and just had the farm back here with the Industrial units going, the shares were valued at £3.2million.
Then land prices dropped, and when we split up for James it

was only £2.8million. Not too bad though.

I made a policy of giving shares in the company to the children right from the start. The first shares were £1 a piece, then £2 a piece. I've given away every year what I could give to the children. When they got married they all got £5,000 each as a wedding present. They were offered it in shares or money, Richard took money, James took it in shares, at £20 a piece, when the company split about twelve years later, they were worth a £120 each! That's luck, we had a fair following wind, and we worked for it.

'I bought Richard a gun once, a very nice gun, and then I said to James, 'Do you want a gun or a share in the Dante Group?' He chose the Dante Group, probably cost the same as the gun. I'm proud that he offered to have the Icicle Meet at Savernake, it's nice to have kept it in the family. I don't know if Richard has still got his gun though.

'Muck and money are very similar, both much better for spreading it about. Too much money, or too much muck in one place, stinks.'

David chuckles at that one.

The children now (1998) all live quite close. James and Fiona live at Savernake Farm near Marlborough. Kate and Anthony live at Northfield Farm in Shefford, and Richard and Sarah live at Highclere. Richard met his wife at school, when they were about thirteen or fourteen. Richard went to Reading University and read Agricultural & Estate Management.

'His Headmaster wanted him to go for Oxford or Cambridge but Richard said that they didn't do the right courses there.

'Anyway, whilst Richard was looking for a proper job, straight after University, both he and James got a job with

140

Richard and Sara married January 1977

James and Fiona married June 1980

Kate and Anthony married March 1988

Jo and David on their 25th Wedding Anniversary. May 1977

David and Jo Liddiard, Elaine Bish and Alec Jenkinson at James Liddiard's wedding to Fiona, 21st June 1980

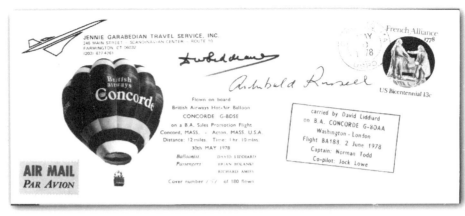

1st day cover flown on board BA Balloon Concorde at Concord, Mass.
Then on BA Concorde Washington - London . 2nd June 1978

David landing Concorde Balloon at Concord. 1978

Practice flight for first Channel crossing by a hang glider.
Flown by Ken Messenger released from a balloon piloted by David Liddiard. July 1977

Marie Antoinette - A hand painted balloon

Laidback cattle
- ballooning

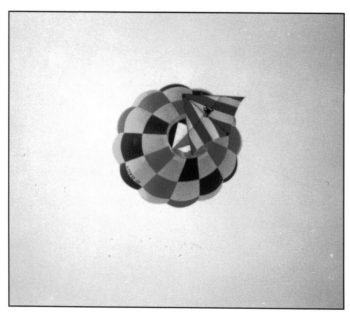

The first hang glider drop from 'Beatrice'
G-BAGY

Inflation

Murphy's. Putting the 'Scotland-Southampton' pipeline through South Oxfordshire and West Berkshire . James was working on surveying, and Richard was working in the office handling all the enquiries and such like. He had to work with the local farmers working out all the 'way-leaves', getting permission for Murphy's to go across the land.

'Richard was very useful to them because he knew nearly all the local farmers quite well, and James was useful to the surveyors because a lot of the parts where they had to go across, he knew the farmers personally, and was able to go and get the permission direct.

One of the Ministry people was going to get James sacked because he was caught off the pipeline, but James said, 'Well, this is a friend of mine, I'm only visiting him.'

So they were quite happy with Murphy's. I think that James earned enough money that Summer to see him through his University in comfort.   He went to Newcastle University and studied Agricultural Economics.

'When Murphy's were going through in about 1976, they came and asked if they could rent a small ten acre field off me, which was really only a reclaimed gravel pit. They offered me about £5,000 to rent it for two years. I mean, they could have bought the field for that!   Anyhow, I went up to the estate, and they said 'Yes'. But when they heard what I was getting for it, they wanted a share, but that was all sorted out amicably.

When they came and started to put the stuff up, I asked them how long it would be before they got going. They said, 'As soon as we can get a telephone, we can't get a line for three weeks!'

I had a spare office on the farm which I wasn't using, so I offered to let them use that, so that they could get started.

So they moved in.

'The boss, Ted Justin, had been brought back from Australia because he was the best line boss they could get. His father was killed putting down a pipeline, his brother had lost a leg laying a line, and Ted had both his legs broken doing the same job, so he knew all about pipelines and the problems. He had put them in across the Sahara, Middle East, Australia, everywhere

He used to arrive about 5.30 in the morning, go and see the cowman, have a quart of milk, that was his breakfast. He then used my telephone, which I said he could.

'After he had been there about ten days, the phone bill arrived I think it was about £1,200! I was a little bit worried, and I went to see him, and he said, *'Give it to me, we'll pay it.'*

'There's some of mine on there.'

'Oh, don't worry, we'll pay the lot.'

Which they did. They carried on there for another three weeks, and the bill was over £3,000, which was a lot of money in those days. There were calls all over the world to get their plant, equipment and the right men for the job ready to start

A long time afterwards he said to me, *'But we haven't paid you the rent of the office, how much do you want?'*

'Pay me what you think it was worth to you', I said.

'We couldn't afford to pay you that much,' he replied. *'It got us six weeks ahead at the start. That, and the better weather, made the job go really well.'*

But they were very good, they gave me a set of rollers, which they made up for me, and about £1000 on top.

'Every night the gang would go down to the Halfway Inn. They had got special steaks in for them, black pepper steaks. They reckoned that Ted would drink the best part of a bottle of Bourbon before he went home, and would take another bottle to see him through the night.

142

He was very hard, but very fair. He would sack anyone for being five minutes late in the morning. He would stand at the gate at 7.00am, and those people who weren't in were told to go back home again. He did it to his two sons one morning! They were late, he said, '*I sack everybody else, if you can't get here on time, you go.*'

'James got a couple of friends to come and work on the pipeline, but they hadn't been taught like James had by his father, and they weren't getting on with the job. Ted went up to them one day and said, '*Right you two. Go up to the office and pick up your cards and get your money.*'
'*What's wrong?*' they said. '*We haven't done anything!*'
'*That's why you're going home*', he said.
James had to be up for work at four one morning, as soon as it got light. The job then was to put a rope across the Thames and pull a rowing boat across, measuring the depth yard by yard. Then they excavated a channel under the Thames.
The way they got the pipe across was to dig a sort of canal, back across the field, build the pipeline the shape it had to be, then floated it in this channel using fifty gallon barrels. They then floated it across the river so that it stuck out each side into the trenches. The barrels were tied on with explosive tapes, and at the right place, they detonated the tapes, and the line sank down into place in the channel they'd dug. They had to wait until there was no traffic.

'When they came to putting under the A4, the Kennet & Avon Canal and the railway line, they had to tunnel using a mole. But where it was too wet, and the mole wouldn't go through, they had miners down there, digging through and sending the soil back out.
It was a big operation. The sleeve was about four foot six, and the pipeline was about three foot six. They finished in time well ahead of schedule and they reinstated the land very well

afterwards. People who don't want these things to go across, don't understand that they leave the soil and ground absolutely perfect, and in some cases better than before.

'Anyway, both Richard and James helped on that. Then Richard got an interview with the Duchy of Cornwall. He got a job as an assistant land steward with them. He had his interview at 1, Buckingham Palace Gate, and he was put on the Royal Staff working down in Cornwall.

'He's done well for himself though.'
'*Do you remember Richard's 40th Birthday party?*' Jo asked.
'Oh yes, it was the 4th January, two years ago. James, down at Savernake, gets two days shooting a year and he can invite who he wants to. One of these days fell on Richard's birthday, and out of brotherly love, James invited Richard along, and four of Richard's' friends. John Norgate was one, Alan Holland, and Adrian Rann the accountant.
It was all arranged, and they went back in and had a nice shooting lunch. A really nice present. But Alan Holland and John Norgate between them, organised a strippagram in a police uniform, for Richard,

'We were all there, Jo was in the room, I was there, Ben was in the room, aged five, a friend of ours from Canada was there, nothing untoward happened.'
Jo, defending him over the stripper, said, '*Richard didn't enjoy it, but said what do you do in the circumstance, you have to go on with it!*'

'James met his wife Fiona at Norlands here, it was just after he left school, and she was a Norland Nurse.
Kate went to the Constance Spry College at Winkfield, so she's a brilliant cook and a good Mother as are both my daughters-in-law.

144

Kate started work in a bank, and if they had a rush or were in a hurry, they always put Kate on the machine because she was the quickest person on the machines. They wanted to put her on the front. This was Barclays. Funny that, Jo worked at Barclays, and Richard's wife, Sarah, was also a Barclays Bank clerk. Three in a family.

After the bank, Kate worked for Memrad Optics before moving to a firm selling Cherished Number Plates.

She met Anthony when she was at school. She and Anthony bought me my number plate as a present to say thank you for the wedding. I would never have splashed out all that money on myself. I had always looked around to see how much they were, but I would always spend money on other people, never on myself.

'Kate's wedding was not everything I wanted, though. We wanted something different and special, everyone thought we would have a marquee on the lawn, so I said, 'We won't do what everybody thinks we are going to do.'

'Richard and Sarah had married at Burghclere Church, James and Fiona were married at Shefford Church, and both boys had their wedding receptions at the Elcot Hotel. So for Kate's, we went up to the Elcot, but they couldn't manage the numbers that we wanted.

The only place we could find which could take the numbers was Littlecote. So we hired Littlecote House for the day.

Someone said, *'You'll be alright there, so-an-so is the catering manager there, and he will do a good job.'*

'The week before the wedding, Peter de Savary sacked him! The chap who was left in charge didn't have a clue really. So much so, that they didn't keep any food back for the Bride and Bridegroom and their parents after the reception line had gone through. When we all went to get some food, it was all gone!

145

'I said to them that there was no restriction on the amount of champagne to be served, but I wanted a bottle of water on every table in the room. When I had the bill, the only thing that surprised me was how little champagne had been drunk. But the quantity of water drunk was fantastic!

'When the people didn't want the champagne, they were drinking the sparkling water, people find it preferable when they are thirsty, I know I do. I was amazed at the amount of water, I just hope everyone had the amount of Champagne that they wanted, the last thing I wanted was people saying, 'Mean old bugger didn't get the Champagne out.'
I did enjoy the day though. Someone said to me, 'You will enjoy your daughter's wedding, you will enjoy taking her down the aisle.'

'I must admit I did. She looked lovely, I was really proud of her, and I like Anthony. Jo was pleased because she got married in the church we were married in, that her grandmother had got married in, it was really nice. Everything went really marvellously, the only thing that I worried about was that everyone had enough to eat and drink. No one complained, but they don't, do they? I just wanted it to be right.

'Jo had a very serious accident at the end of February 1989. She was driving through Woodspeen, on her way back from Newbury. The Land Rover coming in the opposite direction, lost control for some reason or another, came across the road and hit her BMW head on. Jo was on the pavement trying to get away from him, she had only had the car for about eleven months. I didn't know anything about the accident, I had come home tired out and had gone to sleep in the chair. I didn't miss her, then somebody rang me about seven o'clock.

146

'I got up to the hospital whilst she was still in the X-ray room, They were cutting her clothes off at the time.
They said, *'We want to take some X-rays, would you mind holding the plates?'*

So I held the plates. She had a broken neck, five broken ribs, she lost part of her jaw bone with six teeth attached to it, fifty six stitches she had in her face, she has no saliva ducts on that side now. She smashed her kneecap and broke her femur.
She was on life support for twelve days. She recovered remarkably quickly, and was driving again by May.
The driving force behind the recovery was that Kate was expecting Georgina. She was determined to be home for her daughter's first child and she was, by four days.'

'I spent six weeks in hospital, three and a half at the Royal Berkshire Hospital, and the rest of the time in Dunedin', Jo remembered.
David continued, 'It annoys me when all these people run down the National Health Service, it really does. They keep saying this is bad and that is bad, but the Intensive Care Unit at the Royal Berkshire Hospital is superb, second to none. There could not be better service anywhere.
I went up and thanked the consultant when Jo was getting better, thanked him for the way she had been looked after, and I said, 'I would also like to thank you for the way you have treated me.'
He said, *'You were our concern as well.'*
Brilliant people there, there was Mr Ray for the jawbone, Ears, Nose & Throat department, Mr Copeland, and an Indian Doctor whose name I really can't think of for the moment. There was no way and nowhere else she could have had better treatment. They were absolutely marvellous.'

Jo then told how the night of the accident, they had been due to
147

go out for a meal with Dennis Day and his wife. *'We were going to eat at La Riviera as it was the owner's last night. It was Dennis' wife, Pam, who rang David. Apparently the Police don't ring the next of kin anymore, the hospital has to. Anyway, she rang David at about twenty to seven and said, 'Look, Jo's had an accident.'*

David had gone to sleep as is his habit at about five. We were having people for the weekend, and I had had lots of food in the back of the car.

David rang the boys and Kate. They all went up to the hospital. Kate rang the people who were coming for the weekend and said 'Look Mum's broken her leg, we'll have to cancel the weekend.'

When they got to the hospital, it was much more serious than they thought. Kate was pregnant, and I came out of hospital on the 9th April, and she had Georgina on the 13th April.

I didn't know this at the time, but Kate and Anthony moved lock, stock and barrel into the Mill to look after David, until I was out of intensive care which was sweet of them, as they had only been married nine or ten months or something like that. But it all turned out alright in the end!'

'I remember Jo's remark when I got there, she was conscious, and she said, *'I don't feel very well.'*

'We didn't know how bad it was until the next day really.

The first night, they couldn't do a lot, they stabilised the neck, put her neck and leg in traction, decided not to send her to Stoke Mandeville and tidied up the jaw.

When she came round, she was getting a lot of pain from the five ribs. She had five tubes going into her, putting stuff into her in measured doses, she was pretty well out of it at this time.

'I used to go up three times a day in the first week. I used to get up at five in the morning, then come home and have some lunch, and then go back again, come home for tea and go back up in the evening.

I used to help get the mucus off her chest. She got pneumonia, there is still a scar where they had to do a tracheotomy, she couldn't breathe. She was still in pain through the five ribs being broken as well.

I remember an Australian Doctor there, he said to me, ' *There is something they've tried in Australia, I've never tried it, but I think it might help.'*

He actually put a needle into the chest cavity, and injected something directly into the cavity. I think she was on as much morphine as she could have. She had dreadful withdrawal symptoms when she came off it. Seeing worms and such like, dreadful. They had her on a ripple bed to prevent bedsores as well.

'Because you couldn't have flowers in intensive care, I asked people to send donations, if they wanted to, towards a special bed that the ward wanted for 'backs'. The Rotary sent a £100, and between them, the family and all our friends, we raised the money for half a bed, which was very nice. The Royal Berkshire hospital were very pleased.'

'Oh yes they were, David, I remember that,' Jo said. *'I have actually still got the book they made me write as I was recovering. They were trying to make me write and I did from quite early on actually. I think it is that although you are half conscious you might see figures or hear voices when you come back, you know.'*

'You couldn't speak could you. You had to write it? '
'No, I started to put things down.'
It took quite a time for Jo to recover but knowing that Kate was about to have a baby really helped. She knew she had to be there for Kate.

149

Years later, it is difficult to believe that Jo had her jaw rebuilt, or ever went through such traumas. Both Jo and David make the most of life together since, and enjoy entertaining at home, as well as going out for a meal in the evenings.

'I'm lucky in that I've got nine gorgeous Grandchildren. Emma, Rebecca, Laura and Benjamin are James, he's got four. Richard has got three, Elizabeth, George and Henry, and Kate has got Georgina and Edward, and they all get on really well.
Fiona said the other day that Georgina was five going on fifteen on the phone. I mean, I rang up the other day, and Georgina answered the phone. I said, 'Hello gorgeous.'
'I'm not gorgeous, I'm Georgina', was the indignant reply!
'She is very practical as well. They all are really. James has two at St Katharine's school in the village, and the two oldest at St John's in Marlborough.
Richard's Elizabeth is the third generation to go to the Grammar school, now St Bartholomews. The boys both go to Horris Hill School.
Georgina is now at Thorngroves in Highclere but she used to go to the village school in Shefford. Edward goes to Stepping Stones in Froxfield and is moving to Thorngroves this September.

'When it comes to nephews and nieces, my eldest sister has got one boy, John. Barbara has got two boys, both millionaires, one is a serious millionaire. Tony started a shop called Panthouse, just off High St Kensington, he then bought out Jean Machine, and then sold it on. We go over to his house in Florida to keep Barbara company sometimes. He lives down in Reigate in Surrey, he bought a house, pulled it down and rebuilt it. It is quite something.

'John Liddiard, who now lives at Shefford, has got one daughter and three sons, the boys are all farming. Peter has

got two boys but neither of them are farmers.
My sister Susan, Lady Bradbury, has got two sons, John and Ben.

'Both my boys wanted to work with the land.   I tried to instil discipline into their lives, for their future. It's difficult when they grow up. They think they know it all . I think one bit of advice I gave my boys was, 'If you find something you think I didn't, come back and tell me about it!'
To Kate I said, 'Well, I trust you, but it's the little sods around like me that's the problem!'
It's not a case of **'will they?'**, it's a case of **'will they be careful?'**
My sister says it's not a case of *'Packets of three'* anymore, as she found a gross under her son's bed!

'I mean we laugh now, but when I used to help move farmworkers, we used to go with a lorry to help them move house when they came to work for us, you very often saw them (*condoms*) under the bed where they'd been chucked, when you lifted the bed to move it out!
I mean, there was one place I went to where he didn't have a lot of furniture, so we got it all in one lorry.
I said, 'Is that everything?'
'No, I have to get the chickens.'
'Where are they, in the shed down the bottom of the garden?'
'No, I've got them in the bathroom.'
We went into the bathroom, and this is no exaggeration, there were two perches tied on the top of the bath, tied to the taps so they didn't move.   The chickens were roosting over the bath, and there was about six inches of chicken shit in there! As well as that, there was a cleft of hay in the washbasin!
That is a true story.

'I like giving things, surprising people with gifts.

151

For Jo's fortieth birthday, I arranged a surprise party for her. We had just moved into the Mill at that time. It was at a pub called the Yew Tree out near Highclere, and the landlord and his wife belonged to the 'Sealed Knot', you know, dressing up and having mock Civil War battles.

'I went down to see him one day, and said *'I would like to do a really old fashioned party. Would you dress up in your costumes, and have serving wenches and all that?'*
He said yes, and I said that I would arrange for him to have a suckling pig, and to have some ribs delivered, really good ones, well hung.
He did it properly in the old fashioned way. I arranged for about thirty or forty people, to be there, and cut a long story short, I didn't tell Jo what was happening, I got Alan Snook and his wife to ask if we would go out for a meal with them , down to Overton , to a place where we've been a few times.

'I said we'd love to, and on the way there, I said that I had to pop into the Yew Tree first as they owed me some money, which was not unusual, so Jo did not suspect anything.
We went in through the back entrance and bought a drink. The whole thing was nearly spoilt by my brother and Geoffrey Wallis coming in dressed in doublet and hose!
I said, 'Where the hell are you to going to?'
'Ah, - we're off to a fancy dress party!'
'Oh, jolly good show.'
The landlord suggested that we went out of the other door and of course everyone was waiting for us.

'There was mead, mulled wine, and all the meat was put on the tables with daggers, and we ate things with our fingers. It was really fantastic. They brought on the suckling pig, and it was great.'

152

Jo remembers it well.

'It was a real surprise, totally unexpected, and then on my fiftieth birthday we went to Richard and Sara's.'

'Oh yes, they laid on a party for you, didn't they? Then on her sixtieth, I arranged for everyone to go to the Elcot. That was a complete surprise, she just could not believe it, I have a photograph of her walking in. A complete surprise. I can't do it any more, she expects them.'

'I did a few surprise parties for David as well. For David's sixtieth, which was the year of my accident, ' Jo remembered 'I had to do something special, he had been so good to me. Anyway, I arranged to have it at the Five Bells. Dot wanted us there at 8.00pm.
We had a cocktail party at home, 6.30 - 8.00pm or something like that, which David knew about. We were getting our wine from Dominic Elwes along at Easton, and he had agreed to deliver the wine at lunchtime, and quite by chance , and it was quite by chance, James rang up and asked David to go to Savernake, it hadn't been arranged, but he was out of the way until about five thirty, so Kate and I could get our hair done, I hadn't asked James to keep David out of the way but it worked beautifully!

'I had someone from Letcombe Bassett doing the food and she had done the most beautiful canapés, they were lovely, expensive but beautiful. David being David, came in at 5.30pm, and all the glasses had been laid out, he looked at the food and the glasses and said
'I've counted the glasses, eighty, you haven't got enough food for eighty.'
'Typical David! Typical! Trying to take over. I said 'Well it's enough for what I want David.' And I paid for it, not David!'

153

David came in here. 'The trouble with me is that I'm so practical, I look at everything, and work things out, you know!'

Jo continued. *'The party was a cracker. They closed the Five Bells to the public. Although the landlady was not a close friend, Dottie was more of an acquaintance, she had been very supportive to David after my accident. He used to go there and have supper after coming to see me in hospital. She was very good to him and fed him every night. Eventually he said 'For goodness sake, I love coming here for supper every evening, but you must let me pay you.'*
For this party, I hadn't organised a cake, but she had had a cake made.'

'In the shape of a balloon,' David rejoined. 'Beatrice. Beatrice was my favourite balloon.'
'Yes that's right, and it was a really good party, it really was. A cracker.'

'Yes, that's right, but then on my sixty-fifth birthday, I organised my own party. We went around and invited people. It wasn't until the day of the party, that I was counting up who was coming, and it was just 65, For my 65th birthday!
Someone said, *'Coo, that's clever of you!'*
I said, 'I don't take any credit for it , it just happened!'
Then it struck me, so I rang the Elcot which is where we were having it, and said, *'I want a candle on each portion of the pud.'* So I had 65 candles lit!
Everyone blew their own out, I didn't have to go around doing it!
My son got up to make a speech, during which he said, *' My Father must be the only person who on their sixty fifth birthday had sixty five blow jobs!'*

154

I suppose we are a family that enjoys parties, a real open house.

'I had my twenty first birthday when I was living away from home. I went down to see my sister at Burford, and they took us to the Swan at Minster Lovell.
I think that was when I asked you to marry me Jo?'
'Might have been!' Jo said *'I really can't remember, isn't that awful!'*

'We like to entertain, and we regularly go out and eat. One place for a good meal is a pub in Hungerford called the Lamb. It is run by a chap who was a keeper at Bradfords for a few years. Nice chap.
He said to me the other night *'I always regarded you as the best farmer on the estate because you were ahead of your time. You always had everything up together and going forward. You were the Alan Holland of your time.'*
After he left Sutton Estates and Bradfords, he became an actor, got a couple of parts on Eastenders and suchlike.

'Then he got a cancer tumour of the throat. He's got another one behind the ear which they can't operate on. They got the other one out but it messed up his vocal chords. He couldn't talk at all. They actually injected him with Teflon!
He started off then with a bit of pine furniture in the shop in Hungerford. Then the pub across the road became available, and he packed in the pine furniture, and took up the tenancy.'
'The pub he took on had a dreadful reputation.' Jo chipped in *'I mean, some of the goings on! Dreadful! There was a donkey in the bar! It was very, very rough. But they are trying, aren't they David?'*
'Yes'
'I quite like a pubby atmosphere sometimes. My Uncle used to have that pub many years ago.'

'That's right, and Jo's Grandmother used to have the Oxford Arms, or the 'Tally Ho' as it is now known. Jo's Mother and her aunts used to serve behind the bar. They had a good time during the war when the Americans were around.

Anyway, one of Jo's aunts married an ex-jockey and he used to have the Lamb. Another of her uncles had the Plough at Thatcham. Comes from a long line of publicans, my wife does!'

David had to raise his voice at this time as this conversation was taking place in their spacious kitchen at the farm, and Jo was furiously mashing potatoes for an elaborate meal she was preparing for twelve friends.

The whole discourse was peppered with Jo's banging, the noise of which rebounded off the Chinese slate floor.

'We used to walk up from town to see Grandma at the Oxford Arms', Jo yelled. *'I remember 1947 was a bitterly cold winter and we wore sacks on our feet to stop us slipping, coming up the hill. In those days we lived at Northview in Hungerford which was quite a walk.*

In those days, there was pink petrol for business or white petrol with tax on it. My Father didn't like to take us up the hill with pink petrol, so we had to walk. He didn't want to get caught for misappropriation of fuel.'

It all seems a long time ago now.

Early Ballooning.

David is not only known as a local farmer, rally driver and councillor but also as a balloon and airship pilot, and at one time, a balloon instructor.

'The start of my ballooning I remember very well. I had this ambition to farm 1,000 acres by the time I was forty. One day, John and I went up to Sleaford to look at this farm, it was just off the flat bit in Lincolnshire, but although it was big, you had to be a special sort of farmer to farm that land. On the way back, John and I were driving through Weston on the Green and we saw this balloon, red and white stripes, in the airfield.

It was the first time I had ever seen a balloon. I remember watching this red and white striped round thing whizzing down the runway, and being fascinated.'

David turned to Jo.

'I can't remember the date, can you remember Jo? When we went to see that farm in Lincolnshire, Father was still alive? It must have been late 60s. Father died in 1968, didn't he?'

'1969, I think', she answered.

'Ah yes, so it must have been 67-68. When we saw it, we stopped on the side of the road and watched. Then for ages, we never heard anything about ballooning, and we forgot all about it.

'In January 1972, Richard went back to school after the Christmas holidays, and one of his friends came up to him and asked,

'Do you know anywhere where my uncle can fly his hot-air balloon?'

Richard said, *'Oh yeah, at our place, Dad won't mind.'*

(Richard was at the Newbury Grammar School, now St Bartholomew's). Richard came back from school and asked

157

me if it was alright for this bloke to fly his balloon from our fields. 'Yes, that's OK', I said, never thinking much about it. I was given Alec Jenkinson's telephone number, and I rang him, told him that he was welcome to use my field whenever he wanted, and I'd ring him when the weather down here was OK, as Alec lived in London.

'Very early one Sunday morning, not long after that, I fed the cattle as usual, and realised it was a beautiful day. I went back in and rang Alec, I don't know what time it was. I rang him and said, *'Look, if you want to fly your balloon, it is absolutely perfect. A beautiful morning, crisp, clear and the sun's shining, lovely frosty air, frost on the ground, the ground's hard and there's hardly any wind at all.'*
I knew nothing about ballooning but I knew they didn't want to go too fast or have too much wind. I just used common sense.
Alec actually had the balloon in his drive, and he managed to get hold of Peter Langford and arranged to meet him down here and down he came with the balloon on the back of his little Mini.'

Pete Bish and Celia came down as well. Celia cannot remember much of David's involvement then. It was the first time she had seen a balloon on that day. She vaguely remembers him quietly standing in the corner of the field in his raincoat, puffing on his pipe, with that sort of look on his face of *'That will never catch on.'*
Peter Langford was the only one available to the group with a licence then, and because it was only a 65,000 cubic footer with single type of burner, Peter flew with Alec, and Peter Bish retrieved with Celia in Alec's Mini with a trailer. That was the 30th January 1972 and the balloon was G-AZIP the BOAC balloon.

'In fact, I helped celebrate the 25th anniversary the other day *(January 1997)* with Alec. He came up and we got him a ride in a balloon with David Smith. Alec is in a wheelchair now, so it was a very special flight.'

Back in 1972, BOAC had sponsored £500 towards the cost of this balloon, which cost £1,500, on condition that their turquoise speedbird was on it. Pete Bish and Phil Dunnington had the logo screen printed onto the envelope. In those days you were not allowed to advertise in the air except with logos. They had to find eight other people with £100 each to join them in a syndicate to be able to afford the balloon.

David's field was the answer to the newly formed Dante Balloon Groups' prayers, the field was much easier to reach than the airfield at Dunstable where the London Balloon Club was based.

David remembers that first morning well.

'I got the family and we all went down and helped, and I got the Newbury Weekly News out and got a picture in the paper. The balloonists came back after the flight, and it went on from there really. One of them wanted to know who was taking the balloon back that time, and where were they going to put it. 'Well,' I said. 'You can put it in the shed there if you want to. I'm not using it, put a lock on the door and you can have the use of that shed.'

So they did, keeping the balloon there most of the time. It eventually became the Dante Group's stronghold.'

Celia remembers that David also gave them two rooms in a loft, one of which was turned into a club room and bar area, and because there were so many people coming down there then, it was a viable proposition to keep beer on tap.

'There was a room behind that where we actually slept sometimes because we were so keen! We used to bring our

159

sleeping bags. There was a chemical toilet there and everything. If we slept there we could get up early for the morning flights.'

Celia didn't get her first flight until July as there was fierce competition for basket space in those days, and at that time she wasn't a member of the Dante Group.

'News spread though, and before long we were getting up to sixteen balloons flying from there.'

'It seems a long time ago now, 'mused David.

'Although it was a dairy farm, and cattle and balloons are not supposed to get on too well together, we had no trouble, well, except once, which was when I flew a balloon off the lawn. When I got back I got a real roasting I can tell you, they were milking, and I was low in the air, and when I turned the burners on, they couldn't see us. I got into a hell of a lot of trouble over that from my cowman.

But the only trouble we had with the cattle at that time, was stopping them eating the balloons, nothing else. We had no trouble with pigs here either. They weren't outdoor pigs, they were in the barns and we fed them swill. They weren't bothered.

'The balloonists kept coming. It must have been in about June, they came down as usual, and I said, 'What do you have to do to get a ride in one of these things, what does it cost?'

'I thought farmers weren't interested!'

'Well this one is', I said.

'Alright then, we'll do an intermediate and pick you up', they said.

They landed at Hamstead Marshall, and I'll always remember Phil Dunnington looking at me up and down judging my weight, and said, *'Well we won't want this, and we won't want that.'*

Out went the altimeter and other things, adjusting the weight

160

for me. We took off and landed the other side of Hamstead Marshall towards Ball Hill. He came into land, and knocked over a few heaps of bales which I picked up. That was the first balloon flight that I ever had. It was absolutely marvellous, I had always wanted to fly. I don't know what date it was, I might have it in the logbook, but I doubt it.

'After that flight I had wanted to join Dante, and if you look in the Dante book you can see that they made me an associate member until they had a vote around everybody and then I became a full member. I was the first outsider to be taken into the Dante group. But I didn't really seriously try to get my licence until after harvest, October I expect.'

Jo added, *'I found all this very difficult to accept because I'd never heard of ballooning, and we were very much a farming family whose routine was breakfast, lunch, tea, then supper. Ballooning upset this routine. In the early days at Bradfords, I mean quite honestly, a lot of the balloonists were exceedingly arrogant, they would just walk in your house - this is before we had a phone in the farm buildings - and sit down*

'I would find this happening on a Sunday, and honest to God, I found this most difficult to accept. I wouldn't care nowadays, we have lunch whenever, but in those days with the family, when the boys were doing 'O' Levels and 'A' Levels and this sort of thing, and we had a routine, so I objected strongly!
But you were so besotted, David. Nothing would stop you.'

'Yes, but there weren't many people in those days who got their licence in two months.'

'Yes but David, you didn't HAVE to get your licence in two months!'

161

'I did! I hadn't got any time to do otherwise. The only reason I have fitted so much into my life, is that I have made everything a priority.

Dungcart. It had to be organised like a military thing. A lot of people use dungcart like, *'I don't know what the men can do, I'll put them on the dungcart.'*

But to me if you did your dungcart, you went and got it done and went on to the next thing.   You didn't want jobs hanging around.

'I think you have to trust your men.   One of them said to me when I came in one day, and he was sitting down having a cup of coffee.

'You always come in when I ain't working and I've stopped and having a drink.'

I said, 'What are you worried about? I haven't said anything.'

'No, but you always come in when I'm sitting down!'

I said, 'Yes?   But I don't go by what I see now, I know where you started this morning, I know where you should be now, and I know where you should be tonight.   As long as you do that, then I don't care what you do in the middle.'

'You see, I know the time it should take to do a job. This used to fox them. I used to say, 'If you go and do so-an'-so, then you'll have a couple of hours to spare and you can then go and do so-an'-so.'

'But how..?'

I said, 'I should think that job should take you until three o'clock and you can do so-an'-so afterwards.'

I could calculate things in my mind and work out the time tasks took, my Father could too.'

David Rabbitts remembered David when he was young. *'I also remember when they were drilling, and David.L was supposed to be helping, and he would be lazing around, but the minute*

162

he saw his Father driving up, he would throw a sack around his shoulders and run up towards the tractors as if he had been working non stop!'

David L. continued,
'I used to wear an RAF Flying suit for ballooning. I got it from one of those surplus supplies places, I just thought that that was what you had to wear when you flew, you know. I thought that if I wanted to get some flights I would dress right, so that's what happened.
I found out later, that it was best to get tractor suits, so I used to get red tractor suits, they were much better. They all had Massey or David Brown logos on . The best one I had was a black David Brown one, I used to wear that a lot.

'Actually, Alec Jenkinson and I got our licences on the same day, and that is when you think you can fly a balloon, but of course you can't. How we never killed ourselves in those early days, I'll never know. I think, really, that some of the things we did were really pushing our luck.

'I remember this flight with John Emery. We took off and landed right by a place for the mentally disturbed near Basingstoke, Park Prewitt. I remember the farmer coming up, roaring over the field, bellyaching like hell at John Emery. He started going on at him, and at that time I had my old RAF flying suit and a crash helmet on. I took the crash helmet off, took off my flying suit, put my Harris tweed jacket and flat cap on and went up behind him.
He was saying *'You've given all my cows mastitis and I won't get any milk, and I'm going to sue you.'*
'I tapped him on the shoulder and said, 'Look here old man, I've just taken off from the middle of my milking herd, and you're talking about balloons giving your cows mastitis. You're talking bullshit. This won't give your cows mastitis,

163

and there weren't any cows in the field when we landed and I know more about ruddy cows than you do!'

'The argument collapsed after that, and we went down the pub and he bought us a drink. One minute I had an RAF flying suit and a crash helmet on, and the next I had my flat hat and my jacket on talking farming language!

'It has been an advantage being a farmer, because you can talk their language, but if you do happen to make a cock-up, you feel a bigger fool than ever. Landing next to a lambing pen for instance - ask Robin Batchelor.

'When I first got my licence, and I was on site all the time, people were coming down and saying *'Will you fly me, will you fly me?'*
'There was a big map up on the wall in the club room at Bradfords, and I started marking it up. I suppose it was the first marked-up map for balloonists.
We started off with 'UF's, Unfriendly Farmers. Then 'VUF's, Very Unfriendly Farmers, and eventually FUF's !'
I suppose you can say that I was the first Landowner Representative! It helped that I had been Chairman of the Newbury NFU a few years before, I had also been on the Executive of the Berkshire branch for a few years as well.
Then Tom Sage, who wasn't Dante Group, gave me a ride in July of that year. G-AZVT, that must have been 'Jules Verne' We probably flew in the evening. I didn't really get started until I became a member of Dante.

'I went to Ireland, with Laurie Ryan, Nigel Tasker, Mo, and Paul Keane. I supplied the Land Rover and we drove to Ireland with two balloons, and we did two retrieves with one vehicle. It was the Irish Meet and Anne Lewis-Smith was there then as well.

We were flying G-AZVT most of the time, but on one occasion I flew in G-AZNT with Nigel Tasker, we dog-housed a bit I think, but that wasn't too bad.

To dog-house a balloon upon landing was quite common in those days, there were no rigid poles holding up the burner from the basket, and if your landing was hard, the basket could tip right upside-down!

'But the last flight we had there, Laurie Ryan was flying, it was the shortest distance within one hour and we were flying over the river and we didn't see the telegraph poles because they were in the trees at each side, we couldn't see the wires because of the background of the river, and all of a sudden we stopped! There was this 11,000kV wire, it was at eye level when we saw it. Laurie had seen it just before we hit it and burned to try and get out of it and it skidded down the flying wires and caught on the edge of the basket.

'I had rubber boots on, and I put my boot on it, and pushed it off the side of the basket. At that time we always did the cylinder strap buckles up on the outside of the basket. The wire slid down the outside of the basket and caught on the buckle.

'I hung onto the burner frame, and put my foot out and shoved it off that buckle and it slid down to the next buckle. That was too far down then. I didn't really think I ought to climb out that far, so I got my knife out and cut the strap on the inside. We bounced out of that and landed shortly afterwards.

'The London Balloon Club were there, and they got caught in a tree. The flying wires were caught. There were three pilots there, two in the basket and one on the ground. One was saying, 'Burn', one was saying, 'Rip', and one was saying

165

'Cut the tree'!

I came along and said, 'Give me the bloody saw.' I climbed up the tree and as I went up, branches were breaking off underneath me, it was a bit rotten. I sawed the branch off, and they got the balloon off it. But there were no branches left for me to get down, they had all broken off! I got back down again somehow.

'It was the same meet that Noel Lewis or Terry Adams was flying over the Newcastle Inn, and somebody undid the buckle on the trailrope by mistake. It wasn't attached to the basket and the whole trailrope came down and nearly landed on top of the landlord's wife!

At that same meet, the Irish balloon 'Tar Baby' was trying to do a fast descent and pull out. It hit the ground, and the flying wires came down, they coiled, the balloon bounced, the wires snatched up, and the balloon went up with, I think, three flying wires broken on the basket!

'Roger Barratt tried one of those at the Icicle Meet, and there was a bit of cloud, and as he came out of the cloud, he was coming down like a brick, he didn't have enough time to burn out, and came straight down into the wood. The next day was spent with tree surgeons trying to get the balloon out of the wood.

'I got a lot of rides in Ireland, one was with Nigel Tasker, and this is where I knocked up the hours. When I got back from Ireland in October, I had twelve and a half hours flying in my logbook, not bad in three months. I was getting up for enough hours for my licence.

'Then I had training flights with I don't know who - oh yes, there was one with Phil Dunnington to Wallingford. I know that was Phil Dunnington because I didn't like his landings. On

166

the 5th November, I'd gone with Phil, and we flew from Marsh Benham across to Wallingford, and of course you go over the downs towards Aldworth.

Well I know the area very well, and Phil was giving me a training flight, then he took over. We were flying along under the cloud, well not actually under the cloud as we were in the fog. We were over the hills by Aldworth, and I said

'For Christ's sake Phil, look out, the National Grid is just ahead of us!'

We did actually see it. I was worried to death, and just then we came down over Carmel College at Wallingford.

Phil said, *'Crikey, we're in RAF Benson's control zone, we'd better land!'*

'We came over these trees, saw a field and he took the top out at about seventy feet. We didn't drag very far, but digging the basket out was a problem! I don't think we had a trailrope, anyway it was rip out and go. That was the old velcro rip.

'A bit later on that month I flew with John Collier and we went to Dunley. Dave Munson and John Collier were in the basket I think. We had a committee landing, someone did the trailrope, someone did the rip and I was on the burner, heavy landing though. You don't want committee landings, you want to be in charge yourself.

'The day after the committee landing, I went up with Tom Donnelly in Dante. So it was us two and my daughter Kate was in the basket with us.

After flying for a bit, we decided to land over the other side of Boxford, and as we were coming in, we flew over this house, where there was a chap sweeping leaves into the river.

I shouted out, 'Good Morning.'

'It was a beautiful, crystal clear ideal balloon day.

After I cried Good Morning he looked around and couldn't see us.

So I said, 'That's pollution, chucking all that stuff in the river!'

He kept looking round and but still couldn't see us.

I said, 'Look up to heaven, my man, look up to heaven!'

With that I turned the burner on, (you can't be cool for too long).

He dropped the broom and ran indoors. I thought he had run indoors to get someone to come and look at the balloon.

I landed the balloon a bit further on, packed up and went home. It was about ten days, a fortnight later when a friend of ours, Phil Sullivan, said, *Did you fly over Boxford about two weeks ago?'*

'Yes', I said.

'You nearly killed the poor old retired vicar, he thought his maker had come for him!'

'It turned out, with the roar of the burner, the poor old chap went and had a heart attack! Of course the balloon was Dante! Dante's Inferno! Rather naughty really but you don't know it all until you hear the rest of the story. There are one or two things that have happened like that.

'On the next Saturday, Anne Lewis-Smith, who was at her daughter's wedding in Henley-on-Thames, arranged for Mark Westwood, who was also at the wedding, to come and give me a check out flight the next day!

Now I don't know anyone who Mark Westwood has checked out - there can't be many. Anyway, he rang up on the Sunday morning and said that he would come and give me the check out flight. I remember like it was yesterday.

'We took off and he said, *'Right, you're flying very well, where do you think you will land?'* and I said,

'Well, if that field wasn't so muddy, I would land in that field,

168

in the middle of it.'

'You wouldn't get into there. You do an approach and see where you would get in.'

It wasn't until we were about two foot off the ground, exactly where I said we would land, that he said,

'Well that's fine, you're right. Go on, burn away and you land where you think you will.'

'I remember coming up over this field, looking down and seeing a telephone box. There was about a three acre field with trees on both sides, big trees, and I thought, ideal spot to get in, so I put it down into this field, very nice and gently.

'That'll do,' he said.

'I thought you'd say that, Mark. I can drop you by the telephone box and you can ring up the retrieve to pick you up.'

He was quite impressed, I think, and he told me to go on and do my solo. So I did. I took off again, solo, and landed on a spot near Coombe. I held it inflated, on top of the hill for a while, but no one came along. So I took off again and landed down in the valley at Coombe village. No one came along then, so I took off again and landed right on the top near Linkenholt. Nearly two and a half hours. Took off at 12.30pm and landed at 3.00pm. I had landed about five hundred yards from the National Grid, and I had been thinking that if they didn't come along soon then I would have to rip out and Alec wouldn't get his solo.

'Anyway the retrieve arrived, they put another bottle of gas in the basket, I got out and Alec Jenkinson got in and did his solo flight, but the wind changed as Alec got in, and took him straight down the National Grid. Alec eventually landed at Hurstbourne Tarrant, he could only do that because the pylons changed course there!

169

'So Alec Jenkinson and I got our licence on the same day, 26th November 1972.'

David continued looking through his logbooks,
'I look back at some of my flights and there are a lot of memories. In fact the first flight I did after I got my licence was the time I gave my daughter Kate her first flight in a balloon. In 1972 she must have been about 9 years old. I don't think that I actually had the piece of paper saying that I was a pilot. But, 'I was a pilot', I had been checked out and I was going to fly. It was the 10th December 1972 and I had checked out on the 26th November, just over two weeks before.
I inflated, took off and had just got out of the field, climbing away nicely when, at about five hundred feet, I heard this terrific noise. There was a Galaxy, the largest US Cargo plane built then, coming out of Greenham Common, the US Air Force base! There was this bloody great plane, coming out of Greenham, screaming smoke and I thought 'Oh Hell!' There was nothing he could do about it, nothing I could do about it!
Well he missed me, he went off at the side, not very far to the side. He must have missed me by half a mile, but as he had approached out of Greenham, it looked ominous. But Kate loved it.

'The next weekend I flew in G-BAGY, taking of from Bradfords and flying to Wantage, a forty-five minute flight. Sally Smith, from the Farmer's Weekly was the passenger. She wanted a flight because she was writing an article about me being the first Farmer to get a Balloon Pilot's Licence.
It was a fast flight, with low cloud, the wind was fifteen to twenty knots and we dragged seventy yards! That was a stupid one. We were literally flying over the downs at Woolley, in low cloud, fog, I remember going over this line of guns, all friends of mine, out at Woolley Park for a days shooting. That was just before Christmas.

170

'Forty-five minutes to land on top of the hill at Wantage, we weren't hanging about I can tell you. But I've done faster flights than that. Anyhow, that was an interesting flight. I don't think I kept the article she wrote, I might have done. She is still writing for them. I saw an article in there the other day by her.

'I think there were only about forty pilots or so then. When you look at it, there are not many pilots now who are still flying who got their licence before me, you know!

'Also that month, I did a flight with Mike Norton-Griffiths and got to Devizes from Bradfords in two hours, just south of Devizes in two hours. We tried an intermediate but it was too windy, we just bounced along the field. An intermediate landing at speed – silly idea. We were nearly on the Salisbury Plain ranges when we landed.'

Looking further through the logbook, David's eyes lit up.
'This is the one. Bradford to Ham. That was the first Icicle meet, on the 6th January 1973. The Icicle Meet was a balloon meet just for balloonists, not a public one. It is still a big event in the ballooning calendar, it takes place on the first full weekend of the year.

'I took off, with G-BALD again, and it was one of those days when the Meteorological forecast wasn't quite right. The cloud base was supposed to be twelve to fifteen hundred feet, and the wind was supposed to be ten to twelve knots. The speed was about right, but the cloud base was wrong. The cloud base was about eight hundred feet. I remember climbing to miss this tree, and then not being able to see the ground! There were four in the basket, the balloon was 84,000 cubic feet, with a Mark 1 burner, and we were there, very quiet.

One of the passengers said, *'I fly helicopters, and we couldn't fly helicopters in this! I don't know how you can fly in this!'*
I didn't tell him that I didn't know how we could fly in it either! But I didn't have an altimeter on board, in fact, we didn't have a thing on board except three people and me.   I lit a cigarette to think about things, and I put my hand on the side of the basket, and the smoke was going down.
I thought, 'Aha'.
So, if the smoke was going down, I was going up, and if the smoke was going up, I was going down. If the cigarette was glowing, I was going down too fast! That is how I brought it down. As soon as I could see the ground, I could cope.

'We landed in the middle of this ploughed field and hadn't got a clue where we were, we couldn't even see the edge of the field, it was that bad. As it was a ploughed field, I did have a straight line to follow, so I walked down the line until I found a track.   I went left, then I realised that there were less wheel marks than when I was on the track when I started, so I turned round, and eventually came out on the road.

'I was on Gerald Broad's farm at Wansdyke, so I went in and telephoned the retrieve from there. They eventually came and picked us up, and I got the second prize for the longest distance that year, probably about ten miles!'

'The next day, they wanted me to fly Franco Segri, a well known, eccentric old Italian balloon pilot. I also had Celia's Father, Mr Redhead with me. Segri could understand English if he wanted to, but he was deaf, and he took his hearing aid out if he didn't want to hear anything. He was a maniac when it came to flying! It was a low level flight to Burbage, landing in the same field as Jules Verne, quite uneventful really.

'You know, when you look at it, the fact I survived to carry on

172

Little Governor's Camp, Masai Mara Game Reserve, Nr. Nairobi, Kenya. 1985
Post flight breakfast with Peter Langford

John Coleman showing David crocodile eggs.

Jo and David in Gstaad. 1982

Splash and dash - Lake Nevasha, Kenya. October 1992

Dante Group in Philadelphia. 1980

Dante Group in Budva, Yugoslavia. 1978

FIRST HOT AIR BALOON
FLIGHT: GRAND CAYMAN

On the 10th November 1978,
a British Airways Hot Air Balloon
G-BEND flew for approximately
50 minutes from Newlands to
Owen Roberts Airport.

CAYMAN ISLANDS

NEW HARBOUR AND CRUISE SHIPS 3c

VIA AIR MAIL

George Town Post Office
Grand Cayman, B. W. I.

David Liddiard was the first person to fly a balloon in the Cayman Islands. 1978

Inflating the BA Balloon, Plymouth, Massachusetts, USA, in strong winds. (also see over)
Notice the handheld burner with separate cylinder. August 1987
David and Jo Liddiard, Jackie and Chris Smith

Inflating the BA Balloon , Plymouth, Massachusetts, USA. August 1987
Mayflower in the background.
(also see previous)

ballooning is amazing!

'Now if you really want to know about a good one, it was the week after the Icicle. Mike Norton-Griffiths rang me up, and asked if I would take him for another training flight in G-BALD (Puffin) again.

I said, 'Yes I'll do it', but I had promised someone that I would take the balloon and blow it up at the Fair Mile. (The hospital for the mentally disturbed at Wallingford.) 'So I'll meet you there.'

'So we met up, and flew from the Fairmile Hospital at Wallingford to Lockinge. About half way, Mike landed it, near Harwell, and he said, *'Look, would you give my friend a flight?'*

I said, 'Yes'

He said, *'He's done some ballooning, but he doesn't have a licence for hot-air balloons.'*

So this tall chap with a bald head climbed in. I was trying to 'teach' him to fly a balloon!

Anyway, we came to land, and I said, 'I'll take over the landing.' I put it down in an area about the size of my garden. My passenger said, *'God, that was a damn good pocket handkerchief landing. Have you read the book 'Dangerous Sort'?'*

'No' I said.

About three days later, I received a copy signed '**Anthony Smith**' (the famous international balloonist and pioneer). I must admit, he was very good, he let me down gently.'

David had a good chuckle as he remembered this flight, and added that Anthony had been a great friend ever since.

'I didn't know who Anthony Smith was from Adam in those days, I hadn't got a clue. Evidently Anthony often smiles about that one.

'In March that year, I flew with Bob Burns, in 'Contrary

173

Mary'. I remember poor old Bob. He built his own balloon. G-AZYV. He lived in Plymouth, and used to come up to Bradfords for training flights.

He drove and old ex-Post office van, he'd drive all the way up overnight, sleep in the van, and I'd give him a flight the next morning.

On that particular flight (it was a home-made balloon, it hadn't got the dual fuel pipes on it) we were flying along towards Burghclere, and in-between Highclere and Burghclere, there lived a local magistrate, Parker-Bowles.

'Anyway, suddenly, we had no pressure, and we had to do a quick bottle change and turn the burner on again. We had to do the change-over pretty quickly and we had the burner going full on, but we were going down straight down towards the roof of this house. We pulled out probably about thirty to forty feet above the roof of this house.

I turned the burner off, and this voice said, *'I thought you were going to go through the roof!'*

I shouted back, 'So did I!'

We landed fairly soon afterwards!

'Poor old Bob Burns, he was killed digging a trench to lay the drains to his house, the trench collapsed onto him. He was a real nice chap. Did everything himself, even built his own house.

'Robin Batchelor's first flight was with me, teaching Jenny Greaves. to fly, and we landed next to a lambing pen. Right next to a lambing pen! Jenny was in control, and she was not doing too badly then, and I said to her,

'If you keep up a bit, 'cos there's sheep in this field, and if you go over that wood over there, there's a valley. You can come down over the wood, into the lee of the wind, and land before you get to the National Grid. '

174

'We came over the top of the wood, coming in nicely, and right below us was a lambing pen, right in behind the trees. I said, ' Leave the burner off and have a heavy landing!'
We did, very heavy!

'The only damage that was done was that the Farm Manager seeing us coming in, and knowing where we were, came roaring across the field in his four wheeled vehicle, and went straight through the new fence that the shepherd had just put up! He got it all wrapped up around his wheels, and the shepherd was not amused.
The Farm Manager came roaring across to me, and I said, 'Well actually you are the only one to have done any damage really.'
Which he didn't like at all. It's one of those things, it happens. The shepherd and I got on quite well.
Anyway, the landing with Robin Batchelor and Jenny Greaves was in actual fact probably only about five hundred yards from the flight I had with Jo. Her first flight was with Jenny Greaves on a training flight.'
'That's why I gave up ballooning,' Jo commented from the other side of the kitchen.

'Oh yes, that one was in Beatrice, we gift wrapped a bloody tree! Well Jenny was ground shy in those days, she missed about four good landing sites, you know, coming in from way off and going off again. Eventually I said, 'I'll fly it'. Jo was with me and I said, 'I'll land.'
Mike Adams was flying right next to us. We came into land, and I yelled, 'It's all right to land here, it's just been planted, we won't do any damage.'
We both came down, and we were both just taking out the rips, when a thermal came through, Mike went one way, I went the other, both with partially open velcro rips, up over

175

the hedge, down the other side on top of a fencing post, the post fell over, the basket fell over, we all fell over on top of each other, the balloon collapsed against this big tree, and tore about two panels. They all fell on top of me, I was all right, there was Chris Smith, Jenny and Jo.'

'I took Jo once more, I'll tell you about that story. She said she would come with me. I had the balloon 'Gemini', with John and Shelagh Green, and Blackie, the usual crew for the retrieve and the blowing up.
So we blew it up, it was the middle of Summer and it had been a really hot day, and this was the evening. When we took off, it was an easterly wind, so I said, 'We'll try and land at Hungerford.'
We got to about five hundred feet and we ran straight into a blast of air which shot us straight off to the north! A sea breeze, at about twelve knots.
Jo said, *'Don't go too high, don't go too high, mind those trees, mind those power wires, shall we land?'*
We got down nearly to Winterbourne, and I put it down in the valley, put the balloon down beautifully and we stopped.
'Ooh!', she said.
I said, 'You can get out now.' So she got out, and I turned the burner on, and as I took off, I said to her, 'I can see the road, it's about half a mile from here. I suggest you walk, dear!'
That was the last time Jo flew with David. He really chuckled as he remembered the incident.

'As I flew over the road, John and Shelagh Green were there about to follow me again, and I shouted, 'You'd better go back, I've left my passenger in a field back there!'
Yes, that was her second time - and her last.

'Another flight with Jenny Greaves, David Rabbitts and Alan Snook and I was flying it, we landed in the car park of the

176

Crossways pub, four people in G-BAGY. I put it down right in the car park of the Crossways Pub, in Kintbury. Then we went on to have a drink in the pub.

'Here's another one, I took G-AZIP, Steve Burman and Jenny. We landed at Littlecote Park Farm, where I used to farm. I saw Barry Side, and for a bit of a wag, I yelled to him, 'Come on Barry, I'll give you a ride, I'm going to land up here', and I landed about a mile from the road. By the time Barry had run that far, he was all out of puff. We changed passengers, and Barry got in with me, and the other two went off back and the Greens carried on retrieving. As we flew across the hill towards Marlborough, a chap got out of his tractor and looked up, and Barry shouted,
'Good morning. Which way is Bristol?'
The chap yelled back, 'That way!' and pointed down the valley.
Coincidentally, the wind came around the side of the wood, the balloon changed direction and we went off down the valley!
So somewhere on the hills is a tractor driver who can say, 'They can steer balloons!'
We'd lost height and as we came down low we had changed direction to the left. We landed down in the valley near Marlborough.
My longest flight was Canterbury to France, I've not done a lot of long distance flights, I've been up to four miles high though!

'I did well over a hundred hours in my first year after I got my licence! Teaching people to fly, you see. I remember Rodney Whittaker ringing me one day.
'David? You know signing that people are fit to fly is a serious business?'
I said 'Yes?'
'You know, you shouldn't sign them out unless they're fit?'

177

'I know.'

'Well, everyone who comes in fit to fly has been signed by you! You're signing more people out than all the rest put together! Do you know it's a very serious business?'

'Yes I do.'

'I just wanted to let you know.'

I said, 'How many people that I have signed out fit to fly have failed their final tests?'

'Well, none.'

'So what's the problem then?'

'There were more flights out of Bradfords than anywhere else, but I think that people didn't like it because I was a farmer and shouldn't have been flying a balloon. I've stopped being an instructor now, I just didn't want to do it any more.

Some of them on their instructor flights put you down like a sack of potatoes. One particular chap, put me down at Leckhampstead, and he had a camera around his neck, he'd been taking photographs. He put down, we hit the deck, bounced, the camera went over the side of the basket, and dragged along underneath the basket. He was lucky it didn't take his bloody neck off, I told him. I didn't suffer fools gladly.'

Dave Baker, the British Telecom pilot, remembered when David did his check out flight. 'British Telecom had had a raffle locally, and the first prize was a trip in the British Telecom balloon. Although it was a local raffle, the guy who won it lived in Glasgow. Anyway, this guy came down to fly in the balloon during my check out flight, and he brought his young son, a lad of about 10 or 11 years old. He said that he wanted the boy to fly instead of him. We had to do it really, and the boy climbed in, and I took off, and I was very nervous obviously, being the check out.

Suddenly the boy starts crying and saying he was scared, and

178

wanted to get out. David took the boy, and cuddled him so that the boys face was hidden, and told me to, 'Get the bloody thing down as fast as you can.'

Well, I was in a bad enough state as it was, being the check out flight and all, but I managed to do an almost cold descent, and landed the balloon in a pocket handkerchief sized farmyard.

The retrieve were there almost instantly, as we were only about half a mile away from take-off, and the boy was handed over to his father, and we asked if the father would then come and do the rest of the flight, which he did. David just re-lit his pipe and told me to carry on.

Evidently, the boy, when he was safely sitting in the landrover, then went on and on about what a fantastic flight it was! I couldn't believe this when I heard about it.

I passed my check out, but I don't think I have ever managed such a perfect landing since! I'll never forget that.'

David Liddiard went back to his logbook.

'Here's another one. G-AZRN (Gravida, Supernews) Tim Stafford. I did a lot of training with him. He brought the balloon down to Bradfords, never flew it on his own. The first time he flew it without me, he went into electric wires. He never did like to fly on his own.

But this one here, 18th March 1973, we took off from Bradfords, we were flying across a field near Bullington Cross, we were literally going across the field at fifty feet.

Wide open spaces, cornfields, and suddenly I saw this Police car with a blue light flashing, tearing up the road. They put their headlights on through the gateway. Flashed their lights, and shouted through a loud hailer, 'Would you please land? Would you please land, would you please land immediately?'

It was too late to land in that field so we went over the top, and landed just by the crossroads at Bullington Cross. About one field away from the road.

This policeman got over the fence, and came roaring across the

179

field, goes to get over the next fence into our field and got his wedding tackle hitched up on the barbed wire! This did not improve his temper at all. He came rushing up to us.

'You're not supposed to be flying here, you're in controlled airspace.'

I said, 'I'm not in controlled airspace.'

It was one of the few times I had a map with me.

I said, 'This is where I took off from, this is where I've landed, I've come straight across there. The controlled airspace is down there.'

'Well I've been told you're in controlled airspace and you've got to land.'

They pulled down another pilot, Tim Godfrey, and somebody else who was ahead of me, it was controlled airspace they were told. It turned out they had put a purple air lane in.

That meant there was a Royal Flight, a helicopter which Prince Philip was flying, and, in fact we were in the way of the helicopter. I don't know how many balloons were up that day. You could see sixteen balloons up in the field at Bradfords sometimes for no reason at all!

'The next day, and the day after I flew in G-BAMA, who was that with? Oh yes, Joe Starkbaum. I remember, I gave Joe lots of his training flights. Joe Starkbaum was an Austrian Airlines Captain. He came out because wanted to get his hours up in a week and I gave him two or three flights. Two of them are registered down here.

He wanted two hour flights, nothing less than two hours, he wanted to get his hours in. The first flight was two ten, and the next was two twenty. We went to Fosbury one day, and Heckfield the other. He came here because there was no one out in Austria to teach him.

'On all of these flights , I would have been training somebody. I might have taken a few people up for fun , but most of them would have been training flights. In those days, with a Mark One burner and no parachute rip, you really learnt how to fly, you had to.

'Robin Batchelor said, *'You gave me my first flight.'* and now look at him, well up in ballooning. Pete Bish said that I gave him his best lesson in ballooning. I said, 'I can't even remember giving you a lesson! What did I teach you?'
'You didn't actually teach me anything,' he said. *'You just got in the basket, lit your pipe and went onto farming talk, and left me to fly the balloon! It gave me a lot of confidence.'*

'I think I've only ever once had to grab the burner from someone, I thought we might hit the ground rather hard if I didn't. I had to turn the bloody burner on - both taps!

'Have I told you the one about the young couple?
I was teaching someone to fly, and we came over this wood, and I was telling the pilot to land. He said, *'Oh look!'*
Everyone looked over the edge of the basket, and there was a couple down below. It had been a hot and sunny day and they had taken all their clothes off. The young lady saw us first - for technical reasons!   The trouble was, no one landed the balloon after that, it landed itself - heavily!

'Another flight here in G-AZBT (Hermes) with Jenny Greaves. We landed at Maidencourt, Shefford. It was quite late in the evening, when we flew off, it was in March so it wouldn't have been very light. We took off at six and landed at ten past seven. I took a friend of mine, Mike Hogan on that flight. I remember Mike was wearing one of the hard hats, we used to wear from building sites.   They're dangerous, because I found that the peak can cut your passengers, so I used to bend the peaks up.
Mike Hogan had one of these on, and I had one on. He looked

181

over the edge of the basket and his hat fell off!

I said, 'You can watch that bloody hat, see where it lands and walk back and pick it up.'

Then Jenny Greaves shrieked, '*A big black cloud, look a black cloud, we shouldn't be here!*'

Then she sat in the bottom of the basket! I remember that flight.

'We went to Spencers Wood on one of these flights, that's a long way, it's over by Reading. Two hours fifteen, low level flight, thermic conditions on landing, Tim Stafford and friend as passengers. Tim Stafford did a lot of flights with me. He's in Boston, America now. When he retired from flying balloons, I sold his balloon for him.

Do you know, that was the only time that I've ever made any money out of ballooning. He wanted to sell his balloon and I sold it for him. I found someone who wanted it, and he gave me £500.

'*Keep it*', he said.

I can't remember how much it was, £250 or £500, but it was a lot of money. I never thought about money when it came to ballooning, you just did it. No I think I can honestly say that that was the only time I got any money for doing anything for a balloonist.

'One of these flights here, I gave Tim's daughter a ride in the balloon, when she was only three weeks old, in July 1976. They lived in London and his wife, Tot, was a Doctor, they were both Doctors. He studied to be a Doctor after he took up ballooning. His wife specialised in 'Port-wine stains', birthmarks, and their eradication with a laser, she pioneered that.

I had more flights in his balloon than he did, he would bring his friends down and I would fly them.

In April I gave my future daughter-in-law her first flight, Richards wife Sarah, she wasn't married to him then. Landed at Inkpen, fifty five minute flight, we didn't get home until 11.30pm.

'Here's one. We went from Bradfords Farm to Park Farm Ramsbury. We landed in this Farmers field at 8.15 in the morning, and I knew him. He helped us pack the balloon up, and he said,
'Come inside and have some breakfast if you haven't had any.'
We hadn't. I remember going inside with him, and he yelled
'Come on, missus, get out of bed, we've got some people for breakfast.'
He made her get up and cook us eggs and bacon whilst we waited for our retrieve crew to come. It was Frank and Penelope Clothier, a couple of real good sports. It was one of those mornings that you will always remember. It was a wonderful way to finish up a flight, a wonderful sunny morning. A lovely flight, and we landed in a field and had eggs and bacon supplied by the farmer. It just shows that there are a lot of good farmers about.

'Here's another flight with Tim Stafford, I remember this one because it was the only time that I've flown over Aldbourne. It's a lovely little village, I remember coming down over the hills there, dropping right down into the valley, flying over the village, right over the church tower, right over my Mother's grave. I remember that one as clear as anything. We landed just the other side of Aldbourne. That was when I lost my pipe.
When I wanted a smoke on the way home, I couldn't find it and I thought I'd left it in the field. The next time we got the balloon out, we found it. It had been packed up in the balloon. It was a good job it was out! I used to smoke in the basket in those days.

'I remember one flight, I had Chris Smith as a passenger, and as we flew over the wood at Linkenholt, we counted forty six deer in the wood!

'In June that year, I flew G-AZKK, a 56,000cub foot balloon. We were doing some filming for something called the 'Final Programme' They wanted to get some shots of the top of the balloon. So we went to a very deep valley on the farm at Ashmansworth. They wanted a man and a woman in the basket.
Helen Meehan, Kevin Meehan's wife, was the woman in the basket.
We took off, down in the bottom of this valley. Of course there was no wind in the valley, but as we came up through it, the wind sheer made the balloon whip like a pregnant nun! It didn't half kick!
From that moment on I was looking for somewhere to land, we flew for fifty minutes, and landed at Baughurst. There was no retrieve when we got there. I tried to land several times, but the fields were gone before we had a chance.
We were coming in to one field, and I thought, 'We've got to get it into this field.'
There were 11,000kV power wires on the approach, you know, and then there was a five acre field. We came over these power wires at about seventy feet and I ripped. It was one of those occasions when we didn't drag very far, but digging the basket out was the biggest problem. Helen said that she had wickerwork bruises on her backside, but I never saw them!

'We just got up, and I was just thinking, 'Thank God we're down', and a car comes screeching into the field, pulls up, and this bloke jumped out. He was a Major in the Parachute Regiment.
'Is everybody alright, everybody alright?'
'Yes.'

184

'That balloon candled', he said. 'That balloon went into a candle! Are you sure you're alright?'
'Yes.'
'Well I've never seen anything like it!'

'On 21st June, Pete Bish and I flew from Bradfords to St Mary Bourne, and we had a really interesting example of curl-over at Beacon Hill. and we must have dragged about two hundred yards I think. The only time when I've been flying the balloon, climbing hard and still in contact with the ground!
Pete Bish was under training. We had four up in an 84, with a Mark One burner. We got this curl over, and all I could say was, 'Keep the burner on! Keep the bloody burner on!'
We screamed up this hill, picking up hayseeds all the way, but finally got airborne and made quite a nice landing at St Mary Bourne. That was in G-BAGY.

'Later that month I took off from Norland College, the nannies college, I live next door now. Helen Meehan was finishing college there, she wanted to leave the school in style.
I flew from there and we landed at Clatford, the other side of Andover. But I couldn't find anywhere to land. It was all crop, crop, crop. Eventually I flew it across this field of corn, straight at a hedge. I let the hedge stop me, and the balloon flopped over the other side.

'This is still '73, it was a vintage year, a good flying year.
Next day, we landed at Greenham Common Airbase in G-AZKK, a big orange balloon which is highly visible. We landed on the Airbase, just past the bomb dump. Our retrieve crew drove to the airbase gates and asked if they could come and pick the balloon up. To which the security man said 'Balloon? Hey man, there's no balloon on the airbase!'
'I've just seen it!'
'No man, if there had been a balloon landed on the airbase our

185

security guys would have seen it!

Eventually someone agreed that we had landed there. When they did come round with an airforce truck to pick us up, the chap didn't know how to let the tailboard down on the truck, I had to show them! Good sort of security blokes there. They didn't think we were a threat, we just said we had a burner failure!

'The 30th June was the maiden flight of the 'Jack o' Newbury', G-BAXK. Tom Donnelly delivered it, and we had to fly it from the Hamstead Marshall village fete. It was almost too fast, Tom Donnelly said he would come with me as a passenger.

'We took off, and we got about half an hour into the flight and there was a hell of a bang! Frightened the life out of both of us. One of the fuel pipes had burst!

What had happened was that there had been a pinhole in the inner pipe, and gas had leaked into the outer lining. We hadn't noticed and it had burst and we had a restriction on the other line, a blockage. So there we were with two fuel lines, one had a hole in it and the other had a restriction. It was not a very happy flight that one!

Anyway it was put right, and on the same night, I flew John Dunne from Deanwood Farm, to Woody Park. That was John Dunne the Radio bloke you know. Nice landing, a good one.

'In July I got a ride in the Goodyear Airship, N2A. The pilot was Captain John Moran, he actually brought the airship down right over Bradfords, into a field and out again. That night the Goodyear reps came out and had a balloon trip. We had a nice slow flight, forty-five minutes, and we got to Parkhouse School.

'Later in July, I flew in 'Gemini' from the Middle Wallop Airshow. The first night, they wouldn't let us fly, but the next day, I took off as the last thing of the evening. I had a trailrope on board, and we had a running inflation, you don't hear about them nowadays do you? It was so windy, you didn't need a fan - mind you we didn't have them! The wind blew it up, and that was the longest running inflation I've ever done, it was about five hundred yards!

My crew were dropping off like flies, all out of breath!

Jenny Greaves, grabbed hold of the trailrope and undid the clip, so we had to undo the rope on the burner frame and away we went. I had to land without a trailrope, and I remember the barbed wire which tore out holes in four panels. That was the first time I had ever had to pay a landing charge, I paid £10 for landing. I wouldn't give it to him, I made a cheque out to the church steeple fund.

That's the first time I had ever had a problem with a farmer. It was only because he was right next to Middle Wallop, he had had to put up with helicopters and planes all the time, and then there was this balloon landing on his property. The last straw really.

'Here another. The Battle of Newbury, we took Jack o' Newbury, and we had a problem because the pilot light kept going out, and it was thermic. I hated that balloon.

'This is a good one. We took off from Bradfords, and I did an intermediate at the Mill, East Shefford, where Jo and I lived for quite a few years. When we took off again, John Green, my retrieve said,

'Where are you going this time then?'

and I said, 'Tell you what, I'll meet you at White Horse Hill., Lambourn.'

We played around with the wind, and as we were coming up to the White Horse Hill, I could see John sitting in the car park, so I landed in the car park next to him. Jammy wasn't it?

'Now, John Green used to come and help an awful lot, and there was a balloon, G-AZKK (Gemini) and it belonged to Alan Boyd. Anyway, John wanted the balloon, so Alan said, *'You can have it.'*
So they paid the deposit. I think he wanted £1,200 for it, and John paid £1,000 and sold shares at £250 a piece. He stored the balloon at Bradfords, and asked if I would teach them, so I did a couple of flights for them.

What happened then was one day Alan Boyd came down and asked for the other £250. But they hadn't been able to sell the other share, so he said,
'Well if you can't pay it, then I'm taking the balloon back. What you've paid can be for the hire of it whilst you've had it.'
I heard this, and I said,
'Look, anybody who does that on my farm is not allowed on my farm in future. Here's two hundred and fifty. Get off!'
That is how I came to have a share in Gemini!

'From this logbook, and it looks like it was December, I picked up Clive Povey from his farm at Winterbourne and took him for a flight, we hit some barbed wire when we landed . I remember the flight now. We landed at Marshall's farm at Winterbourne, the winds had been getting very funny, it was near the end of the day when we landed.

'Then there was the Icicle Meet, it doesn't look like I flew at the Icicle Meet that year. I don't know if anyone flew, I probably didn't fly because I was organising it. I didn't need to fly because I had flown such a lot, it didn't matter. You've seen the amount of hours I'd done in that first twelve months, you know, I was getting a bit blasé about it. British Bacon brought a balloon out to Bradfords and I started teaching that crew to fly.'

188

'One weekend, I remember I flew on Friday evening, Saturday morning, Saturday evening, Sunday morning, and Sunday evening. On one occasion, I remember flying from Bradfords, landing in a field near Leckhampstead, and as the balloon touched down, a car drove in. 'Come on, jump in', I said, and I had to fly so and so. I don't know who it was, I can't remember. But you know, it was another flight on the same day.

Here's three flights on the 2nd December, they must have been training flights. To get three in on one day is quite a thing. It looks like Tim Woolard, Colin Boseley, and then I took Clive Povey for a ride. It's a job to remember going back that far.

'I don't know which flight this was, sometime in January 1974, but I remember flying over Beacon Hill and getting down draft. What happened was that they had chopped all the trees down in this wood except about six.

With a Mark 1 burner going full blast on a 56, and we still kept going down, so we thought we would chuck out the trailrope to try and stop us. It didn't. If you chuck the trail rope out, and dump it, it doesn't give you lift as you'd think it would in a down draft.

We were just going between these two trees and the flying wires caught, one on one tree, and one in the other. The balloon went out like a windsock, and we were left hanging up there.

'Well the next thing is, usually when you have a trailrope and you're stuck in a tree, is to climb down it. But the trailrope was in the road. Luckily, we had a handling line which we dangled it down to John Green. He attached it to the trail rope and we pulled it up, so that we had something strong to climb down.

I told Colin to go on, but he said, *'No, no it won't be safe!'*

So I did something which I never should have done, which was to leave the basket before my passenger. It was just to test the rope. 'If it is strong enough for me, then it's strong enough for you Colin.'

So we came down the rope.

It's surprising how big a tree you can cut down with a bushman's saw. We cut this tree down to get the balloon. There were only two panels damaged, and the basket bounced when it fell. All it says in the logbook is, **'Landed in tree near stud at Beacon Hill.'**

'I flew with Frank Barnes next. Frank Barnes was a great character. I remember Frank coming into the field one day and got the balloon out on his own. No one to help him, and remember, we didn't have fans in those days. He blew the balloon up on his own, tied his bike to the crown line and he flew his balloon, and cycled back to pick up his vehicle! He had a puncture on the way back, and the AA mended it for him! That was Frank, completely potty type, you know.

The last time I really had anything to do with Frank was in the Serengeti, when he helped us, we got a ride in one of the big balloons out there. Then he got permission for us both to fly from Naivasha Country Club. That was when we flew together, he flew alongside in his balloon.

'Now we didn't have fans in those days but I had a fan for ventilating hay and corn, and I think I was the first person to blow a balloon up using a fan. It was on the back of a tractor. The only trouble was that it nearly blew the balloons across the field! You didn't want any wind to take off with if you had that!

First Hang-glider Drop, 7th May 1974

'Ken Messenger and his sponsor came and asked me if I'd drop a hang-glider from the balloon, and I said, 'How do you do it?' and they said, *'I dunno, it's never been done yet'*

190

That was a Saturday, we did it on the Tuesday or the Wednesday. If someone suggests something new, you don't hang around and think about it, you get on and do it, otherwise you'll never learn. They showed me how a hang-glider worked, and Ken said, *'It's alright, I've tried it from a beam in the barn just to see if it worked.'*

'So the day before, I rang the CAA to ask what the rules were for dropping a Hang-glider from a balloon. Typical of a government department, they had never heard of it, as it was a grey area and they couldn't give us an answer. So I said, 'Would you let me know?'

'The next night was absolutely perfect, hardly a breath of wind, a lovely May evening. So we got the balloon out, and a three hundred foot length of line that they used for towing water-skiers. They made up a special piece to go on the balloon for the glider, with a metal bridle attached to a twenty foot of this cable, so that it wouldn't be affected by the heat. That was attached to the burner frame in the shape of a 'V', and then down about twenty feet with a ring at the bottom.

'I told Ken I would do it on one condition, that he would release himself, and so they put a glider release on the top of the king post of the hang-glider, so that when he squeezed the handle, like a clutch, it would release the pin and release the cable. I said I wouldn't cut the cable, because if you're going to release, you release yourself. I didn't want to be in the Coroner's Court when they said, *'How did he release himself?'* and have to say, 'I cut the rope.'
So I said, 'You do that or we don't do it'. So they did it.

We put the balloon up and we went up on a five hundred foot tether, lethal! I advise no one to do that. He only just got control of it before he landed.

191

In those days, it was a different sort of Hang-glider, a great big Rogallo wing, a big triangle thing. Nowadays they've hardly got any wing at all. Had he been using one of the modern ones, it would have killed him.

'It was a hell of a long tether. When he released, we were attached to a Ford Estate car, and it lifted the back off and dragged it right across the field making everyone else scatter. We had to then bring the balloon down. I remember John Green saying, *'Shall I cut the rope?'*, and I said, 'No, you'll bloody well cut someone's head off if you do! '

'Anyway, we had the dump open, but dumps in those days were so ineffective, but we landed. *'Wow'*, Ken said. *'That was good, I'd like to go a bit higher.'*
So I said, 'Alright.' John Green and myself had just got in the basket and this bloke said, *'Can I come up with you?'*
So I told him to jump in. Now this is a Mark One burner on Beatrice, and the way you take off for this sort of thing is you weigh off the balloon with three passengers, and you have two people on handling lines. They let me go up very gently on the handling lines. You have to be very gentle with these things, so you just rise gently, and they just let you up bit by bit, and the hang-glider walks in underneath, and he's already attached.

'When he's right underneath you, he takes up the cable, and then you have to do a complete weigh off again.
Then I said, 'Let me go.'

'We undid the handling lines and threw them out and we were climbing away. But there were these big trees to the west of the site.
'Oh Christ, we're going to hit the trees!'
The balloon cleared the trees all right but the hang-glider said

192

he felt like a bird coming into land, he walked over the trees. We got him clear and climbed to two and a half thousand feet, then he released himself.

It was rook shooting time, and as he flew back towards the farm, all my mates were shooting rooks in the clump of trees over the road. The glider circled this clump of trees, he didn't realise what they were doing down there, but I could see that they were all down there with their guns.
One of them said afterwards, *'It wasn't half tempting when he came round over the top of us, but we had to stop shooting.'*

'Reminded me of the joke when the hang-glider went over, and this guy raised his gun and shot and afterwards said, 'I don't know what kind of bloody big bird that was, but I made him drop that man!'

'The following morning, I had a letter from the Civil Aviation Authority saying that in no circumstances was I allowed to drop hang-gliders from the balloon. I had to ring them up and tell them, 'Too late, I've done it.'

'They actually sent someone down from London to take statements from me and from Ken Messenger, twice, with a view to prosecuting. The first time they were going to prosecute me for dropping something over the United Kingdom other than sand or water. I told them that wouldn't work because I didn't drop him, he flew away. They came back down again, and they were going to prosecute me for carrying a passenger in an aircraft in other than a seat that was designed for passengers and he wasn't strapped in his seat.
I said 'Well he was strapped in his seat and he was in his aircraft. You wouldn't want him to have taken off in my basket, slid down a rope, climbed over the wing and inched

himself in.   He was actually in his aircraft, strapped in his seat when we took off.   What's more, I consider that I had permission as I had an Aerial Work Permit, and I consider towing hang-gliders as Aerial Work.'

'The chap who was interviewing me said, *'Mr Liddiard, I don't think we should prosecute you, because I think you would laugh us out of court!'*
Then they wrote to me and told me that I was a very naughty boy and I shouldn't do it again.
In-between writing and telling me that I was naughty boy, they had also written and given me a licence to drop Hang-gliders from balloons for experimental purposes for the following year, and could I write the rules for it, they had also rung and said that they would like to come and see it being done.

'So on 4th June 1974 the CAA sent two people down to see a take-off and release. It was a lovely evening, with a southerly wind.   The two blokes were very interested with how we hitched up, and the whole thing was text book, absolutely text book.
We flew towards Boxford and actually I flew to five and a half thousand feet, and technically four and a half was as high as we could go. We let him go and he flew back to the farm ,and I remember my wife saying, *'Ooh it was lovely, he circled round, switched off the engine and landed.'*
I said, *'he didn't have an engine!'*
There is one thing about hang-gliders. The minute you release them, you're on your own. No one is interested in you, it takes the glare off you really. They are all watching the hang-glider. I definitely found that out a few years later.'

Still Airborne.

'In May 1973, the BBC rang me up and said they wanted to do a ballooning programme with Fife Robertson. They asked me if they could come down, and could I get two or three more balloons. We didn't know much about it in those days. We charged them £25 per balloon just to cover the cost of the fuel.

I flew Fife Robertson, and Jenny Greaves flew the cameras . The camera team followed us. We flew down across my farm at Ashmansworth, towards St Mary Bourne.

As we flew across the farm, I shouted down to the foreman, Alan, and his wife, *'Come on, come and follow us!'*

When we were over Alan at St Mary Bourne, I dropped the trailrope, and Alan and his wife, who were both large people like myself, good to have at the end of a trailrope, grabbed hold of us and pulled us almost to stationary, and pulled the balloon down. It was absolutely like putting a baby in a cot, you know. It was a beautiful landing, one of the most beautiful landings, Fife Robertson wasn't a young man you know, but he turned to me and said,

'Ach well, I'm a little disappointed with the landing you know. There should have been a bit of a bounce and a drag, it would have looked better on the film you know!'

'They put the whole thing in the can, and they were delighted with it. The programme was **'Fife to Nine'** it was called. **The Most Useless Hobby or Sport**, that was the one we did, ballooning! Completely useless, of no use to anybody!

They did a ten minute slot on that. So that was another thing, ten minutes on television with that one.

'Later that month, I did the maiden flight of Marie Antoinette from Bradfords. It was a beautiful balloon, all hand painted, actually it wasn't the real maiden flight, because that was whilst she was still being painted. But I was worried to death because it was so beautiful.

195

'We took off from Bradfords, we flew to just South of Newbury, to Ecchinswell, I remember the flight quite well. She belongs to the Balloon Museum now, the painting is still lovely but very faded.

At the same time, Tom Donnelly was flying a new balloon of his which had aluminised fabric on it. I came into land in a very small field and I was well in control, no problem. I landed at the end of this long narrow field and walked it up to the gate.

Tom Donnelly tried to make it, missed, and when they came into land there were power lines they hadn't seen! Their balloon being aluminised, Tom said, *'jump'* and they both jumped, and the balloon went on by itself, landed without any damage!

'Later on that month, we flew G-AZRN (Gravida 1 / Supernews), Tim Stafford's balloon, and we landed in the car park of the Crossways pub. That was the second time I'd landed there. We had to do it , because someone had said that they had landed closer to the bar than I did. This time we got someone to hold the trailrope, and we actually put the balloon down on the flat roof of the bar! No one has got closer to the bar than that unless they went through the roof!

'In April 1974, Frank Barnes was one of the people I was instructing and I was also teaching John Green to fly. John and I went on a very fast flight with a heavy landing, a very heavy landing. That was the only flight I didn't walk away from. We took off from an unusual place, it was over the road from Marsh Benham. It was early in the morning, 6.45am, and we flew down to Upavon, and that was in only 50 minutes!

John Green tried to put down on the edge of a golf course, and he ripped out, hit the road and bounced, and we went back up again about 50feet. The only problem was that we were on

196

the top of a hill and the hill was dropping away about 100feet, so as we came down we were in free fall for about 150 feet!
I stood on my toes to take the sting out of it and tore the ligaments in my calf muscle.
I remember jumping out the basket to deflate the balloon and my legs folded under me. That was the only time I've hurt myself on landing I was limping for weeks after that.

'Then actually, I gave Alan Dorman one of his first flights. I introduced Alan Dorman to flying, I'm not quite sure when that was. He came down and watched one day and wanted to fly.

'Then there was the Cirencester Balloon Meet, and I had permission from the CAA to do a hang-glider drop. But they wouldn't let me do it. Don was doing a double. He dropped a two seater hang-glider. But they wouldn't give me permission because they said they weren't insured. It didn't worry me, once you've done a lot of flying, it doesn't really matter one way or another.

'That was in June, I flew G-AZRN at Cirencester. That was the balloon meet when they had a double decker bus as the control tower, and Anne Lewis-Smith was there with Malcolm Forbes. Oh yes and that balloon flew into a tree, they were yelling 'Burn, rip, burn rip', and doing both at the same time! Quite well documented that one.
I remember my brother, Peter, took a caravan there, and Alan Snook was just in the process of getting the balloon Jack O' Newbury going. We stayed in the caravan, and I remember waking up the next morning with a hell of a headache, the blimmin' gas cooker had been on all night!

'Oh yes, then I was asked to go to the Grammar School, to fly at their school fete (Newbury Grammar School, now St

197

Bartholomew's). I took off in the middle of the playing field,
In July I took the Assistant Headmistress away from the Girls
School. I said if anyone wanted to pay, they could give it to the
school funds. I think she paid £25, which was a lot of money in
those days. We landed at Stroud Green, which is just over by
the racecourse. She had a gammy leg, so I had to get her
down pretty gently.

'September is the Newbury Show. We didn't fly balloons at a
Newbury Show until it moved back to the Shaw showground.
It had moved out to Elcot, then to Turnpike Road, then to
SeigeCross, and then to Shaw. The first time we flew a balloon
from the show was about ten to twelve years ago.
There was a little bit of dissension between the secretary and
myself, owing to the fact that when I was Chairman, he had
applied for the job and I'd turned him down and put somebody
else in, then he took over. I know I was right in what I did, but
the other chap actually used us as a stepping stone to go to the
Southern Counties Show.

'After that I went to the Irish Meet. I took David Rabbitts,
Barry Side and Renee Thornton. This was in Ballymahon. We
stayed in the Newcastle Hotel, and managed seven flights
there. I can't remember how many balloons were there.
We did twenty miles on one flight, and twenty three miles on
another landing in twenty five knot winds!
We had a good time, but the last task was the first one to get
to Noel Lewis. He was going to be in a pub, so we had to fly
there, land and get to the pub, and be the first one there.
As we were coming across this Irish bog, we got a hell of a
down draught from somewhere on the bog, and I had the
burner going all the way down.
'We hit the ground and bounced, and a branch of a bog oak,
went through the balloon, and it ripped the balloon from the
dump valve in the middle down to the bottom.

We went up to about a hundred and fifty to two hundred feet with a side of the balloon torn out!

We came in to the following field to land and I said to Barry Side, 'This is going to be a bloody hard landing.' I ripped out and we stopped.

Now this was a competition, we had to get to the pub. I said to Barry, 'You run, I can't, I've got to see to the balloon.'

There was this guy leaning on the gate *'What do you want?'* he said.

'I'm looking for a pub.'

'I know, you'll be looking for Noel Lewis, jump in I'll take you there.'

So we won first prize. Oh yes, Ireland was a very friendly place. We took David Rabbitts's BMW as a retrieve vehicle on that one I think.

'Back home, Ken Messenger rang up and said, *'the Yanks have done it!'*

They had gone up to do a Hang-glider Drop, and they had been up to 7,500 feet. He said, *'Do you think we can go up higher?'*

I said, 'Yes why not!'

So I took him up from Ashmansworth and we went to 8,500feet. I landed at Bull's Bushes Farm down near East Oakley, Basingstoke. He came down and landed close to me. I used to get down quicker than he did. That took an hour and ten. Not bad really, to take a hang-glider up to eight and a half thousand feet and back down in an hour and ten, was it? We were flying Gemini.

'Then the next flight I did was from Savernake during the Icicle Meet in January 1975. There was a competition to fly back to Marsh Benham. Strange thing is, that it was from the field next to James' farm, so the first time we flew from Savernake was 4th January 1975. I don't know whose balloon

199

it was, G-BCAN. That was when I nearly put all the telephone wires out near the railway line. We had four in an old 77,000cubic foot balloon and they didn't climb very well in those days. We only just cleared the wires, and landed back at Marsh Benham.

The joke was that they had wanted to put the cross in the field at the farm, and I said 'No, we don't want anybody coming up by the farm. So put the cross in the field the other side of the woods of the launch field.'

Well I flew about a 100 yards North of that, and landed in the field behind the farm! So if I'd let them put the cross where they wanted to, I would have been right on target!

'I was just picking myself up after landing, and Ken Messenger came rushing across, yelling, *'Look, the Yanks have taken the record away from us again, they've gone up to 11,000 feet!'*

'How about taking me up a bit higher so that I can get the record back?'

I said, 'I haven't got any fuel in the balloon!'

I went into the yard and British Bacon had just refuelled and were just going to launch again. I said, 'Lend me your balloon?'

I told them what I wanted it for, to take the Hand Glider up.

'Oh that's alright, as long as one of us can come up with you.'

Frank Barnes came up with me, and we went up to 13,000 feet The stupid thing was that we didn't take off until five past three, in January (!) and we actually landed at ten past four. It was just about dark. I remember releasing him, and looking at my watch and there were twenty minutes before it got dark! We came down fairly fast. Frank Barnes tapped me on the shoulder and said *'We're only 2,000 feet up now.'*

I said, 'I know, but I don't usually fly this high.'

He said, *'But we are going down at a 1,000 feet a minute!*

I wasn't looking at the instruments, I was looking at the

200

countryside. Anyway, we pulled out and made a perfect landing.

I've never believed in a cold descent, I always keep putting the burner on to keep it warm. I keep putting the heat in, so that when you want it, you don't have a bag full of cold air. Anyhow, I put the burner on just after that, pulled it out and landed with about a minute before it got really dark.   A minute to spare.

Our retrieve had seen us coming in, and we landed in a field next to the road, I think it was a stubble field.   They came in and had to put the headlights on to help us pack up, and to help guide the hang-glider in for landing.

'Oxygen?   No. It doesn't bother me, I can survive, and if I can't breath well that's that!   I'm not too good at breathing anyway!'

Jo shrieked with laughter.   Between guffaws, David said,

'I know someone who used to share a room with me on some of our trips, he said *'David doesn't snore, he makes a hell of a lot of noises all night like a big hedgehog waking up!'*

This really tickled David and he laughed even more when Jo added with glee

'No one seems to clamber to sleep with David on these trips, no one really wants to share with him.'

Both of them fell about and Jo carried on *'I don't have any trouble with it but they do!'*

David continued 'I remember one night in America, Niall Duncan had been chosen to share my room, but when I woke up in the morning his bedding had all gone! He was in the next room. I was sleeping on my own.'

Some of David Liddiard's ballooning trips with Dante were to very interesting places. Celia Kunert as a member of Dante Group, has been on many trips abroad when David has been one of the team.

'It was on an overseas trip, and although David is very popular, everyone who shares a room with him, has horrors about what's going to happen. It got to a stage when they would say 'I'll only go on a trip if I'm not sharing with David.'
On this occasion, it was Chris Smith. They were in a twin room, and they went to bed and in the middle of the night, Chris was woken up by this horrendous noise from the bathroom. He woke up with a start, 'Oh my God, what's that?' Leaped out of bed, turned on the light, to find David standing in the bathroom in only his underpants, holding the towel rail in his hand!
Chris said, 'What's happened, what's happened?'
'Oh' said David, 'it's the towel rail, I just reached out and it came off in my hand!'
Chris said' Why didn't you put the light on?'
'Because I didn't want to wake you up..
He wanders around at night, going to get a glass of water and things, and makes wonderful snuffling noises in his sleep!'
Roger Kunert remembers hearing how David got up in the middle of the night and went to leave the room and ended up in the broom cupboard. David always has a good chuckle when they tell him these things.

'Back to ballooning. One event that happened was that I was asked by Andrew Lloyd-Webber to go and tether a balloon for the launch of 'Aspects of Love'. He doesn't live far from here, he owns Watership Down. I had to go over and see him, I was ushered in to the lounge next to the piano room where he was re-organising a bit of music, and I had an hour of him playing the music and rewriting it. I was the only one there.

'Then when we actually did the tethers for him, there were all sorts there, John Gummer, Aled Jones, and one or two other stars, I can't remember their names, all came up for tethered flights.'

202

Zanussi Airship -ANUS I

Gordon Passey, best known to the locals of Newbury as a canny Merchant of Scrap Metal and car parts, is a good friend of David's. David knows that he has Romany blood and that his word is his bond, like Skylark, the king of the Gypsies who sold David his first milking machine

Gordon Passey has always been good to David, Jo calls him a rough diamond, his bills are sometimes three years late. You don't mess with him allegedly. *'No scruples, he either liked you or he didn't.'* Jo said

He rang David up one day and said *' I've got something that might interest you!'*

'What's that?'

'Half an airship.'

'So Jo and I went in together. Actually, the day before, I'd been into hospital to have an operation. I'd had a little lump at the base of my buttock, and whenever I sat in a chair for too long, my leg went dead. So I went and had it removed - not the leg, the lump!

Anyway, it was one of those rare mornings when I hadn't got out of bed early, because I thought I had an excuse to stop there. But Gordon rang at about 8.30 - 9.0'clock so that made me get up. Jo drove me into Newbury and we went to have a look. Gordon and I had a bit of a laugh about why I was a bit fragile, having a lump removed from me arse! *'Are you sure it was the right one they removed!'*

'David roared with laughter. 'I said it was about that big Gordon, and it was in a bottle when they showed me! I hope it was the right one!'

Anyway, the airship seemed in quite good condition, but the envelope/canopy wasn't with it.

'How much?'

'To you David - two and a half.'

203

(*Thinks £2,500!!*') Christ! That's a bit steep Gordon! How about one and a half?'

'*OK £150.*'

David thought he had been talking thousands! He handed over the three £50 notes in his pocket immediately.

'I don't usually have £50 notes in my pocket, but someone had paid me for something in notes, very unusual.'

He then wanted the envelope. Gordon said '*Zanussi have got that, they're going to burn it, it's got their name all over it.*'

'When I got home, I rang Zanussi, in Newbury, found out the name of the guy who had it.

'Have you burned it?'

'*No it's still on the shelf,*'

'Well,' said David, 'You ought to give it to me, I stored it for you for many years.'

'*Oh no can't do that, it's got our name all over it.*'

'That's only stitching, we can take that off,'

'*Oh no you might hurt yourself doing that and blame us,*'

'No, tell you what, I'll give you a letter saying that I do not hold you responsible for anything after I have it.'

'*OK come and pick it up.*'

So within twenty four hours, I was the proud possessor of the whole airship! I didn't even know I wanted an airship, and now I had one! '

That was 1988, the same year as Kate, his daughter, got married to Anthony.

David sent the airship to Cameron's to get it checked out as there were a few burn marks in it. David considers himself very fortunate that a friend of Anthony's worked as an aeroplane engineer, and he was able to check out the engine. By the time he had paid Cameron for the bits etc., the whole airship only cost him £500.

The BA Balloon outside the Pegasus Hotel, Jamaica. November 1989
(Left to right) John Baker, David Liddiard, the BA organiser - Ian Brereton, Dick Plume

(left to right) Don Cameron, John Christopher, Alec Jenkinson, David Liddiard, Phil Dunnington, Sheila Christopher
at RAF Hull Avington, Wiltshire. 5th December 1991
20th anniversary of maiden flight of Dante with Alec Jenkinson.

David at the Mill, East Shefford.

Photograph by Reading Evening Post

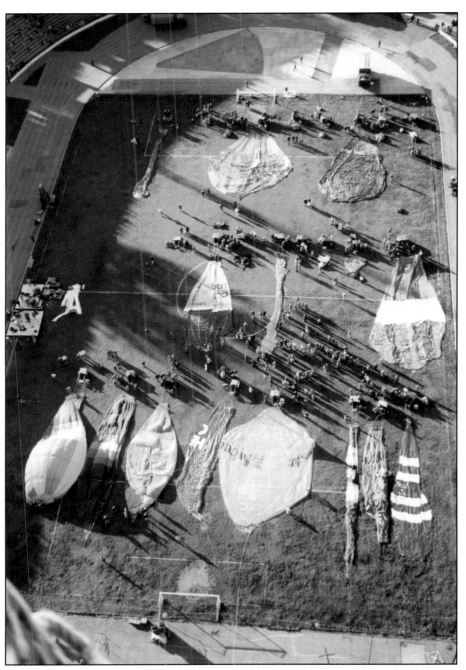

Laying out in Rayzan, Russia. 1990
(No vehicles allowed)

Soldiers carrying balloons into Rayzan Stadium. 1990

Take-off from Russian stadium

When they got it back, they took it up and laid it out on the lawn in front of Kate and her new husband's house. Kate, Anthony and David , then set about removing the lettering. They removed 'ZANUSSI' completely from one side and then Kate went in to get some food. David and Anthony rolled the fabric over, and he took a letter off the front of the word, and Anthony off the end. It got too dark then, and so they packed it up and put it away.

'The next day was perfect for a trial inflation. They dragged it out of the barn and laid it out. Inflated it and had it standing there on two tether lines. They drove it backwards and forwards on the tether, and in the end, David said, *'This tether is a blimming nuisance, let's get rid of it'*
So they did, and off they went. David was flying an airship, no instructions, no nothing. When he landed, someone came up to him and asked him why he had used that name for his airship. David was a touch non-plussed until he was told that the letters read '**ANUS I!**

But there was no instructor available to teach David how to fly that sort of Airship, the Cameron D96. All the people who had been instructors, were out of hours on that type. Alan Noble, now the Marketing Manager of Cameron Balloons used to fly it for Zanussi, some time before. So David taught himself to fly it. He got so proficient with the airship, that he flew over to the Savernake Forest from Marsh Benham to see his son James on one occasion.
'There can't be many people who can say that they visited a relation in an Airship!' he chuckled.
'It was a hard thing to fly, a pig, a real pig to fly' he said.

'When I was in America, at the time I was flying the airship, I bought a set of transmitters for people riding bicycles, they had a range of up to two or three hundred yards. They were a voice activated microphone in your ear!

'They worked. I bought them for when I was flying the airship, but I didn't fly it very much really. There was no way with the engine and the burner that you could communicate. I flew it only eight or nine times. But you needed so many crew to get it up. This is what killed it. When two of my crew went to Australia, Jo had her accident and Kate had a baby, that was it. Jo didn't like me flying it either.'

Jo has not been up in the airship, in fact David said it is difficult to get her up in a balloon!

'I suppose it was more dangerous than a balloon in that you had two systems to contend with, and you had two ropes, one to pull left, one to pull right. Keep it up in the air using the burner and so on. Nothing happened for twenty seconds after you done it.

'In the end, I sold it to Malcolm White, poor old Malcolm, he spent such a lot on it.'

When asked if he had found it sad when the Airship crashed into the tree at the Icicle Meet in 1995. David's voice fell to a whisper.

'I wasn't there, I wasn't there, and it was the first and only Icicle that I've missed. We were on a world cruise.'

'When I first got it, I flew with Phil Dunnington to get my licence. When we landed Don Cameron came up to Phil and asked about the flying, and Phil commented that I could fly it better than he could.'
David chuckled again, 'I thought that was a compliment until he flew it into the tree.'

Most balloonists belong to the BBAC, the British Balloon & Airship Club which was formed in 1965.

'G-BBAC was the Registration of the first British Airways Balloon, and September 16th 1973 was it's maiden flight. The reason it is not in the museum now, is that in July 1976, we were doing a show from Greenham Common. Dave Munson was P1, well he was the only person on board, it was a bit windy. It took off and went to Kingsclere. He forgot to put the pilot light out when he landed. He landed in a field of straw, dragging through it, piling up a huge heap which caught fire. Dave learnt to do the four minute mile! The firemen found some burnt out tanks and a burner frame!

'In April, there was a Dante trip to Kingston, Jamaica, with G-BBAC. Jo came with me, Alan Snook and his wife paid for their own air fares and came with us. We had the old British airways balloon, and Pete Bish, and Phil Dunnington, from Dante were with us as well as it was a BA promotion.

We were staying at the Pegasus Hotel, but we couldn't stay as long as we wanted to because there was a Commonwealth Conference going to take place at the Hotel, all the Heads of Government were going to be stopping there . So we moved up to the North of the island. Someone we had been introduced to, said that she would show us around. It was a wonderful week. That was my first time ballooning abroad.

'One flight was from the Caymanas Airstrip in Jamaica and the next one was from the Caymanas Estate and we landed in a sugar plantation. Interesting flight that was.

We flew out from the Caymanas airstrip and flew across an old quarry. In this quarry was a shanty town, houses made out of flattened out oil barrels, cardboard, bits of tin. There were children , goats and dogs running everywhere. I reckon if we'd landed there we wouldn't have had any balloon left, they would have used it for clothes! It was a real shanty town.

'We flew on, flying over a big brewery or distillery or something. Finally we were looking for somewhere to land, looking down at these sugar fields, and it looked like a lot of black ants running in and out of them. It was all these little children following us.

'We finally found a field that had been cut, and we landed, and as it was all short sharp stalks, we couldn't let the balloon down in it, it would have damaged the envelope fabric. So we kept it up and stood there waiting for the retrieve to come and walk it out of the field for us. There were children all around us about thirty or forty deep. They were all jabbering away at us, and I realised I had to turn the burner on to stop the balloon cooling.

'I reached up, never gave it a thought, and turned the burner on and it frightened the life out of them! They were all knocking each other over all trying to get away! I felt ever so sorry for them. To be knocked down on the sugar cane stumps, there must have been some of them really badly hurt, but they all got up laughing, smiling and joking!

'The next time I said something, but I did feel sorry for them, I didn't think the first time. But I will always remember and feel sorry for those little kids. Pete and Phil flew home and then the four of us stayed on for a week's holiday afterwards.

'I don't photograph while I'm flying. My view is, that you are either flying a balloon or taking pictures, you can't do both. Even a conversation can destroy your concentration. You have just got to concentrate the whole time.

'Back in England, on 14th June, we did a sponsored hang-glider drop. The local newspaper sponsored us, and Ken Messenger was sponsored by BP.

We got a tankard for this one. We took off from Bozeate, near Northampton. I dropped Ken from 5,500 feet, and he landed back where they wanted him to. We flew for about two hours, it was quite fast, I could see Cardington in the distance. So I thought I would make for Cardington, and if they had opened the hangar doors I could have landed in the hangar!

'I landed right in front of the doors to the hangar, but at 7.00am, there was no one there to let us out of the compound. A bit of a problem, but we coped.

'I flew G-BBAC from Sudely. I was not supposed to do a show flight, just a tether, but they only had handling ropes, and they let me go. I had to burn really hard to miss the fairground. I had Pete Hornfeck on board with me for that flight.

I remember seeing my retrieve crew doing about sixty miles an hour to catch up with me. I also remember that when we got up in the air and looked round, there was a glider up in the air with us. I remember thinking, 'one of us shouldn't be up here' I kept looking for somewhere to land. It was fast, we were fair cantering along. I remember the glider came into land at the racecourse, Cheltenham Racecourse.

We were still high then looking for stable air. I would not say I was frightened, but I was suitably worried. I knew by looking at the map that we were going to be in Wales very soon unless we did something about it. We came over the top of this hill, and I said to Pete, 'you're in charge of the trailrope. When I tell you to drop it, drop it, but don't drop it before.'

We came over this old apple orchard, and I said 'Let it go!''

It is a marvellous thing to drop a trailrope over a lot of old trees, slows you down beautifully.

Pete said, 'There's a small field with power wires the other

209

side!'

I said, ' I don't intend to land the other side.'

As soon as we were clear of the trees I took the whole top out. We were about twenty five foot up. We landed and stopped. Well we didn't drag very far. I remember that as being a very good fast landing.

'I haven't seen a trailrope for ages., big heavy things, trailropes. We have handling lines only now. Trailropes had their uses then but now, no. We used to fly in conditions that we wouldn't dream of flying in today, and then they had their uses. I don't think you need a trailrope at all, if you fly in the right conditions.

Back to the logbook. 'Oh here's one, half way through June. You'll love this one. I was asked to fly the bride and bridegroom away from their wedding reception. I was stupid enough to say 'Yes I'll do it'

'It was a beautiful day. We got permission from the farmer to take off from the field at the bottom of the garden.

'I said that I wanted £25 for the fuel, a bottle of champagne and three paper cups. It was for the daughter of a retired Colonel or something, she had come back from Africa to get married, and this was a surprise for her. I blew the balloon up in the field, and there is a photograph of Barry Side lifting the bride into the basket somewhere. She evidently said to him when he did it, *'Ooh be careful,. I haven't got any knickers on!'*

'But that's beside the point. She was a bit apprehensive, so I climbed very slowly away, the day was absolutely perfect. We flew from Peasemore, and we flew over the old airfield at Hampstead Norreys. The sun was at such an angle that when we flew over it, you could see every runway, every perimeter road, every building, in the crop! They all showed through

210

with the change of colour in the crop, It was just before it got cut.   Of course I remember it during the war, there were Wellingtons and all sorts of planes there.

'We were floating over it, and I served the champagne, and she said - remember it was her Wedding day, *'Do you know, this is the nicest thing that's happened to me today!'*
Her husband looked a bit crestfallen and said, *'Yet..'*
She turned to him and said, *' What's going to be different about that tonight then?'*
He said, *'Well I have changed your name!'*
'At that I turned the burner on!   Anyway, we were coming up to Pangbourne, and we landed quite close to the National Grid there. I had made the decision to land, and it was a bit heavy, and as we landed they were facing each other, and as we went over, there was a sharp exclamation from him as her knee went somewhere it shouldn't do. So that was not very good for his wedding night.

'Coincidentally, a few years later when we went to Zimbabwe with the balloon, we went down to Bulawayo.   It was too windy to do anything there so I went to a Rotary Club meeting there. I was talking to my neighbour sitting down there in the meeting, he asked me what I was doing there, and I told him. He said *'Ooh that's interesting, do you ever give talks?'*
'Oh yes, quite a few at home,'
 and he stood up and said, *'Mr Chairman, you can cancel our speaker , (Mr Bloggs or someone), I've got a much better one here!'*
So I ended up giving a talk to the Bulawayo Rotary Club, and I mentioned this particular incident with the Bride and Groom flight. Afterwards, this bloke came up to me and said was the bride and groom's name so-an'-so? I said yes. He said did I know when it was, and I looked it up in my logbook, and he said, *'Oh yes, they are both divorced now, and have gone off*

211

with other people.'
Funny how you can tell a story half way around the world
and the people knew them. Amazing!

'Did I tell you about the Nationals in America?   When I didn't
know until two days before, that I was going?   At the
beginning of August 1975, I said to Niall Duncan, *'Oh you're
off to America on Thursday?'*
 and he said *'No, we can't go, we haven't got a pilot!'*
I said 'What do you mean?'
'Well we can't take the balloon without a pilot!'
'I said 'I'll do it!' Now it was just at the beginning of harvest
as well!

'So they rang me up, and said if I had to go up to London the
next day, get a visa, get the balloon to Heathrow and catch a
plane early the morning after.   So I packed the balloon up,
dropped it off at the airport on my way up to the Embassy, I
had to be there at 6.00am I think. I dropped the balloon off,
drove up to the American Embassy, queued for my visa, and
got home at about 3.30 in the afternoon. Sorted the farm out.
Told them which bit was ready for combining, told them to get
on with it. Then caught the plane to America the following
morning! So it was a bit hectic. All arranged in 48 hours!

'Anyway, we went to America, to Iowa and I flew in the US
Nationals there. There were about 150 balloons there. I did
eight flights there, but I can't tell you much about them except
that I won the competition for the Hare & Hounds. Quite by
accident of course!

'It was lovely flying out there. I was trying to teach Niall
Duncan to fly. One flight, I said *'Right, do an approach on
that lovely big grass field, (it was about 100-150 acres) then go
up over that maize field and land the other side'*

212

Well, we missed the grass field completely. We didn't half cut a good swathe in the maize. I remember going through this maize at about 15mph, about a foot off the ground! bump, bump, bump. Anyway we had the burner on and we went up and I looked back and there was this great big swathe through the middle of this maize!

I said *'I'll land it'*, so we came down towards the next field on a down wards slope, and I just took the top out. It was just as well, the river was in front and I couldn't see a bridge for miles. It was a tiny field, and I ripped out at about 100feet! It was one of those positive landings.

'Another flight, I was with Niall Duncan, and we landed in this field with a few cattle in the next field. We were confronted by this very, very angry farmer. I mean VERY angry, he was ranting and raving. I told Niall to go out into the road to meet the crew, and I'd sort it out.

'So I started talking to this farmer, saying what nice cattle he'd got, talking farming language. We finally started talking farming, English farming and such like, and we were getting on very well. His son came up and we were talking, my crew came in and packed the balloon up quietly, and carried it out of the field. I eventually shook his hand and said *'Thank you very much for your hospitality and that.'* and at that he started shouting

'Don't you ruddy well come back here, you tell those balloonists to....'

He was ranting and raving.

'I went out of the field and there were two other balloon crews in the road with ours, and they said *'How ever did you get your balloon out of there! We had a balloon impounded in there for three weeks once!'*

They said he was the kind of farmer who puts barbed wire

213

across snowmobile tracks! They said he was the most vicious unfriendly bloke in the area!

'Then the last flight of the Nationals, which was 7th September, was the Hare & Hounds. Don Cameron came up to me and said '*I want you to take the reporters, it will be good for British Airways if you do.*'

'So the Hare took off. All the other balloons were blowing up, and they all took off one after another, and I was still waiting for the reporter. By the time he had got on board, and sorted himself out, there wasn't a balloon in sight, let alone a Hare balloon!
'I said 'It's OK, we'll have a bit of a flight.' So off we went. I remember flying down a railway cutting, and suddenly all the men on the track below leaped off the track, and I looked around and there was a train coming! I was only at 15 feet, I had to go up a bit! The train passed, and we went up to about 700 feet, and as I looked forward, I could see the Hare balloon laid out ahead, and there were a few other balloons packing up in the same field. I said to the reporters, 'This is going to be a heavy landing!'
I dumped and we went straight in and my balloon collapsed over the top of the Hare balloon. So we won that by accident.

'That was the first time I saw chipmunks. There was one chipmunk getting very upset because the balloon had landed over his burrow. He was going '*chink, chink, chink.*' He was upset with us, but not scared. I had to hitchhike back, complete with balloon because my retrieve couldn't find me, as I'd gone in and landed so fast, my retrieve missed me!

'I've had to hitch-hike two or three times over the years. Anyway we had to cut and run from the Nationals before the presentation, because my son, Richard, was getting engaged.

214

He was getting engaged on the Saturday evening, and we got back on the Saturday morning.

'I was with two members of the Dante group who shall be nameless, and we were stopping in a University campus. They made my room the British Embassy, innocent little sod that I was. No alcohol allowed on the campus, they all came and drank in my room.

'I had a room to myself originally, there were bunk beds. Anyway I had Don Cameron sitting on the top bunk, he tipped Southern Comfort on me or something, it was most uncomfortable that night.

'Anyway, on the last night, a couple of the American female balloon crew groupies took out two of my crew. They had too much Tequila, and they were a b s o l u t e l y comatose in the morning, and one of the mattresses was hanging out of the window. The chap on the bottom bunk had dreamed it was raining, until he realised that rain wasn't warm. So they had to hang the mattress out to dry. Unfortunately, Thunder Balloons were there with a balloon advertising something American, and in all the photos there is a mattress hanging out of the window behind it!

'Anyway the next morning, we had to get a flight out of Des Moines in Iowa to Chicago, and one of the crew was still suffering from tequila, and was not responding to us trying to make him get up and get dressed! So I lifted him with a fireman's lift off his top bunk, carried him stark naked down the stairs to the showers, put him on the floor, turned the cold shower on full blast and left him. I believe there is a photo of him , stark naked with a beer can propping up what would not stand up on its' own!' That was quite an interesting trip.

'Back in England, I flew G-BAGY from Inkpen to the Mill? That's a funny one? I wonder why we went to Inkpen? Oh yes we had to go and fly someone. That's right. We ended up at the Mill where I lived, which was rather nice. I've managed to land there about four or five times which is nice.

'G-BDSE, the Concorde balloon, her maiden flight was from Marsh Benham on 14th June 1976. I took up two of the British Airways 747 pilots, and we flew from Bradfords to Thatcham in fifteen minutes. I remember saying to one of them, 'When I tell you, you can let the trailrope go.' We used the trailrope in those days.
'How do I do that?'
'You pull that little catch up.' I said
'Like this?' and he pulled it up and let the rope go, straight into some electricity wires! He was a pilot - of 747s. A couple of days later I flew the same bloke down at King's Somborne, near Stockbridge, and he was fiddling around with the tether line whilst we were on a tether, he wrapped it round his neck for a joke at one point!

'I flew that balloon a terrific lot. It had the same insurance as a Jumbo, £250,000,000! It was part of the British Airways fleet, and all the fleet carry the same insurance. I flew it for the BALPA Group, the British Airline Pilots Association. I had to fly it anywhere they wanted me to fly it. All over the place, America and everywhere. They made me an honorary life member of BALPA for doing it, I am still a card carrying member. It comes in handy when you're flying.

16th April 1976, I was teaching Ross Page in G-BDNZ we took off from Bradfords and flew to Collingbourne in one hour fifteen minutes. Ross did the landing. Afterwards he said *'How was the landing?'*
I said 'Pretty good, all four of them!'

This one ought to be forgotten, it was a couple of days later. Kintbury to Ludgershall in thirty-five minutes. Down on the tank ranges!

'We were doing a demonstration from the health hydro in Kintbury in Gemini. It was too windy. There were two or three other pilots there and they all helped me blow it up, and threw me in the air. You couldn't tell how windy it was because you were sheltered by the trees. I said I would do a demonstration flight only.
But the minute I was clear of the trees, I was away! My retrieve reckoned they were doing sixty miles an hour to keep up! It was very, very fast, I could see the tank ranges coming up and thought I would put in there. It took me ten minutes to find a field big enough to land. I rounded out at about fifteen feet up, and I took the whole top out quickly before I hit the ground.

'If I'm flying fast than I adopt the policy that I land ten to fifteen feet up, and then do the rip, in other words, don't come in and hit the ground. Then, by burning out at fifteen to twenty feet, by the time you hit the ground you've got the whole rip out. But I took it out too quick.

'We were going that blimmin' fast that as I took the top out, but being a velcro rip, it was fixed at one end, and the balloon inverted in itself and formed a petal. The amount of air trapped in the front of the balloon held it up and became a spinnaker, and we sailed on for 180yards! 180 yards across the tank ranges at about 20mph! Luckily I was on my own, in conditions like that I fly by myself.

'At the end of May I flew my first Viva. G-BDUZ ~Hot lips I think, That was Debbie Warley's. Anyway, Ashmansworth to Kingsclere in one hour fifteen minutes.

217

'Here's another one, when I took the inimitable Clive Jenkins for a ride in G-BDSE, the Concorde balloon.

We flew from Bradfords to Wootton Hill, and it was one of those stupid flights when the winds were light and variable towards the end. It sort of dropped off, and we were over a lot of trees and a lot of houses and suchlike. I could have landed on someone's lawn. I shouted down 'Can I land on your lawn?'

'No you may not! What are you doing this low over the houses?'

I said, 'Looking for somewhere to land.'

They reported me to British Airways for flying too low. He was evidently something to do with Air Traffic Control, or Bristol airport or something.

I mean, it was alright, I was just looking for somewhere to land, I had to get it down.

'Not only that, but it made the William Hickey column! What was it? Oh yes,

'The vociferous Clive Jenkins, and Hot air. Hot-air balloon kept up by Clive Jenkins, strange to relate that his pilot was none other than a farmer and Tory District Councillor, David Liddiard!'

So we got that in the Hickey column.

'In August, I did a 55 minute flight and we landed where we took off from. We went off and came back in again! Winds can be funny sometimes.

On the 18th August I did a check flight in Smirk, with Dave Smith. I'll tell you an interesting thing about that one. There were three balloons up. The next morning, I got a telephone call from a very irate farmer. One of his cows had got a broken leg caused by the balloons making it run around.

I said 'Right, where are you? I'll be right round.'

I rang my vet, and he went straight up there. He was there within the hour.

He rang me back in an hour and a half, and said that cow did not have a broken leg, it had a fox wire around it's leg and it had probably been there two or three days. It was right round and into the bone. The farmer did ring up and apologise.

'I then took the Concorde balloon down to Bassington, near Stockbridge. It was for a BALPA garden party, held in the grounds of John Fairey's house, the Spitfire pilot.

'I did the maiden flight for Rob Fuller of Snapdragon, he was an auctioneer chap, a real Sloane, lives in Surrey now. He was the same age as Richard, he went to University with him. He stayed here a while.

'Oh yes, Wantage. I went to a party one night, and someone came up and said 'We're running a race from Lockinge to Winchester. We'd like you to take part. It is to get from Lockinge to Winchester by any means other than combustion engine. We thought that maybe you could fly by balloon.' This was three weeks before the race. So I said 'Ooh yes, I'll take part.'
Now, the chances of the wind blowing from the North West are very remote. So we thought that what we'd do, is to take a hang-glider up, let the hang-glider go, and the hang-glider could do it! So this is what we had authorised. Christopher Lloyd was organising it.

'Anyway, on the day, Ken Messenger couldn't do it, so he sent his side-kick along. It was blowing far too fast really, so we were going to have to abandon the hang-glider. We had to bike from the square with King Alfred's statue in it, out to where we were going to blow the balloon up. The crew were already there with the balloon, so when we got there it was all ready to blow up.

219

'We got there, blew the balloon up, turned the burner on, put the hang-glider pilot in as a passenger, and took off! Then after I took off, I realised that the bloody maps were still on the ground!

So I tried, on the downs by the Wantage memorial, to land and pick them up! It was the only time on landing that I've been thrown out the balloon! I actually bounced out of the basket but held on to the burner frame, I think I got back over into the basket at about sixty feet.. My passenger had never been in a balloon before!

So I decided not to put in for the maps. We flew on, and I was flying high to get a right, and we were going quite fast. I remember seeing two other competitors, one on a horse, and one on a bike and overtook them quite comfortably.

'Then I saw Winchester coming up, but I was far too much over to the right, so I came down very low. I could see the road going down into Winchester, and there was a wood, and there was a clearing in this wood. So I came down, brushed the basket through the wood, came up to the clearing, and it was full of people!

'Get out the bloody way,' I yelled and they did. We landed, a nice landing. We ran up to the road, found the crew with the two bikes, biked down into Winchester and won the competition! The retrieve crew came down into town to find us, swearing like mad, and I said, 'What's the matter?'

'Next time you put a balloon down, don't put it in a wasp's nest!'

'I had landed over the top of a wasps nest, and when they pulled the balloon off, the wasps were not happy! That's how we came to win the race, the 'Wessex Challenge' it was called. I've still got the cup upstairs I think.

'In October that year, still 1976, I went to Boyle, to the Irish

Meet. We had six flights in Boyle. I believe I was still teaching Alan Noble then, anyway he was my co-pilot.   I was driving an old Wolseley.

'We had a Hare and Hounds out there, and Kevin Meehan was piloting the hare balloon, and I was following, and he went up through a hole in the clouds. The clouds were solid!
I tried two or three times to come back down, it was really solid. I finally saw a hole, saw the ground and went down through it, We were near the side of a mountain, well a fairly steep hill, if you had landed, you would have rolled down! A bit further on, we landed.
Anyway, it was in Ballygonnelly in County Fermanagh in Northern Ireland! We landed, went to see the farmer, but he wouldn't open his door to us! He just peeked out the window. We had just missed his farm buildings, and landed there. We got some strange looks driving back into Southern Ireland through the checkpoint.

'I think that was the meet when Tim Godfrey landed on the far side of the river. It was pretty deserted, and he said to his passenger, 'You walk that way until you meet somebody, and I'll walk that way.'
So off they went. After half an hour they met!   They had landed on an island!

'One of them had to swim ashore to get a retrieve I think, you'll have to ask Tim for details.

'On another retrieve, we went into the pub at the end. We needed some Irish whiskey, and we asked for a hot toddy. The Irish do a hot toddy really well. But he poured it out, and went and put it in the microwave! Microwaving the whiskey to make a hot toddy! I'd never seen anything like it, and that was twenty years ago.

'On the last flight, Alan Noble was piloting it. We came into this field and we hit these bloody great Irish rocks, doghoused, and my hand went right back over and my watch went in to it, and I couldn't use my hand! I drove all the way back from Ireland, changing gear with the wrong hand!

When we got home, I went to see the Doctor, and said I've really hurt my hand you know.'

He said, ' *Well yes, you've hurt your hand, but do you have problems with your fingers?*'

I said, 'Yes? I do get pins and needles.'

He said,' *Well you'd better go and have an operation.*'

That's when I found out I had 'Carpal Tunnel Syndrome.'

Well where I had been working all those years ago, had affected all the muscle and gristle where the nerves to the fingers go through. The nerves had been trapped by all the muscle and gristle. So I had to have both hands operated on soon after.

'It affected my farming and ballooning. Well, I'd been paying into BUPA all my farming days, never used it. Always used the National Health. The Doctor said, *'I'll do both of them together'*, so I had a surgeon one each side, of course I wasn't awake to see it.

'I went in on the Thursday night, the night before, so that they can do all the preparation stuff. I remember being in my room, sitting on the bed reading, and the door opened *'Everything alright?'*

'Yes thank you Sister'

The door shut. The steps receded down the passage, then they stopped. They came quietly back and the door opened.

'Mr Liddiard?'

'Yes'

'Oh my God!'

'You don't remember me?'

'Remember you!! I'll never forget you! You were my worst patient ever!!'.
She remembered me from when I had my back done, nine years before!

'Anyway, I had the operation on the Friday morning. But afterwards, I remember waking up to find my hands tied up to a pole at the top of the bed! Well, you know, you can't move like that!

'Well because of the call of nature, I called a nurse over, and she went and got a bottle and started to help me out! Then she complained that 'we' had wetted the bed!
I said 'Well don't blame me, it wasn't my end that caused the trouble it was your end!' which she didn't think was very funny.
Anyway, I managed to get my hands unhooked after that and did it myself.

'She was not very happy with me, but I got on very well with a few other blokes on the ward. There was one bloke down the other end of the ward, moaning and groaning and making a lot of fuss. I said, 'What's wrong with that chap down there? Is he dying?'
'No he's just had a disc removed.'
Well' I said ' had a spinal fusion in here a few years ago and I never made that much noise!'
She said I've never had a recovery ward like this in my life before! I wish you lot would keep quiet.' We were all chatting.

'Anyhow, I was wheeled back to my room, and I was uncomfortable in those operating gowns with the strings all down the back, so I managed to get it off and put my pyjamas on. A little nurse came in and said 'Oh! Who's been in and dressed you?'

223

'Nobody' I said 'I did it myself!'

'You're not supposed to get out of bed!'

'Well, I did. I had to get my pyjamas.'

'Oh, well, I'm going to give you a shave.'

'No you're not!' I said 'The surgeon complained that you did an awful job when you shaved my arms! You're not going to attack my face like that!'

I said, 'Go and get me two plastic bags, two rubber bands, and I shall be quite happy to get out and wash and shave myself.'

'You can't do that!'

I said 'I can.'

The nurse scurried off.

The sister came in.

'What's all this about?'

I said 'I want two plastic bags, and two rubber bands so I can get out and wash and shave myself.'

'I've never heard anything like it!'

Anyway, they did it eventually, and I got out and washed and shaved myself, and that was within fifteen hours of the operation!'

'I had the operation on the Friday morning, and a friend came to see me on the Monday evening, and the Doctor said *'There's nothing much we can do for you here, you might as well go home!'*

So I said 'Alright Barry, I'll come home with you!'

So Barry drove me home on the Monday, and on the Tuesday, I got the car out and drove around the farm! I'd gone into hospital the previous Thursday, not bad eh? Blimey I only started talking about how I had my hand operated on!

'I needed some therapy, and having done up the Mill, what was the next one we did? James got married seventeen years ago, and they moved into a house at Bradfords, it was the worst house on the estate that I was responsible for. There were two cottages, and this was the worst one. It was 121 Marsh Benham. When he said he was getting married, I said well you had better do it up. He spent £7,000 doing it up. They were still knocking a lot of buildings down on the farm then. I said to James, 'Do you want a porch on this house?' He said 'yes'.

'Right, get the fork lift. Let's go round to where they've knocked this building down.'

'It was a Saturday when we went round, and having measured it up, I took the chainsaw and chopped this bit off here, another bit there. Cut through the timbers, picked the whole roof of the porch up with forklift, drove round and put on the front of his house. We did the whole thing over the weekend. On Monday, I got the carpenter to tidy it up, we put some old tiles on it, build a brick wall round it, and it made a lovely porch.

'Inside, we knocked down a wall so that they could make one room out of two. Originally, it was a real state. There were mushrooms growing out of the ceilings. But we knocked the fireplace about and made two lovely big ones by returning them to their former glory.

'We ended up turning it in to quite a nice house. There was a bathroom downstairs, we left that there, because I couldn't work out how to move one upstairs simply because James and Fiona wanted a certain width for their bedroom. Eventually I suggested that they moved rooms and made the other one slightly smaller, and they agreed. I had actually already put the pipe there!

'The drainage was different though. Some of it would go to the septic tank that was already there, but where this bathroom was, I couldn't get the bath-water into the same tank, so I took the pipe under the concrete across to the pipes down to the dairy, and it went off down to the fields. The joke was, the day after they had moved in, I went down, and found James outside.

'I'm having problems with the drains Dad. But I've shifted it.' James said.

He was outside and he was rodding it like billio.

'James' I said 'you're rodding it the wrong way!'

'But I've got rid of it!'

'You're rodding back into the house, you should be rodding it that way!'

'But it's going Dad!'

I looked in the bathroom, and he was right, he'd shifted it, and the floor of the bathroom was inches deep in you-know–what!

I have never felt so sorry for anyone in my life as I did for Fiona.

'Right where is the dustpan.' I said.

I helped get it all mopped up, and we put down sawdust to soak the rest up. My sons are not practical. I cringe sometimes at things they've done. But because it was always quicker to do it myself, I'd never taught them., we called James Dyno-Rod after that!

'When we went to Bradfords, we had to empty the septic tank every six weeks, two months or so. It was terrible. So I said 'We'll put a new soakaway in to stop this lark.' So we started to dig this soakaway and found that there had been a hole knocked in a pipe from the A4 and we were getting all their drainage! We blocked that up and it was OK after that. No problems.

'Northfield Farm was after that I suppose. Although Jo and I had lived there when we were first married, in fact both boys were born there, we didn't do anything to the place. We didn't have the time or the money. There was no central heating, only open fires, and a back boiler for hot water, if you didn't have a fire, you didn't have hot water.

I did Northfield up after I had finished doing James's place. I did it in the evenings for occupational therapy. It was all gash labour, I got a brickie if I wanted one, a plasterer if needed. We did all the basic knocking down and getting it ready. It has always been natural knowing which were load bearing walls.

'With Northfield, cleaning off all the paint was the biggest problem. We cleaned all the wood. There is no painted wood in there now, the beams and doors are all stained. Then we started on the rest of the buildings there. There is a cottage now on the end of the main house, I didn't have time to do at first, I just blocked the door up and left it derelict, that's a nice place now. Then I did the industrial units, and then I made the old cowshed into two houses, that was about 1986, before Kate got married.

'I suppose I've been building all my life, I mean all the farmworkers cottages, as they fell vacant, I have done them all up, and now they are all let. I have been lucky though.

'Take Pete and Elaine Bish's place. I designed that, I pulled half the house down nearly. I said to them one day, you don't need a hole here, here and here! Why don't you prop it up, knock the whole wall down and put a steel beam in and make the rooms bigger. It is all RSJs, we got enough bricks out of the fourteen inch wall that was there, to build the whole of their extension without buying any second hand bricks. The round window frames came from a barn that James was pulling down, and the two wooden beams came from James's silo barn. All the oak on the ceilings, the oak upstairs, and the oak on the walls, came from fencing along the Bath Road,

227

when they were replacing it.

'Take this place College Farm. It was derelict when I completed buying it on March 6th, sixteen weeks later on June 26th, we moved in. No sense in hanging around. Just get on and do things. OK so the organisation had to be fairly tight, decisions had to be made. I think this is the reason the men like working for me.

After I did Pete Bish's place, *'Buy another one governor, we like working for you!'*

I got this place, and they said *'Ooh yes, just what we want, get in there.'*

I think of it is a case of *'What do we want done here? '*

'I think we'll do so and so, what do you suggest?'

What about so and so?'

'I don't like that.' or *'Yes, that's good we'll do that then.'*

'I have one firm where I use the brickies, one firm where I know the chippies, I knew what they did, how good they were, they worked for me before. The man who did the roof, I'd used him before. They all know, that if they give me a price, as long as it's sensible, I don't hold them to it if something goes wrong.

If I change my mind, or want a bit extra, I'll pay a bit extra. If they say it won't be in the price, I'll say 'I know you did a bit extra, how much is it going to hurt me? ' As long as it's sensible I'll always pay.

'I was also lucky in that if we were running short of materials, I would ring up and very often it would be there the next morning. We have a very good firm I always pay on time. I mean there was one firm I used, never used them before, they were recommended. They sent me a bill, and at the top it said 'Credit Limit £2000'. The bill was for £7000!

I rang them up 'Look - £2000 credit, and my bill is £7000!'

'Oh well, we weren't really worried.'

'I'm coming in with a cheque now' I said, and took the cheque straight into them.

This is what people respect, when you realise they've done you a favour and you turn round and do them one. 'You stand your word, you pay your debts and look everyone straight in the eye.'

'Anyhow, back to my logbook and ballooning, we come to the Icicle meet, January 1977. Flying from Bradfords at Marsh Benham. This is where I won first prize. I was flying Smirk then, It was called that because of Mr Smith and Mr Kirk. I was flying Mr Kirk at the time.

We went up to 3,500 feet to get as much right as we could, and we had to land in a set triangle as far away as you could from any other balloon.

We were just underneath the cloud you know, at that height and just coming up to the edge of the triangle, so we started coming down, very, very fast. We came down and landed from that height in 7 or 8 minutes. I believe Mr Kirk never flew again!

Anyhow, we won the competition, but my retrieve crew took two and a half hours to find me. One minute I was a dot in the clouds, and the next time they stopped to look, there was no sign of me. They thought I had gone into the cloud. They went on driving all the way down to Salisbury, waiting for me to come out of the clouds!

'The next day I flew G-BALD, That was Norton-Griffiths wasn't it? We landed on the main runway at Greenham Common Airbase. Not supposed to of course. Well we had major burner failure -didn't we?

'In May that year I flew the Concorde balloon, from Bradfords to St Mary Bourne. I started a friendship with Jack Jessop from that trip, Flight Operations Manager for British Airways, and he's been a good friend for years. About a week later, I took the Concorde Balloon to Farmington in the USA. We did one, two, three...four flights from there. I went out with a crew from BALPA, which consisted of two secretaries, and Jock Lowe.

Mark Young who had arranged it couldn't come because his wife was ill, which is why he'd sent the others, and his wife died of cancer whilst we were there. We had not been there very long, but they all had to go back, and they left me there.

'I remember arriving in America, and a U-Haul truck had been organised, and I had been designated driver. We were driving out of Boston Airport on the evening of the one of their holidays, it was pandemonium. It was my first time driving in America, on the Freeway and with the 4th July coming up, everyone was going home to celebrate.

'Jock and I had a flight, and then we were refuelling from a pump tanker and were getting far too much pressure really. During the flight, I changed cylinders because I couldn't get the gas out! It was full up, but the gas wouldn't come out!

The 'O' ring had slipped along and jammed. Luckily, I had the other cylinder connected, but I was down to the Master cylinder and had to land to sort things out. It was then I discovered you could unscrew the inside, and the slip the 'O' ring off which was interesting.

'Anyhow, before I left England, I'd said to Jack Jessop that I ought to take the Concorde Balloon, and fly it from Concord. He thought it was an excellent idea.

He rang me up and said, *'I've had a word with our people, you'll never be allowed to fly out of Concord, the Americans won't let you.'*

I said,' What if I do? I bet you I can, and if I do, I'll come back on Concorde!'

He said, *'If you manage to do it, yes you can come back on Concorde.'*

To cut a long story short, my crew had all left me, and I was staying with Brian Boland. Brian built a barn to house his fire engine and his balloon, and they hadn't moved the tree, it was growing right through the middle of it. He had built it around the tree!

Brian came with me up to Concord, and we not only flew the balloon out of the Golf Club in Concord, but we had the front page of the Concord Journal, a hell of a good write up, a hell of a lot of good publicity.

'My neighbour at Ashmansworth, she lived in what used to be the Farmhouse for Ashmansworth Farm. She was in the Girl Guides with the Queen, was a quite well known opera singer and coincidentally, her sister was married to someone in Concord! She had asked if we would call in and see them, and they put us up for the night. Then we went up to Newburyport, but it was too windy to fly a balloon up there, so we went back to Concord.

'I left there and went down to Boston and saw British Airways, and said that they had promised me a flight back on Concorde. They said, *We'll check on that. Sorry no.'*

Whilst I was there, I had rung to Jack Jessop in his office in the UK. They then said, *'Come back in the morning.'*

I went back in the morning, and off the telex machine had come the message *'Concorde Pilot Liddiard to be given seat from Washington back to England on Concorde. Please execute this without further hiccups.'*

The balloon went back in the hold of a 747 from Boston, and I flew down to Washington at my own expense, but I got to Washington, I flew back here in Concorde! I spent most of the time in the cockpit with Jock Lowe. So that was the beginning of June 1977.

'Then we went up to do a job for Concorde at Heythrop Park, the NatWest College, Chipping Norton. We stopped the night up there. I had the Chairman's bedroom! Really nice, big with a lovely bathroom and everything.

'The next week we went to Balleroy, Malcolm Forbes' chateau in France. He was an American millionaire, and had a museum of ballooning there, holding a balloon meet for a few invited guests every year. Alec was asked to go, and he was just starting to suffer from Multiple Sclerosis then. Alec and I flew from Balleroy to St Lucs, our first free flight in France which lasted about an hour and a half.

'On the third of July, Ken Messenger had a brand new hang-glider. It was the one he was going to use for the Cross Channel Flight. There were two hang-gliders, one was for Brian Milton, and one for himself, Ken had built them in his barn. We tested them and we dropped him from 4,500feet.
It was a fifteen minute flight, a brand new hang-glider, we've got photographs of that one haven't we Jo?'
'Yes upstairs somewhere.'
'There were two balloons up Phil Hutchins in J&B Rrare and his hang-glider pilot, Brian Milton, a Disc Jockey. They were trying the new hang-gliders out. Anyway they all worked well, and it was the build up to the Cross Channel Crossing.
15minutes at 25mph was what he achieved, and from that he was able to work out how high he needed to be to be dropped and clear the English Channel.

Cross Channel Balloon Flight with Hang-glider
21st July 1977
This adventure is well documented in the press as well as in David's memory.

232

Ken Messenger wanted to be the first to fly over the Channel in a hang-glider, although he was already the champion.

'We got permission to do it with a slot of three months. There were two balloons who were going to do it. One was Phil Hutchins in J&B-Rare and Brian Milton was going to be the hang-glider pilot. We were going to do it in Beatrice, with banners on for Olympic Holidays who were sponsoring Ken.

'We had one false start when James and I drove to Canterbury but the wind didn't change. The people who were organising it were more interested in getting money for themselves than anything else. Although the cameras were supposed to be arranged, there were no good shots of any of it. I've got a few muggy ones, but there were no good photos of the whole attempt.

'I left home with James at 6pm, drove to Canterbury, we had a bite to eat, bit of a discussion about where we were going to do it in the morning, one or two other things, and went to bed. Don Cameron shared a bed with Dick Wirth! There was a shortage of beds that night. Someone called us at 2.30am and did a Met check.

'We left the hotel just after three, got to the field at four and put the equipment together. I remember I was wearing winter woollies although it was July, my crew was James, Chris Smith, and Graham Stagg.

'It was the first time I'd seen my parachute, you had to put it on, pull the red handle, and if the chute doesn't open, you come back and they give you another one. That was my entire parachute training! I remember trying to jump into the basket with everything on: Mae West, Immersion suit, Oxygen bottles, flying suit, and parachute. I really looked like a Michelin man! I remember going to jump into the basket, and

233

my feet didn't leave the ground! I was way overweight!

'I had seven gas bottles, all that equipment, hang-glider and a pilot. There was no one in the basket with me, there wasn't room! We took off at five in the morning and climbed for 55 minutes. We were the first off. There were two other balloons, Phil Hutchins and Brian, and the Thunder team with Tom Donnelly and Dick Wirth.

'Of course, one of the first things you do before you take off is to give your crew a telephone number. Never gave it a thought until I was about 50 feet up, then I yelled, *I'll land as close to the coast road as I can, and I'll see you in France.*'

'We climbed really hard for the first few minutes, and the heat link and streamer went at 3500feet! It landed on the top of the Hang-glider, and Ken wondered what it was. We carried on climbing a bit slower after that. Anyhow, we had agreed prior to this, that you would need a minimum of 14,500 feet to get across the channel. We got to 14000 feet and the other glider was launched, so I yelled down to Ken, 'What do you want to do?'
I want more height, give me more height.'
The other balloon was alongside us about a mile away, and they also released at 14000ft.
I said to Ken 'They've released! Do you want a bit more height?' *'Yes, I'd like a bit more height.*'

'I climbed to 20,000 feet within the hour, a 350 feet a minute climb, a consistent rate of climb. Pretty good really if you think about it. When we reached 20,000 feet, I started descending, and released him at about 18,700 feet at 6am.

'When the rope stopped swinging round, I looked down, and we were right over Dover. Ken was about a 150 feet below me for an instant and then flew right up, and actually went up

234

above me. I kept going down and eventually pulled out and carried on across the Channel. Jo wasn't with me on that day, were you?'

'No, there were reasons why I didn't go. I have regretted it since, but there were reasons why I didn't.' She answered.

David continued.

'On the way up I got my oxygen equipment tangled up when I was changing cylinders, so I was without oxygen at about 15,000 feet for a while, which gave me a bit of a headache. I took the oxygen off at about 10,000 feet and went down to 6,000 feet, and I was on top of a cloud. It looked so solid, the balloon basket was just floating along on the surface. I put the basket down through the top of the cloud and it looked really solid, I felt I could get out and walk on it. I had a terrific urge to get out and walk on the cloud!

'It could have been because I had suffered from lack of oxygen a short time before. I'd never thought of it before today. It was quite frightening when you look back. Then I knew I had to get through the cloud, because I had to be down to 3,000, but I had no idea how far down the cloud went. I think probably in all the time I have been ballooning, it was my most frightening experience being on top of those clouds, and knowing I had to be below 3000 feet because of French airspace.

'I tried calling up on the radio, we were supposed to have a boat in the Channel. But nobody answered me, I only had the radio and an altimeter for company.

'Then the second frightening thing happened, I went down, and broke cloud at about 2,500feet and I was looking straight down into the Atlantic! I thought the wind had changed and I was going down the Channel instead of across it, I was completely disorientated. All that had happened was that the balloon had rotated. I carried on down to 500 feet, and saw a big Townsend Thorensen ferry change course to follow me, he obviously thought I was going to ditch it, but went back onto course when I pulled out.

'What I didn't know then was that the other hang-glider had ditched in the channel, and had been picked up by a Russian boat, but Ken had got right across.

'It was fast. I didn't get to 20,000 feet until gone 6am, I got across the Channel in about 55 minutes, and the whole flight was two hours. I did contemplate landing on the beach but I was going too fast.

'I came in nearly touching the sea, burned, climbed up over the dunes, and there was an acre or so cut for reeds. I took the top out of the balloon and the basket dropped onto the reeds, and the balloon fell over on top. I was about fifty yards in from the road. I got out and kissed the ground like the Pope does. Mind you, he does it every time, he must have a terrible pilot! I was just to the left of Cap Gris Nez, a village called Wissant.

'Anyhow, I took my parachute, the Mae West and the oxygen equipment off, but there was no way I could get the immersion suit off because the zip was down the back. I staggered into the road and eventually a little 2CV came along and stopped, I spoke no French, he spoke no English. But I got him to take me to the Gendarmerie, and he did. They didn't speak English at the Gendarmerie either, but they helped me out of the suit. They asked someone else, and he couldn't speak English, the fourth one came in with pips on his shoulder and he couldn't speak it either!

Nearly 'Zanussi' airship

Landing in the desert, Israel

Bedouin hospitality, Israel

Israel 1989

David in the Dead Sea. 1989

Jo helping at Rotary Club event. 1990

Maurice Bond and David barbequing at the Mill.

'Eventually, they took me down to a local hotel where the owner was English. He explained the score to the Gendarmes, and they said to go back to the balloon and wait for the customs to arrive.

'I borrowed his phone, rang home and told Jo where I was and that I was alright. I think I had a large scotch, a coffee and a croissant, then the owner took me back to the balloon.

'I got back to the balloon at half past eight, and I was just wondering what to do when the retrieve vehicle came up and found me, and helped me pack up the balloon, they were one of the best retrieves you could ever have. I had been told by the Police to stand by the balloon and wait for the customs to arrive. No one did, so we went into Calais for some breakfast.

'Ken landed where Bleriot first took off to fly the Channel, but Ken overshot the landing site at 6,000 feet and came back upwind, landing with all the press and photographers looking out to sea, looking the wrong way for him, and no one got any pictures! We did meet Ken in Calais, but we couldn't get onto the same hovercraft. He had to get back for a radio interview. We got on the next one and travelled back to Ramsgate, then drove home. We did stop for a bite of lunch on the motorway, but we were home by six o'clock!

'The whole trip by the balloon was missed by the press, no one asked me for an interview, it was all Ken in the hang-glider. I was just the taxi driver. That was twenty four hours in the life of a balloonist!

'That was on the Thursday, and Richard had just moved down to his new job in Cornwall, and had asked us down for the weekend. So off we went down to Cornwall. Now I've always had trouble with my chest, and that weekend, I had dreadful catarrh, and my ears were very painful. So on the Monday, when we came back, I went to see the Doctor about my ears because they still hurt. He said that they were pretty red and inflamed but he didn't think there was any damage. He gave me something to calm me down.'

David was still on a high after his achievement. Not many farmers had crossed the English Channel in a Hot-Air Balloon by 1977!

'It was the first time that three balloons had crossed the channel together. Phil Hutchins landed just down the beach from me, and Tom and Nick flew right inland before they landed. We were travelling fast. Now Brian, the other hang-glider released at 14,000 feet inland, and I've heard this since, he was picked up on radar, because when he got into the cloud he just went round in circles! He was disorientated like I had been, and he was heading for Le Havre not Calais. He was the only one who wouldn't wear an immersion suit, 'I don't need one.' he said.

'When he put down in the Channel, he lost all his hang gliding equipment, all his recording stuff, his oxygen equipment, all his cameras, the lot! He was picked up by a Russian cargo ship and landed at Le Havre. He was lucky to be alive I should have thought, landing in the Channel.

'He then tried to be the first microlight (motorised hang-glider) across the Channel, but he accelerated too fast at take off and went wheesh-bang and landed up-side-down. But today, July 21st 1998, I read in the paper that he has successfully flown around the world in a Microlight, days, beating the American record. It is quite a coincidence that it was 21 years to the day when he tried to fly the Channel, 21st July 1977.'

Councillor Liddiard.

'The first time I took an interest in being a councillor, was just after I started ballooning about 1974. God knows why. I was running two farms of a thousand acres, and flying balloons. Somebody asked me if I would stand for Newbury District Council, I think it was George Wallis, another farmer, I never gave it a second thought, I said 'Yes', and then had to carry it through. I stood for the Lambourn Ward. I had to be elected, I remember the count was at Hungerford.

'I did a term there, and being a Councillor, and with all the balloons flying from the field all the time, I thought we'd better legalise it. So that was when Marsh Benham became the first field ever in the United Kingdom to be given planning permission as a ballooning site. 1976 I think it was. It was quite a famous field you know.

'But I resigned from the Council in the end over the Leisure Centre being built in the wrong place, under the wrong management. Everything was wrong about it. It should have been built between Newbury and Thatcham, where it would have covered everything, not at Northcroft. It was like a committee designing a horse and it ends up a camel. The ground, the soil was not suitable, and the access was stupid. There was only one road in, it was so stupid. It was a combination of Liberals and Conservatives who were very keen on it so it went through and of course the Council owned the land.

'When I was looking into it, I needed to know more. I asked Kevin Meehan, the balloonist, for advice, he was running a leisure centre at that time. He said, 'Well, it won't make a profit, and it'll cost them £2,000 a week to run it.'

So I used his figures and facts when I was talking against it in the Chamber.

239

'You see, this is the thing, there is so much information available, but people don't use it. I left school early, without all this education, but I found that all these people who are highly educated, are dying for someone to let them use their knowledge, and make them feel they're wanted.

'I did a lot of flights in the balloon to raise money for the Northcroft Leisure Centre despite my feelings about it. A lot of those flights were in G-ZUMP with Mike Allen, an Estate Agent in the area.

'I was farming, being a councillor and flying with the Dante Group and I know I was wrong. I should have stayed on the Council, and fought it longer, for another six months. But basically, I hadn't got the time. Not only was I doing the councilling, the farming, and the ballooning, but the overseas trips were coming in too. I was going to America, Jamaica and everywhere. So I really hadn't got the time. I'm one of those people who when I do a job, I like to do it properly.

'So I left the Council. Then in 1994 I did try to get on the County Council, but it was a by-election and the Conservatives were wiped off the council. The trouble is, the grass-roots are Conservatives, but they don't come out and talk enough. I don't know if farmers will do better under a Labour Government. Some say yes, they said they did after the War. But everyone did well after the war.

'Take inflation for instance, if we get high inflation, then people, farmers, who own a lot of land, get richer because the value of the land goes up so quickly, I can remember when it was fifty pounds an acre around here.'
'I heard on the radio this morning that Set-aside might be abolished ,'Jo said.
'I hope it will be. Basically farmers don't like this idea, they

240

would rather work for their money.

'Well it does seem ridiculous ,' Jo chipped in, 'Getting money for weeds. It doesn't bode well, does it.'

'On the other hand, you've got to do it, and farmers never look a gift horse in the mouth.   Set-aside was only brought in about five or six years ago, and as I've already said I consider the best years in farming, were 1939 through to 1989.

'In 1962, I became Vice Chairman of the Newbury Show, and Chairman the following year. I believe at that time, I was the youngest ever Chairman. I've always been involved in the organising, this year I'll have been on the committee for fifty years.

'It was Israel Sieff who taught me quite a bit. He was a wonderful, wonderful man. He took it upon himself to help me as much as possible. He told me that if I had any problems, to ring Marks & Spencers in London, ask to speak to his secretary, 'Tell my secretary what you want, and she will see if she can find me.'

I did ring up one day. She said, 'Oh Mr Sieff's in a board meeting.'

I told her the problem, and she said, 'Oh, he'll want to know about that, will you hold a minute?'

Within about a minute, a minute and a half, he was on the phone. I said, 'I feel very guilty taking you away from a board meeting.'

'I told them to sit and wait. They can wait until I get back. It's no problem. They can wait, you can't.'

'Anyway, we sorted the problem out.'

'You did have horrendous problems that year, didn't you?' Jo remembered.

'Oh yes, the Secretary, it was his last year and his mind was not quite as sharp as it had been.

The problem was, we always had a Show lunch in the marquee, and on this particular year, Mr Sieff had said that he would hold a cocktail party for everybody the night before, and because it was the Secretary's last year, he could invite who he wanted to.

'So the Secretary duplicated the invitations to the lunch party! He was in the process of inviting three hundred and fifty people to a tent which would only hold a hundred and fifty. I had to go to the Post office and withdraw the invitations! It was very difficult, but it had to be done.

'Mr Sieff came down on Saturday, and I met him, picked him up, took him down to see the secretary, and it was sorted out.
He took the blame, he said, *'Well, it was my fault, I didn't realise the tent only held a hundred and fifty, you were only doing what I said.'*
When we came out, I said to Mr Sieff, 'It was not your fault! I know what was said, it was not your fault.'

'These are the words of wisdom he came out with.
'Little men never make mistakes my boy, only big men. A big man will learn by them, but a little man will blame someone else.'

'That was very, very profound, little men never make mistakes, it is always someone's fault. But a big man will say what a bloody fool I was, I'll not do that again. So that is why little men remain little men! I've remembered that, and if something goes wrong, I always think 'why did it go wrong?'

'It's like I've always said, when someone said about small farmers. A small farmer is a frame of mind. I know people who'll make more money off a hundred acres than some farmers make off a thousand. Because, they organise themselves and maximise everything.

242

'OK, so every aircraft accident has an analysis to it. It is silly if people don't analyse when things don't go right.   For instance, if I'm going to build a cow shed or a piggery, I used to go and see someone who has just built one. They used to show me around and point out all the things that went right.
I would say 'Hang on a minute, I don't want to see all the things that went right, I can see that. What mistakes did you make and had to put right, so I don't make them?'
It was more important, to find out the bad points of a place rather than the good points.

'I was building a piggery once and somebody said to me
'You'll have a lot of trouble with the pigs' feet for the first two or three months until the floor gets worn down. When you make your concrete, there are bits of flint in there, and some of them are like needles and they get put in the concrete pointing straight upwards.' He said *'You will find that that makes the pigs' feet sore. But it will be alright after two or three months when it is worn down.'*

'I thought that was silly. Now just before that, I'd been with Ted Hill down to South Cerney, between Swindon and Cirencester. He'd been showing me the gravel down there. It was very small pea shingle, and he'd said to me, *'If you put this under the microscope, it is all little holes, it's porous.'*

'I'd remembered this, so I rang him up, and he said that it was not quite so hard wearing, but we used it. We actually used it for two reasons. It didn't have any sharp bits in it, and also, it was not so cold as the flint.   Actually when we built the piggery, we also bought a lot of 'Aglite' which is clay which has been fired in little pellets. We put down three inches of that to make it warm. Then we put three inches of this South Cerney gravel down which had no sharp bits in it. So we never had any trouble with the pigs' feet!

243

'That was at Ashmansworth. My strongest attitude in life has been that, I turn my setbacks to my advantage. What other people throw away, I can use. There was a point when I made all the trailers on the farm apart from the tipper trailer. I used to get the scrap from Gordon Passey and turn it into things. Gordon would always let me have things as cheaply as he could. When you're throwing away so much good stuff, you think *'God , it's a shame to throw it away.'*
Someone comes along and turns it into something and he likes to see it happen. This is why he sold me Zanussi, the old airship, for £150.

'I was on the Newbury NFU committee for a long time. After I had finished being Vice Chairman and Chairman of the Newbury Show, I became Vice Chairman, then Chairman of the NFU. Maybe it was 1962, I am not quite sure now. Oh I was thirty two, and that's thirty five years ago, so that was 1963.

'The funny thing is that when I was Chairman of the Newbury Show, the Secretary resigned, nothing to do with me, and then we had to find a new Showground. We were at Elcot then. The year I was Chairman we had the trouble of finding a new showground and a new Secretary. There were about forty odd meetings that year.

'I'll tell you a story. We have a friend, XXX and he lives in a house where the stairs go up, and then split, one flight goes to their bedroom, and the other flight goes to the other two bedrooms.

'Now they had a friend who came to stop with them whose husband had gone off abroad or something, on a course or something for a week. So she was stopping with them. That night, XXX and his wife were just getting into bed, XXX had his pyjamas on, and suddenly said, *'Ooh damn it, I've forgotten to turn the water pump off for the cows. I've got to go down and do it.'*

'He stomps down in his pyjamas, puts his gumboots on, gets in the Land Rover and drives off. About an hour later, his wife wakes up and he's not back. She looks out the window, Land Rover is still not there, but as she looks along the house, in the light of the moon, she sees a ladder up to the spare room window! So she goes quietly down, and takes the ladder away! She then sits on the stairs and waits for him to come out of the bedroom. He did eventually. 'Anyway that got round, and at the next Newbury Show, which was not long afterwards, Oakes Bros had a big stand there, and on all the vehicles, if they'd been sold, was this big notice saying 'Sold to so-an-so   at such-a-such address', you know. All the machinery was sold to somebody.

'Johnny Bach used to organise all of this, and I said *'Hey Johnny, get me one of those notices printed saying Sold to Mr XXX esq.'*

'What are you going to do with it then?' he asked.

'Stick it on that ladder!'

'There was a ladder stand that used to come to the Newbury Show, all sorts of ladders. I think I was Vice Chairman then, doing all sorts of helping anyway. 'So Johnny gave me the sign at one of the cocktail parties that we had the evening before the show. Off I went. Have you ever tried to climb a ladder, and when you get to the top, take a hammer out of your pocket and tack a notice to the top of a 30 foot ladder! It was only the next morning when I looked at this ladder, that I saw that the ladder was only held on with two bits of bent

245

wire like meat hooks, and I'd been right up to the top!

'Anyway, everyone coming into the show saw this ladder with the sign the next day, and those that knew had a good chuckle. Anyhow, I happened to be there when XXX came in, with his wife and child and pram, We had a good laugh, and it was the laugh of the show by those that knew about it, of course that wasn't many. On the Monday morning, Mrs XXX was at home and this lorry turned up with a ladder on top. *'I've come to deliver the ladder.'*

'She told him where he could put his ladder! 'A few shows later, I told the ladder man the story, and he said *'Oh I couldn't understand what it was all about, I didn't half get into trouble when I delivered the ladder. I didn't understand.'* Anyway we had a good laugh about it, he was a West Country chap.

'Going on from the first show, in the Winter, we had the Clay Pigeon or Skeet Shoot Annual Dinner. This is where they presented the prizes for the most points, the fastest, the most doubles and all the rest of it. All these prizes were presented and then the Chairman said *'We have an extra prize this year, for the most outstanding performance of the year. Mr XXX esq.'*

'He trots up, and Dick Wallis had had a silver ladder made, and on the top rung was engraved 'Erectus perfectum.'! As he trotted back, his chum asked him *'What was that for?'*

'More recently, at his silver wedding, he was presented with a pair of kitchen steps as they thought his ladder days were over. Actually, when we went to their Ruby wedding, I had acquired from a shop fitting company up at Northfield, a display rope ladder, not a proper one, the rungs were plastic and ropes were silky. I gave it to his brother, and it was

246

presented to him saying that now his ladder days were over, they were no good unless his wife could hold it up for him!'

'The year I was Chairman of the NFU, 1966, we had all the trouble with Newbury Cattle Market closing, trying to stop that. But that went through and we couldn't stop it from being closed. Newbury District Council closed it because it was uneconomical. All the cattle markets started to close, except a few big ones.'

'After that I took up the Chairmanship of the Newbury Fatstock Society, that was 1967, the year the Newbury Cattle Market actually closed, and that was the last Fatstock Show and the last Dinner as well. Actually, the chap who was Chairman before me, wouldn't make speeches at the Annual Dinners, so they made me Vice Chairman so that I could make the speeches for him, especially at the Fatstock Dinner. The dinners were always pretty ripe, especially when the slaughter men got up and told a few jokes.

'Then the next year when I was Chairman, we had an outbreak of Foot & Mouth. I was in hospital having my back operation, during the Foot & Mouth Epidemic, and the Fatstock was closed the following year. I was back to make the speech at the final dinner. So the Fatstock Society was wound up, and we distributed the cups between the Newbury Show and the Young Farmers and suchlike. The Reading Fatstock carried on for a few years, and I went to their dinners with Alan Snook. I remember I went to one at the Caversham Bridge Hotel.

'Of course that was in the days when I used to drink, and I wasn't driving, so I had a few drinks and they had a raffle at the end. The raffle was for charity, and one of the prizes was a brace of pheasants. Anyway, I won the pheasants, and

247

someone chucked them at me. I picked them up, and said, 'I don't want any pheasants, auction it for charity.' and I threw them back, he ducked and they missed him , hit the guest speaker in the back of his neck and knocked him off his chair!

'It got quite foolish then, someone plucked the pheasants in the middle of the dining hall. The Mayor, who had had a drop of drink, and the Vicar, who had also had a few drinks, retired to the bar where the barmaid had also had a bit to drink. It ended up with a wedding ceremony, the barmaid being married off to everyone! It got so out of hand that the Fatstock were banned from ever having their dinner at the Caversham Bridge Hotel again. 'I felt bad that night, really bad, though I have to admit to overindulging a few times in my life.

'Then I was asked to be Chairman of the Ploughing Match. They had lost money the three previous years, so we took it in hand, shook it up a bit, and ended up making money that year. I remember that I asked the foreman to go out and put 'YFC' with the cultivator right across the field so it showed up from the road. The problem was that the morning of the ploughing match, it was so blinking foggy, you couldn't see across the field!

'We'd had a bit of trouble with people ploughing for too long. So I went and bought two rockets. One could be fired at the start and one at the finish. No one could see the starting one because of the fog, but they could see the finish one!
You get about sixty to seventy entering the ploughing. The Young Farmers Club would probably enter ten or twelve. The categories were the two furrow, the three furrow, the four furrow, the five furrow and over. Then there were the vintage tractors as well. It was quite big. There were some horses there too, and some steam engines around the edge.
You need quite a big field for it though. That was a problem

then. But nowadays, with modern farming, everyone wants their fields planted by the time you have the ploughing match! That is the busiest time of the year, between harvest and before it gets too wet to plough, ninety percent of the crops are Winter crops, Winter corn you see.

'Today ploughing is a different story, and the new Chairman - President of the Newbury Show, Clive Povey, decided to have a ploughing match in 1997. Well someone had to try and resurrect them. and the day was beautiful, and the whole event was a great success.

'I used to do a lot of judging of ploughing matches. You had to judge the opening, the setting up, the compaction, the straightness. Of course nowadays with modern ploughs, they are two way ploughs, there's no opening, you just keep ploughing, you don't have to make a veering, you don't have to measure up so that they both plough out and you just have a small gully. Nothing like that. Its all different today. I don't suppose anybody nowadays has to learn to plough like we used to have to years ago!

'It's the first time we've had a real farmer for President for years. It's rather nice. I've known Clive for years. In fact when Clive got married, I think that was the worst I've ever got drunk. I went to that wedding, and I didn't realise then that I was allergic to brandy! Every time I drank Champagne Cocktails, with brandy, or had brandy at the end of a meal I've been really ill. On this occasion, Clive and Myrles' wedding, I felt really ill.

'Her Father, Roy, was a great character, there was no expense spared, you could drink as much as you want. The Policeman was pissed out of his mind! Everyone was riding the Policeman's bike, wearing his helmet!

249

'When I realised I wasn't very well, I went out and found Father's Land Rover, and lay across the seat, head hanging out the other side being sick. John came down and took me home and I went up and lay on his bed, he gave me a couple of Alka Seltzers. The woman who helped in the house came up and saw me *'Ooh you look terrible. I'll get you a couple of Alka Seltzers.'*
That was four Alka Seltzers. Then Mother came home. She looked at me, and said *'You look terrible! I couldn't find any Alka Seltzers in the house, here's some Andrews Liver Salts!'*

'I was married at the time and we were both going out that night with Jackie Bolton, and Roy Bennett, the Bennetts used to have a tractor firm. But Jackie Bolton was asleep in the bath, Roy Bennett was asleep somewhere else, so the three men were completely pie-eyed you know. Gone. I think that was the worst I've ever been! I've only ever been ill through drinking four or five times in my life. There's no pleasure in it.

'On one occasion, after an Old Newburians Dinner, we'd had a fair old drop to drink. It was before Richard was born, or about the time Richard was born. We had the dinner at the Chequers, we had a good meal, a fairish meal. We didn't pay a lot, so we didn't get a lot! We had a drop to drink, and Francis Wallis came up to us afterwards, drink in hand and said, *'Here you guys, that wasn't a very good meal, but I found some biscuits and cheese.'*
'So I grabbed a plate and popped a piece of cheese in my mouth, at the same time as another guy did, and it was bloody Sunlight Soap wasn't it! He'd cut it into little squares. It was yellow and looked like cheese. You swallowed it before you tasted it you see.

'The other guy who'd eaten it poured his beer over my head, but it wasn't my fault at all! Ooh I was sick on the way home.

250

'I had to keep stopping, and eventually, Francis Wallis's brother, George came up and said, *'You silly young bugger, move over, I'll drive you home!'*
He drove me home and got his wife to drive his car and I spent the night on the settee.'

David was standing for Local Government election during the time we were researching for this book, in fact the General Election, happened right in the middle of this period, with David actively campaigning nearly every day.

'When I'm canvassing, people ask *'Well what are you going to do for us?'*
My answer is 'I promise you nothing, but I will do the best I can.'
I don't promise things I can't do. It works, the last time, I was the only Conservative to get in West of Bucklebury.

'I know about horses, I learned to ride when I was four, I used to go hunting until I started my own farm, there wasn't time after that, I had to give it up.
'The last time I went on a horse was about five years ago.
Somebody had upset me over ballooning, by telling me that balloons could land on his farm as long as we wrote to him and told him which field and what time we were going to land!
He said even his grass was a crop, and had to treated with respect, and certainly not drive across it to pick up balloons, the balloons were dragged across it and caused damage.

'He also complained about the people who followed balloons, and blocked up the country roads, parking up at the side of the road watching the balloons.
He was a Master of Foxhounds. But he took on the wrong bloke when he took me on.   He was actually 'Joint' Master of the Foxhounds. I rang the other two Masters up and I said,

'You can whip him in to line or you can forget hunting across my farm, and my brother's farm, and there are enough of us now that we can put a block on the area of Fawley right through to the Motorway. You won't get through anywhere up there. They'll all back me.'

'Well the next year, the Hunt had what they call, a Farmers' Day or a Ratcatchers' Day. Farmers didn't have to come dressed up in Hunting gear, they could come in Ratcatchers gear if they wanted to. Anything you wanted to wear.

'The meet was being held at this MFH's house. So I thought, 'Right, I'm going to get a horse and ride across HIS farm'. So I hired a horse for the day, although I had not been on a horse for thirty years. I wore my corduroys, my Harris Tweed jacket and my ballooning hat! You know, the old one that looks like a deerstalker. Anyway, I wore that and off I went!

'I had great pleasure in riding across his land, having a glass of lemonade. We then went hunting, and I hunted for three and a half hours. During that time, I came up to a hedge I wanted to jump, but the horse didn't want to do it so it stopped – but I didn't! I went straight over his head! I know now why horses put their ears up, it is where they're aiming! They put their ears up and you go straight through!

'I went straight over his head, did a somersault and landed flat on my back! I never let go of the horse either, broke my finger, and broke the rein but I never let go of the horse!
Not only did I hang onto the horse, but I got back on, on my own and carried on.
Anyway, people said, *'Have you been practising for this?'* I said 'No, but I only want to get stiff once.'
But would you believe it, the next day, I had no ill effects whatsoever. I was not stiff, I had no bad joints, nothing. I

couldn't believe it, nothing wrong with me at all.
Someone said, *'Ooh you wait until tomorrow.'*
But tomorrow came, and not a twinge. Not bad after thirty years, I mean I was sixty then! Someone did say to me, *'You've got a good seat boy.'*
I can handle a horse, not many people realise that.

'I used to enjoy hunting, but I don't think I was ever 'blooded'. I mean, all this bullshit about foxes being torn to pieces, I can't remember seeing a kill all the times I've been out!
'It's a good day out! But what a load of bullshit!'
David roared with laughter 'The safest place to be if you're a fox, is in the Craven hunting area. The farmers don't shoot them because they leave them for the hunt, and the hunt can't catch them.'

'I mean, these do-gooders, they do so much harm. They let all those mink out a few years ago. Decimated the wild life. We caught thirty odd mink down at Shefford. The fact is, you never see a watervole down on the Lambourn, you never see any young ducks, or young moorhens, the mink have ruined the ecology.

'These people don't understand the countryside, they come in with different views. The countryside and the ecology is what the farmers have made it, they want to listen to the farmers a bit. This is the problem, it's the same with local government. The only reason I went into Local Government, if we don't do something ourselves, we get the idiots we deserve! My motto in life has been **'Farm as if you live forever, but live as if you die tomorrow!'**

'Someone came up to me who had just been made the new Conservative agent. He said, *'It's nice to meet you David. I've heard a lot about you. You're the kind of person we want.*

You're the rump of the Conservative Party.'
'Yes' I said, ' I've always been a bit of an arsehole!'
'He didn't know what to say after that! He didn't mean it like that. We had a laugh about that. But that's my trouble, mouth in gear before mind!'
David roared with laughter at the memory of that incident.

'During 1996 and 1997, I have helped to get a new fitness centre at Lambourn, we have looked after the racing industry to provide jobs, and dealt with planning permissions in the best way I could to what I consider to be in the best interest of the Lambourn Valley. My policy all the way through the election was that I would do my best for the Lambourn Valley. If anyone wants my advice, they can have it, if they take it or not is up to them, but we have an ever open door, and an ever open telephone line, and everyone knows it. It's amazing how many people ring me up.
'David, where can I get some railway sleepers?'
'I want some telegraph poles, any ideas?'
'Do you know where there's a bit of old oak?'
'I want some second-hand bricks.'
'They always seem to ring me up because they always seem to think that I'll know where to find things. I suppose, fifty percent of the time, I can say 'Oh yes, I'll see so-and-so or so-and-so.' You know. It's because I go around with my eyes open.

'Like a couple I got some slabs for, don't really want them, but Shefford school want them. So they're stacked up in the wood until they need them. They want to put down a small quiet area for the children. Shefford means a lot to me, it is sort of my home patch. I'm on the Parish Council of Shefford, and the West Berkshire District Council.

'Now because we've moved to Hungerford, I have some
254

interest here as well. I will try and help if I can. I've looked
into it, and you have to live no further than three miles from
the Parish Boundary to be on the council.

'My patch for the election is fifteen miles from one end to the
other, a hell of a big patch. There was no hope of going to
every house, but I tried. I did a fair few. One Sunday night
when Jo and I went out to some of the really out of the way
ones, I was really buoyant. Then when we went around a
housing estate, and people were saying, 'Oh, it's time for a
change.'

'I think that was the biggest decision. The other thing was that
the Conservatives couldn't agree amongst themselves. I have
a feeling, that they didn't want to get back in though.

'Anyhow, on Election Day, I was at one of the Polling stations
just before seven to help start with the telling, because
someone didn't think they could get there on time. As it was
they did. We were very lucky, we had people out to do the
telling at all the stations, and we were going well, but I just
had that feeling that there were lots of people whom we felt
ought to vote and didn't.
There were people coming out of the polling station who didn't
look at me. You knew damn well, that they had maybe voted
for me, but on a National scale? Well, it was one of those
things. It's a job and you do it to the best of your ability.

'That day, May 1st, we went on until ten. I went around
afterwards and thanked each polling officer at each station.
By the time I got to some places they had gone. Jo was with
me, she organised the tellers at Shefford. Kate was wonderful,
she took over and delivered things for me a couple of times in
Shefford. The Chairman and his wife and a lot of helpers from
Lambourn came round with us doing a lot of canvassing.

I was tired, a couple of days before the election, we got home, and I said to Jo, 'I don't think I'm going to get in.'

'Where we had been that day looked terrible. I had a dream too. I dreamed that I was in a running race, there were two of us. I was winning, but someone ran across the track in front of me and I swerved to miss them. When I picked myself off the floor, I realised I had fallen clean out of bed, broken the table by the bed, which had had a glass of water, a radio, the phone and all those sorts of things on it. Jo had had a long night working with the Samaritans, she rolled over, said, 'What was that noise?', and went back to sleep again!

'I didn't go down to Newbury Racecourse for the main count, we went down at nine the next morning for the local count. They did the easy ones first where there were only two people.'

'It was shame that Alan Snook didn't get in.' said Jo, 'He worked very, very hard, that was his first time, and he was only 159 votes behind. That wasn't a lot really David.'
'He was going against the stream, Jo.'
'I tell you what was interesting' Jo continued, 'I haven't been in on a count since Judith Chaplin died, you know. It was so much more sensible to have the count for the District Council on the Friday, instead of doing the General Election and the District all in one go.
They didn't get the results through until about three o'clock anyway, and everyone was desperately tired by then.
It is not the time to start counting straight after the big one. They didn't use the same counters, they used the people who were working on the polling stations the day before.
There were a tremendous amount of people up for the District Council, and there were a lot of recounts during the time.'

'Oh yes', David continued, 'Ours was very complicated. There were six people standing for two seats. They finally got ours counted at about twelve, then the Liberals asked for a recount because they could not believe the result.

The recount came out better in my favour by about two. They finally got through the count for the third time by about half past two. Kintbury had three recounts. The first time they had one Liberal and one Conservative, at the end of the third count it was two Conservatives! So in the end, instead of six seats we got fifteen seats. I don't think the local elections are half so political, I think a lot depends on personalities.

'Anyway, we managed to get fifteen councillors. It's a good thing because in six months time, Berkshire will be run by six Unitary Authorities. Newbury Town Council will be like a Parish Council, and a lot of major decisions will have to be made locally which is a good thing. Berkshire is run from Reading, and over here we do not really have any big metropolis, and the area is mainly rural, and needs rural understanding.

'I feel guilty that I don't get to all the meetings. There is no time. No sooner than I get onto the District Council, then they expect me to go to all the parish Council meetings, and I ought to go to Lambourn, Shefford, East Garston, and Eastbury. They expect you to turn up to all of those, otherwise they think you are neglecting them. The trouble is that the Lambourn ones are on the same night as the planning ones so I can't get to them. Self defeating that one.

'I don't know what Graham Jones will do, I think he wants to get onto Education. I want to get onto Downlands planning and the CCTV scheme and the Police, you know. I don't want to get onto Social Services or Housing because I would be out of my depth.

257

People don't realise, but by the next election I will be seventy! I know I act like a teenager at times, but maybe that's because I didn't really have a life when I was a teenager, I'm still trying to be a teenager. I mean, I left school at fourteen and went to work

I know I am still trying to be a teenager, but the music.! Do you know, when I've been somewhere where the music is BOOM, BOOM, BOOM, my ears hurt for days afterwards. I suppose it doesn't help that I was in an aeroplane that depressurised at 30,000 feet, or hurt my ears going across the channel in a hot-air balloon at 20,000 feet.

'I suppose driving tractors in the early days was bad too. I can hear all the deep sounds like car doors, which Jo can't hear, but I've lost all the birds and light noises. I mean, balloon burners are a sort of white noise, they were worse in the old days. Maybe we should wear earplugs.

'I rang one person up and told them I had got in, and they said, *'Well done, what plans are you going to put in now, now you are back on the Planning Committee.'*

'That really hurt. People don't realise that when you are on the Council Planning Committee, there is no way you can put things through for yourself. It is much easier as an ordinary citizen, but when you are on the Planning Committee, you have got to be whiter than white. I can assure you that you get nothing out of it. You get tired. You certainly do not need it as a status symbol!

'As one old farmer said to me when I asked him why he didn't buy himself a decent car.

'Boy, you don't buy status symbols, you earn them.'

I've always remembered that, just because you drive a flash car doesn't mean you've earned it.

'The other day we had a planning meeting at West Berkshire District Council, and the District Planning Officer is very much against anyone making their gardens bigger from agricultural land. On this night we were looking at an application from someone who wanted to enlarge their garden, as the local sewage plant was closing down, and all sewage was being re-piped somewhere else. They said well it isn't really agricultural land, I suppose it is what you would call a brown field site, rather a green field site.
I said, 'Mr Chairman, from what they had out there before, it is definitely a brown field site!'
That caused a lot of laughs.

'I cannot be serious, life is so serious, and there are people nowadays who think that nothing is so bad that it can't get worse. There are some people who go through life with a half empty glass, it's always half empty. I go through with a half full glass. That's my attitude, the way you look at life, I told you earlier, my biggest advantage is to turn my setbacks to my advantage. Always look for a way out, one door closes and another opens, but you have to look for it.

'The nicest thing after I got elected, was the number of Liberal Democrats who came up to me and shook my hand and said 'We're glad you got back on, we need people like you.'
That meant a lot. I don't go with the herd, if I think some poor individual needs some help and support, I will give it to them. regardless of whether I endear myself to a lot of people, I will stand up for the individual.

'The individual needs to be stood up for. I've upset the planning officers on a couple of things. The planning officers are so used to never being questioned, they think they are God. They are not, they're on tap, not on top. As I said in my Election address, I am always a phone call away, my phone is always open, I will always help people.

'One local farmer rang me one night, it was about one thirty in the morning. *'David I'm in the ditch! Come and pull me out with your Land Rover.'*
I went down, he had got to the level crossing, the gates were closed, so he had turned around and ended up in the ditch. I had about fifty foot of parachute nylon webbing, but it was like elastic. I got it from Gordon Passey, when the Americans left, they had dumped all this webbing, like wide seat belts except it was stretchable. Anyway first I didn't think he was going to come, then all of a sudden his car shot out of the ditch and straight into the ditch on the other side of the road! So I had to pull him out again!

'At the Newbury Show, I pulled a beer lorry out with the Land Rover. Did it exactly the same way , but I didn't think it was going to work, but just as the wheels were starting to spin, the elastic took up and we got it out.

'If you know how to use a Land Rover, they are amazing. Another time, there was a London Brick lorry in Shefford, it had broken down and was being towed by another lorry. But the tow rope had gone under the front wheel as it was going down the bridge the other side of the Swan and there was no way that lorry could go down.
I said, 'I'll push you back over the bridge to get you off the rope.'
'You won't move it with that thing!'
I said, 'Give me a try?'
So my front bumper went up against his front bumper, and I just eased him backwards gently up over the brow of the bridge, the tow rope came clear, and we were able to get him clear of the bridge. He was blocking all the traffic, and actually, after all that, all there was, was a dent in my front

bumper where I had exerted the pressure.

'I knew how to drive a Land Rover. When I was young I did a bit of competitive driving in the Land Rover Owners Championships. I've got five cups for it.
It was the All England Four Wheel Drive Cross Country of 1960 or 61. I used to do a bit of that. We went up to the Land Rover Headquarters, I didn't know if I was going to go or not, so I didn't enter until the last minute. By the time I entered, I was seventy second out of seventy three around the course!

'On one section, the first thirteen got through but from then on there was a winch lorry there to get them out, until I came round, I was the first to get through after the first thirteen! We had the Land Rover stripped down, with no top, windscreen down, and my passenger, Jimmy Gore and I went for it.
I said, 'For Gods sake, hang onto that bar.' (There was a bar in front on the old Series one Land Rovers) 'We're going through on that spot which I can see no one has used, and it's going to be bloody rough!'

'We did, we bounced through it and we were also fastest through the section. There was another section where you went up, turned right and drove along two sleepers end to end, nine inches wide. They were really slippery where seventy one had tried before me! If I'd slipped I'd have been airborne, I did it really fast, so by the time I had slipped, I had gone over!

'But the one where I really, really did pick up the points was where you had to drive a Land Rover up on two steel ramps, and they were balanced on a pole, and you had to tip up the ramps so that both ends weren't touching the ground. People were driving up and sliding the clutch and hoping to do it. A matter of fact they had buggered the clutch up on the works Land Rover, so I said I'd do it in mine, I don't mind.

I had watched everyone, and I knew the point where it stopped. If you drove to that point, it wouldn't go down. I watched and watched. I drove up really fast, jammed the brakes on, it swung up and stayed, nineteen seconds. Then there was an objection that I had used my own Land Rover instead of the works one. So I said 'OK, I'll do it in the works one.'

I did it again, but this time in eighteen seconds!

'I was in that sort of mood that day that I didn't care, I was in it for the fun of it. There was one little thing in my favour, there was a local firm around here called Vacu-Lug, which put new lugs on tractor tyres. It was run by Richard Hill. His brother said he was known affectionately as 'Horizontal Hill.'

Now the year before when I had entered, some people had put dungspreader tyres on, which are like small tractor tyres and they were banned. The rules said that they had to be a continuous running surface with lugs on both sides. So we got four worn out Land Rover tyres, put a continuous running surface around and then put inch and a half lugs on the side so I had one hell of a grip.

'I won the best overall on Saturday, the best overall on Sunday, the team prize, the best individual prize, and the fastest round the course prize. Five cups in one weekend! This was about 1960-61. When I got home and showed Father the cups, all he said was, *'How much damage have you done to the Land Rover then?'*

He never said, 'Well done' or anything.

I did one or two others, with John Goddard or Jimmy Gore, but I had to give up eventually because my back couldn't stand it, all the jolting. The other reason I gave up was that I became the Chairman of Newbury Show which meant I didn't have the time to do anything. Funny how the experience paid off though.

'I was flying the balloon one day, and I looked down and there was this huge nursery for Leylandii, evergreens. Right out in the country. Next day, because I wanted some evergreens, I went out and found it. There was a chap there on his own. I said what I wanted, this, that, and the other. I said 'How much is that then?'
'Normally three pound a piece, but to you, two pound. I shall never forget how you came down at six thirty one morning and pulled me out of the snowdrift in my milk float.'
'I can't remember it!
'I can remember it. I was in the ditch, stuck fast. and you came along and got me out. I will always remember, so you can have them at trade price.'
I like to help people and to do things for them.'

David emphasises this strongly.

'I remember a young couple, Sue and Phil Brittain, I was able to give them an album of their wedding photographs at their reception, an hour and a half after the event! I've done it for a couple of weddings. You have to get up close for the pictures. Unfortunately there are all these people videoing weddings now, and you end up being in the picture a bit more than they would like.
Anyway, I get John, one of my workmen, to wait outside the church, he takes the film into the place where they develop it within an hour, and then he comes up to the reception, and you can pop them in an album, and they can have a record of the day to take away with them. They seem to rather like it.

'Peter Robinson did it for me once, rushed the film into

Newbury, waited and brought it out to me and we hadn't even got to the main course! It's really nice to see their faces. It's always nice to help people. There is far more satisfaction giving than receiving.

'You've heard the story about this girl, this nurse, who used to go in and help this old chap, every week. She used to do things for him around the place. Every week, he used to give her this lovely little tin of almonds. After a few weeks, she said 'You can't keep giving me all these almonds, you can't go on buying them for me!'
'Oh I don't buy them, me daughter buys 'em. But I can't eat 'em cos of me teeth being so bad!'
'Well, tell her to buy you something else.'
'Oh no, I like sucking the chocolate off 'em first.'
David roared with laughter as he regaled this gem.

'If you treat people right, then they will help you through life. You've got to pay your debts, and look people straight in the eye.

'I mean, we had a problem with drainage the other day, I was down there at quarter to eight that morning, went down with a JCB, found the problem. I rang somebody up and said 'How about sucking them out for me as soon as you can.'
Anyway, they sent the chap round, 'Where do you want the tanks drawn out? We'll do it for you today?'
This guy did it and I asked how much I owed, he said 'Alan will tell you.' So I gave the chap a twenty pound note, which was a better taste than what he had to deal with. He'll remember, and they'll come back. But the thing is, you've got to treat people right.'

David Rabbitts was talking about David Liddiard a few months ago. 'He is so open, never keeps anything to himself,

264

it's a good thing in people really. We went ballooning to Ireland with David' David Rabbitts remembered, 'Barry Side and I, we took a BMW I remember that because it broke down! We were stopping in the same bedroom, the three of us, Barry Side was quite amusing. Barry lives Burghclere way now.

David has got a heart of gold, he'll always help, it's amazing how many people I know who have problems, lost their job or something, and David will ring up and say 'Can I help?' Amazing.'

Ballooning Overseas

'In August 1978 we went to Budva in Yugoslavia. Chris Smith, Graham Stagg, Jo, myself and James.

We flew to Zagreb, then to Dubrovnik, and then we got a bus which took us down to Budva. One of the members of the team got a little lubricated on Slivovitz , and nearly took over the bus on the way there, that was quite an interesting trip.

We had to tether the balloon at the Adriatic Fair for British Airways and were put up in a house which belonged to someone in British Airways, and were fed either at the fairground or next door, in the Police Headquarters.

'The chap in charge was called 'Dragon'. He used to pick us up from the house, take us in through the back door of the Police Headquarters to get to the fair or to feed us and then take us back after our tether. He wasn't in uniform, I think he was one of the security or undercover people. When we went in, there was no security, we went through the Police building into the exhibition centre.

'One day, he was having a day off, and he sent another driver and we had to go through all the paraphernalia of going in the right way, through the front door. It took ages because the new guy wasn't important enough, so it took a long time to get into the showground that day.

'When we had a day off, they all wanted to go down to Stefi Stefan, a well known beauty spot island down on the coast with a lovely beach, swimming and the suchlike, but when we do these ballooning trips I always get tired.

So I stopped behind and had a sleep. It was a lovely day and one member of the team, who shall remain nameless, had a little bit too much sun and when he came back that night he was glowing red. He sat in the room with us moaning.

'Has anybody got any ointment, I'm really sore.'

'Yes I have.' I said and went and got it and put some on his bad shoulders.

'Have you got enough to do me all over?'

'I said, 'Yes', and rubbed it in all over.

'Ooh that is lovely, what is it?'

I said, ' Well it's actually called Germaloid.   I've got it for piles but it's just right for arse-holes like you!'

The other two members of the group fell off the bed laughing.

'The last day, Dragon had decided to arrange a special flight for us from Titograd to Zagreb which would save us having to go on the bus. We had to get up at four in the morning.'

'I'll never forget the journey, he drove so fast, and the roads had sheer drops down the mountains!' Jo said, ' He drove SO fast, overtaking on hairpin bends! Oh it was terrifying!'

'Oh Yes', David added, 'Bloody good driver, but Crikey! It was a hell of a journey. The balloon went on ahead in a lorry with the Germaloid smeared member.   The British Airways chap was Dusan Djordjevic, a friend of Dragon, and they arranged it together.

'Titograd is a military airfield and when we got there, there was a long line for the security check-in, but Dragon just drove straight through the guards, saying a few words here and there.   We were taken in and given breakfast there, bread, salami and black coffee.

'It was quite a trip, I haven't put in the logbook how many hours tethering but it was probably two or three hours , I just put the dates.

'It wasn't very long after we got back, less than a month, when we were asked to go back again, this time to Belgrade, they liked us so much. So at the beginning of September, we returned and had to inflate in a sports stadium during a pop concert.

'This time it was Celia, Alec and myself. I think it was the last trip Alec made with Dante, he was really starting to suffer. Then, poor chap. It was Celia and I really, quite hard work.

'Anyway, the next day, before we left, the British Airways chap took us out and showed us where Tito lived, and then took us to a restaurant up in the hills.
I'll always remember, there was this huge semicircular terracotta brick plinth with a fire in it, and there were four whole sheep cooking in there. You just went up and carved a bit off! Lovely meal, I remember that.
One of those things where it's very plain cooking but lovely. That was my second trip to Yugoslavia. That was with the balloon G-BEND.

'I remember that the night I got back from that trip, we got back home very late. I just took my cases upstairs, went to bed, and didn't bother to unpack. I had to be off on the farm first thing in the morning, I woke up, came downstairs, stepped off the bottom stair straight into water! So I went back upstairs and got my gumboots from the bedroom.
My gumboots were still in the case upstairs, just in case you wonder why I have them in the bedroom! Then Jo came down and started crying her eyes out.
'Oh do stop crying.' I said, 'There is enough bloody water around as it is!'
The washing machine pipe had burst, water had flooded the utility room, the kitchen, the television room and was seeping through to the hall. Luckily it hadn't got through to the main lounge.

'Anyhow, the best thing to get water up is a dustpan. It took ages and then it took six of us to carry the carpet out!

Members of the 'Dante' Group at the Mill.

The Mill

Checking the tether points, Tempelhof, Berlin. 1987

David Liddiard, Anne Lewis-Smith,
Anthony Smith and Alec Jenkinson

'The Dante trip at the beginning of November in 1978 was to Cayman Islands. I paid for Jo's ticket, and Niall and Wendy Duncan came as well paying their own way. We went out on a Jumbo via Bermuda, Jamaica and then on to Cayman, and we had the balloon. Pete and Elaine Bish, our James, and Chris Smith were the other Dante members, and they flew to Miami by 747, and then onto the Caymans on a BAC1-11.
There are only two planes which won't carry our balloon, a BAC 1-11 and a DC9. It will go in any other aeroplane. So we had to go that way round.

'Anyway, half way across the Atlantic, Niall, who's an airline pilot, said to me, *There's something wrong with this plane!*'
I said,' What do you mean?'
'I heard something go bang.'
'Don't tell the girls.'

'Sure enough, when we landed in Bermuda, the plane was wheeled off to the side. We ended up being grounded in Bermuda because the plane had a broken spar or something, and we had to wait for the next plane to come through. On that plane was some Royalty, Prince Edward or the Duke of Kent or someone. That plane was taken off sick as well!
While we were waiting, we were held in the transit lounge. The only thing to drink there was warm Coke and cold coffee!
Now we took off on the fifth of November, and we were sitting in the transit lounge, and I looked at my watch and said 'Oh! It's past midnight! It's my birthday!'
I had two litre bottles of whisky in my case, so we opened them and distributed them around all the passengers. I do remember that the Roman Catholic Fathers were not at the end of the queue! There were a couple of nuns who also liked their drop of whisky.

'There was a big black Jamaican lady, a big well built girl,

and I gave her a drop as well. She said *'Oh I didn't think you were going to give me any.'*
'Why not? Everyone else is having a drink.'
Then they announced that they were going to put us all up at the Holiday Inn for the night. As we came out of the transit lounge, she came up behind me and whispered, *'If you sleeping on your own tonight, you've no need to. You can put your shoes under my bed anytime.'*
She was a big girl! Jo laughed her head off, she was next to me and heard everything!

'We arrived at the Holiday Inn, had something to eat and then went to bed. Suddenly, there was a hammering on the door. It was Niall.
'Come on, they've got a plane for us, we're going!' he exclaimed, *'We were just getting on the coach when we realised you weren't with us!'*
Mad panic, Jo left her knickers there in the rush!

'We got down to the airport, and Niall and I helped load the balloon into a DC-8. We got on the plane and it was very hot and sticky.
This big bloke got on, I mean very big, he stuck his fingers in his cowboy belt and said,
'I guess you guys are getting a bit hot, we're going to crank the engines up and then we can get the air conditioning going.'
He was the Captain. This was Evergreen Airways, and the hostesses were not happy because they were supposed to get off in Bermuda, and they had already been on for fourteen hours, and now they were going to have to go all the way to Jamaica and on to Mexico again!

'They couldn't serve us anything because there wasn't anything on the plane, it had been commandeered as it landed!
We arrived in Jamaica at four in the morning, and put into a

270

hotel until a plane could take us on to Grand Cayman later that day.'

'Didn't Brus Henriques and Stella come down and see us?' Jo asked at that point, pausing in her cooking.
'Oh yes, they came down to the airport to see us. We had met them when we were in Jamaica before. He had the biggest agency for GMC cars in Jamaica, we gave him a ring and he came down to meet us. Ooh he was a case, big lad.'
'His wife was Jamaican, but he wasn't was he?' Jo remembered. 'They were a wonderful host and hostess.'
'You had to move quite fast to get away from him didn't you?' David chuckled.
'Oh yes, we went to a barbecue up there once, it was horrendous!'
'That's beside the point. Anyway, we got to Cayman eventually, and the airport was quite interesting. The airport buildings were tin shacks! It's different now, but then.'
'Oh yes,' interrupted Jo, ' On the plane, most of the people had cardboard boxes for cases, they were so poor. Travelling home from England or Jamaica. All with cardboard boxes, tied up with string! I couldn't believe it!'

'One poor guy dropped his box and about four bottles of rum broke! That was messy. Anyway, we ended up at the Holiday Inn.'
'It was nice too.'
'We met up with James, Pete and Elaine Bish and Chris, and were asked to do a free flight across the Cayman Islands. Well, Pete doesn't like flying across water, and we had to fly across the bay. The bay there was horseshoe shaped. So we went down to the tip on the upwind side, and I flew solo, across this water. I decided on a good place to land between two houses on a building plot. What I didn't realise was that it was swamp! I ended up, up to my knees in water! I was in

271

amongst these bushes and a little voice reached me saying, *'Are you alright in there?'*

I said, 'Well not really, I want to take off again, my crew won't find me here and there are some power wires about twenty yards down there.

'Well I've only got my slippers on.'

I said, 'I really would appreciate it.'

'So he wades in, in his slippers and shorts, this little white man. I told him that I wanted him to hold me down as much as he could when I heated it so I could take off straight up. That worked, and as I went up, at about twenty feet or so, I leaned over the side of the basket to say thank you, and he was standing right underneath me, and as I did, a large piece of swampy stuff loosened itself from the bottom of the basket and fell on top of him. Plop!

'Anyhow, I flew on, and then I had to land as we were running out of land. Our truck was coming along on the road, so I decided to put it down on the road, the overshoot was the other side of the white line. The other side of the road were Mango Trees and swamps, then breakers, and the sea.

'Anyway, Pete Bish was there, I landed on the road, and we held the traffic up whilst we laid it out, and packed it away. That was the first flight of a Hot-Air balloon in the Cayman Islands, and probably the last! That night we went to a reception, and I was introduced to the Postmaster General. 'I know you don't I?' I said. It turned out that he was the little man in the slippers who had helped me that morning!

'We had a great time there, so Jo and I decided to stay on for an extra week. We had a really nice holiday, and then we came back via Miami. Jo wanted to have a night in Miami, *(and I got into trouble for this)* but this British Airways plane

272

had been delayed leaving Miami, and when we landed, it was still waiting to be loaded.

I said, 'Any chance of getting on?'

The Ground Staff chap said, *'You can go on standby.'*

This upset Jo, 'cos she wanted a night in Miami, but I wanted to get home. So we sat at the airport, and they called all these people, and we waited, and there were only two left, and we thought, 'Oh well, we've had it now.' Then they called our names, and we were given tickets for two seats.

'We were just walking through, boarding passes in our hands, and someone came up behind us and said, *'What about me, I've got a firm booking!'*

With that, the staff snatched the tickets from my hand, *'Sorry Sir, this gentleman has a firm booking.'*

So we lost the tickets. I went and saw the ground staff chap, and said, *'What about us?'*

He said, *'Hang on,'* went off, came rushing back, thrust two tickets at us and said, *'Run down to Gate 19 and you'll get on the plane.'*

Jo said, *'What's happening?'*

'Madam,' he said, *'Are you not satisfied with two First Class tickets?'*

'We couldn't sit together, otherwise she would have given me hell all the way home, but we came back First Class. So that was Cayman Islands.

'The Icicle Meet in January 1979 was held at Bradfords as usual. Ron Griffin was doing his final check flight before he went for his licence. It was a pilot declared goal, and we were the first balloon off, G-BFOZ.

Everyone else was waiting, and as we took off they shouted, *'You haven't given us your pilot declared goal.'*

'Oh' Ron said, *'Newbury Swimming Pool.'* and off we flew.

'Ron Griffin flew, kept to the height I wanted him to. He was a marvellous pilot, marvellous for his age, only seventeen. We could have actually landed in the swimming pool. We went over the top of it, which was covered in ice, at about fifteen feet, and landed just outside. It was locked up so we wouldn't have got it out if we had been inside. Alan Noble's first wife, Pat, was sitting there waiting for us.

'Look at that' she said, *'Your retrieve has got here before you landed.'*

'Yes,' I said, *'But why didn't you put the trailer on?'*

She was so embarrassed, she had to go back to Bradfords to pick up the trailer to bring us back.

Ron Griffin is one of the best pilots I have ever taught, a brilliant pilot, a Scorpio like me. If I said go up ten feet, he'd go up ten feet, you know. He was good.

'Then we go on to February 1979, and Abu Dhabi. That was the only time I have had to unpack the balloon at Customs when we were taking it in. We were going through Customs, and the Customs Officer said, *'What have you got in that bag?'* I said, 'A balloon.'

'I want to see it.'

Well, being a bit devilish, I had the top of the bag open and half the balloon out before he could stop us. We'd carpeted the Customs hall with balloon from wall to wall. I don't think he could believe what was coming out of the bag. He was waving his hands saying, *'Put it back, put it back, put it back!'* It was stopping everyone from going through customs.

'That was Pete Bish, Chris Smith, and myself, and there might have been someone else, I can't remember now. The next morning, I was designated to take the balloon up on a tether next to the Talking Clock. We tied off the tether lines to two points on the sea wall. We had to have the balloon up in the air by the time the Queen and Prince Philip came by.

274

'At one point the wind and thermals, instead of taking me inland, were blowing me out on these tethers, right over and down into the sea. They said it was the funniest thing watching me climbing the rigging to make sure I didn't get wet feet. Anyway, it went back up again by the time the Queen went by, we were only a few yards away from her.

'We did a free flight in Abu Dhabi as well as lots of tethers. We were given permission to go out and fly from this little spit of land. Pete wanted to get his free flight in, I helped him put it up and he flew, and he landed it on the sand.
I said, 'Why don't you fly on and land on that beach over there?'
'I'm not flying over water.'
So I got in and flew over the little bit of sea, and landed in front of one of the hotels in Abu Dhabi.

Then we went down to Dubai on the 26th February, and I did a thirty five minute flight. We made the mistake of telling the British Airways crew that we were going down there, we were staying in the same hotel as them. We also said, the night before when we were chatting, *'Oh yes, sometimes you can take off and come back and land in the same place you took off.'*

'The next day, we took off from just outside this Country Club in Dubai, from the side of the road. I took a hostess with me, and we flew over the golf greens, (except they have browns), over a rugby club, then I climbed, and the wind took me back. Thirty five minutes later, I put the balloon down on the side of the road within about twenty feet from where I took off from.
'Ooh' she said, *'I didn't really believe you when you said that.'*

'Then it was my turn to retrieve, Pete took off with Chris. I

was driving this four wheel drive truck, drove it into the sand and got it stuck in the desert didn't I? I had to walk back over the sand dunes to find someone.
Eventually I saw this compound in the middle of the desert and I walked up to it. It had a huge high wall around it, and I had to walk right round it to find the gate, it must have been about half a mile square! It was a service station for oil exploration. They had this great big water truck. *'Oh we'll bring this and pull you out.'* they said.

'The tyres on it were enormous, taller than two men, you needed a ladder to climb up into the truck. They came and pulled me out though. I drove off and eventually found Pete, they were standing on the side of the road.

'We did a couple of other tethers, one was on the side of a creek as the Queen opened a Municipal building. We had been given these three great big posters of the two Sheikhs and the Queen to hang on the basket. So we tied a Sheikh on each side, and the Queen on the front. We were up there with a wonderful view of the grandstand and the Queen opening it.

'The Duke was standing there with his hands behind his back, and he looked up, saw the picture of the Queen on the basket. He tapped her on the shoulder and pointed, as if to say, *'They're up there again, look.'*
I waved, and they waved back. I saw more of the Queen in those ten days than I had in the rest of my life. Then I did a tether in front of the World Trade Centre, and we only had one tether rope. All the ropes were tied together, and I tethered on one long line. Probably the highest I've ever done, about two hundred and fifty foot high.

'Then in April 1979, I took the balloon to Bermuda where I did a tethered flight in the Zoological Gardens for the Royal

Bermudan Agricultural Society. Although it was the Royal Agricultural Show of Bermuda, it was only chickens, bantams and rabbits and that sort of thing. We were tied to two palm trees in the middle of the day and it was murder. Really hot and gusty. I looked up at one time and the balloon was out like a wind sock! We actually bent the burner frame.

'There is a photograph from a local paper somewhere of the balloon after it had bounced and on it's way up again and all you could see was my arm. There were no flexi-rigid poles in those days, and if the wind slammed you down, when you hit the ground, the burner came down on top of you. You had to get down in the basket out of the way!

The picture title was **'Pilot's Remark Upon Landing: "Aaagh!"'**

That was Bermuda.

'Then in May we went to Tempelhof, Berlin. That was to celebrate the Thirtieth Anniversary of the Berlin Airlift. We were the only moving thing, all the other exhibits were static. It was a huge place, undamaged during the war.

We were supposed to be tethered the whole time, but the tether rope came undone, accidentally on purpose and Pete Bish got a five minute free flight, and I got five minutes flying across Tempelhof airfield.

'We didn't have any problems about it, it was the Station Commander that had the problems. He was driving round, busy watching us flying across the airfield. There was a big fire truck, and they were busy watching us too.

The station commander stopped, the fire truck were still watching us and there was a big crunch, and there was a big fire truck parked in the boot of the Station Commanders car. By the time they had sorted that out, we had packed up and gone.

'In June, I went to Philadelphia to do a tether, and they put me on the helicopter pad on top of the Holiday Inn. There again, we only had two tether ropes, not three and the wind changed. It was only a 56,000cub ft. balloon, and I had a cameraman, and a sound recordist with me, and the wind blew us over the edge of the hotel, and down the side of the hotel.

'I was a bit worried about the bits of burning scoop which were falling on top of me. When we had set up, the scoop was facing the right way for the wind but when the wind changed, the scoop blew across the burner. I couldn't turn the burner off because I needed to burn to get back on top of the hotel. We got back up on top of the hotel eventually, but I only had half a scoop left.

'The next day we were part of all the razzmatazz of the Philadelphia Hot Air Balloon Meet. We had to do a Hare and Hounds from the centre of Philadelphia. All the balloons were on their trailers, and we went through the streets with all the bands and the people and floats, typical American carnival. We eventually ended up in the Benjamin Franklin Boulevard and were told to set the balloons up in the middle of the road. This was right by the Art Gallery and Library.

'Now that morning, I had listened to the weather forecast. They were advising people who were camping to take their tents down and take cover, and all those with camper vans to take them to high ground because there were severe electrical thunderstorms coming across. So I thought, well we shan't be flying anyhow. I thought we would probably put the balloons up and give the people a show.

'We'd drawn lots the day before to see which balloon would take off first, and I was to take off second.

'Anyhow, we blew the balloon up. There was Alec, Mike Drye and Pete Hornfeck. Alec was not feeling too great that day, but Pete Hornfeck and Mike Drye are quite adequate to hold a balloon down. We were standing there, and suddenly, away went the Hare balloon!

'Look' I said, 'The Hare balloon, someone's let him go!'

Then Wally Gunter, came along and said, *'Right, that balloon is going in two minutes, and you follow one minute after.'*

I said, 'We're not flying are we?'

'Yes.'

Well, as the only Englishman there I thought, I can't let them down. At the side of the road, were lamp-posts, trees and flagpoles, and blimmin' great skyscrapers! The first Hound balloon took off, and Wally shouted, *'Right, go when I tell you.'*

I said to Mike and Pete, 'Right, hold me down, I need to clear this lot.'

Anyway, when they let me go, I went. I rounded out at about 2,000feet I think. I went up like a champagne cork! The Hare balloon chap said to me in the evening, *'What were you flying? A Saturn rocket?'*

'Anyway, I stabilised it and thought, 'What's a nice guy like me doing in a place like this.' I must admit, for the first half an hour I was looking for somewhere to land, I was not interested in anyway in taking part in the competition. I was looking after number one.

'I saw a school playing field coming up, and I saw the Hare balloon which I was overtaking because I was higher than him, and he was coming in from my left, and we were both heading for the same field. We were both coming down, and suddenly he dropped down into somebody's garden. There was actually a bit of a down draft there.

It looked like I was going to as well, so I chucked the trailrope

279

out to slow me up in these big trees, and unfortunately there was a knot at the end of it. It doesn't half stop you. It slowed me right up and my forward speed was transferred into my downward speed. I landed within twenty one foot of him in this person's garden, there wasn't room for more than about three balloons in there. So I won the competition!

'In actual fact, two of the balloons never made it out of the town centre, they got torn on lamp-posts and trees taking off.
As for my retrieve, they took two and a half hours to find me. They kept on driving as they thought no one could land in those conditions, especially in the suburbs of Philadelphia.
Anyhow, I got the balloon packed up, and sat on the side of the road for two and a half hours and waited for them to pick me up.

'I was presented with a very nice handpainted limited edition 'Patriot Bowl', and the crew and I all got gold painted Liberty Bells, I complained about mine - it was cracked! They were presented to us by the Mayor of Philadelphia who said, *'Here we are celebrating two hundred years of getting the English out, and here you are winning the prize!'*

'I replied that shortly before ,'I had flown from a place called Concord, and on the bridge there was a plaque saying, *'From this place, the first shot was fired which set two kindred nations asunder, now happily reunited in friendship.'* So I've come back, as a friend, to teach you how to fly balloons.'
That went down rather well.

'When we went to come home that night, there was no room on the aeroplane. It was absolutely solid, and I wanted to get back. So I sat on one of the little jump seats that the stewardesses sit on, and Mike Drye and Pete Hornfeck sat on the jumpseats in the cockpit.

'The balloon came back with us, but Alec Jenkinson decided to stay in the States, and as he had signed the balloon in, he got into trouble and they were going to fine him because he wasn't signing it out again.

'In September 1979 we went to Hanover, just doing a tether, not very spectacular, and then about a week later we went to Tampere and Hyvinkaa in Finland. I was there for the opening of the new Airport with Pete Bish and Phil Dunnington. That was a lovely trip. All the women in the town were beautifully dressed in furs and everything.

'Next month we went to Hobart in Tasmania to fly at the Agricultural Show in Hobart. For the first tether, I went up in the commentary box and did the commentary. The next day, I was doing the tether in the main ring, and we deflated the balloon so the Cattle Parade could take place in the same ring. We just stayed in the middle of the ring, just sitting on the basket.

'Suddenly a heifer got free, an eighteen month old heifer. She was roaring round the ring creating havoc, and as she went by me, I stupidly caught hold of the end of the rope! It was a stupid thing to do, but I eventually worked my way up to her head, and brought her under control and led her out the ring.

'The whole time it was going on, instead of the commentator telling the people about the cattle in the ring, he was commenting on me doing the rodeo, who I was, where I came from etc. because I'd told them all that the day before!

'The crowd loved it, and the Hobart Times, which came out the next day, had a full page of photos of me catching the heifer. Ian Culley was on that trip, with Chris Smith, and Celia. David and June Rabbitts had paid to come out and so had Jo, and the four of us stayed on for two weeks afterwards. We had three weeks in Australia looking round, and catching up with our sons.

'Our son James was getting work experience in Australia and so was Jeffrey, David and June's son. James was taking a year off before starting farming, and working his way around the country, and although Jeffrey was older, he wanted to do that too.'

David Rabbitts can remember how both boys needed to get the travel bug out of their system. They both worked their way around Australia, working on farms, in supermarkets and suchlike, and they both came back with more money than they left home with..

David Liddiard continued 'We were driving off over Australia, and June kept on that she hadn't seen any kangaroos. Her son Jeffrey had told her there were lots of kangaroos out there, so many that they had to take care that they didn't run into any as they were driving along.
She kept on and on about these kangaroos, and I said, 'June, don't worry, you needn't bother to keep looking for them, you'll hear them when they come.'
'Why?' she said.
'Well, you've heard them on the television. They go 'BOING, BOING, BOING!'
She said, 'Oh yes, so they do!'
It was naughty of me, it really was.

'After that, at Icicle 1980 I just did one flight. Bradfords to Beacon Hill. Then later that month, we went to Austria. Flew to Vienna and drove to Villach, and got there at ten thirty that night. When we got there we learned that the balloon had to be in the air by eight the next morning.

So we refuelled and got it ready, to be told that, 'You will fly at nine o'clock.'

Next morning we got it up at eight o'clock, and at nine they said, 'Fly'.

'But they hadn't given us maps or anything, so I said I would just fly it up behind the hotel and land. But behind the hotel was snow and the Alps, and all these people swimming around in a swimming pool with steam rising from it. I hadn't realised we were staying in a hotel where there were warm springs! So we flew on up the narrow valley with an electrified railway on one side, and power lines and a road the other.

'I was coming in to land by the road, Pete Bish and the retrieve crew were there, and Pete ran to meet me and pull me in, and as he left the road, he fell into a deep snow drift up to his armpits. There was nothing I could do, I was coming down straight on top of him! Luckily I missed him by inches, and as we dragged over him he grabbed the rope handles on the basket and it pulled him out of the snow drift, and slowed us down. It's a good job I don't believe in heavy landings all the time.

'In April we went back to Hanover again, they liked us. When we got there we were met by the organiser, who told us in broken English that there were no beds for us anywhere. 'But do not worry, here are tickets to Berlin, I have booked you in there for the night!'

So we left the balloon at Hanover, and got back on the plane and flew to Berlin for the night. James was with us on the trip, and when we got there, I said to James, 'Come on, I'm going to hire a taxi and show you the Berlin Wall.'

He really couldn't believe it. We saw the museum at Check Point Charlie, you know, and then spent a night in Berlin. The next day we flew back to the Hanover Air Show.

'We did some tethers, and on the 26th they gave me and two other balloons permission to take off on condition that we landed as quickly as possible. I landed at one end of a football pitch when a game was in progress.

'Unfortunately, the balloon trapped the goalkeeper in the goal mouth. He couldn't get out at all. The Germans have got no sense of humour, they didn't see the funny side of it at all. But we were packed up and off the pitch in two or three minutes. I did tell them that they had nothing to worry about because while my balloon was wrapped around the goal posts, they couldn't score any goals! Anyway, I landed, but the two other balloons, both German, flew on for another thirty minutes, and when they got back they were banned from flying again.

'We went on to do three more flights. The first one, I landed in the Army camp next door, that was difficult as they couldn't work out what I was doing in there. The second time was on the perimeter of the airfield. But the third one had a different air traffic controller, and he didn't understand that balloons do not take off into winds like aeroplanes. He gave me permission to take off, and you must remember that this field not only had an airshow going on but there were commercial flights going in and out as well!

'I took off and then looked up and there is a twin engined Cessna coming straight at me so I pulled the top out and dropped into a very, very fast heavy landing, very hard, on the taxiway. The jolt caused the burner to turn on and burned the scoop. We were dragging along the taxiway, and I was hauling away on the rip line which was caught under the basket, and the friction of the drag wore away the rope handles and the rip line! The crowd thought it was spectacular! There was a fire engine and an ambulance chasing me, I was going on a quite a speed, we stopped eventually. Dramatic stuff though.

'In May 1980, we went to Cologne where it was a sort of open day at the airport.

'Two months later we went back to Philadelphia to take part in the Philadelphia Balloon Race again, but we only came fourth on that one. We were put up at a hotel near the airport. There was Niall Duncan, Dave Munson, Pete Hornfeck and myself. We had adjoining rooms, and my room became the British Embassy, it was a standard arrangement. Anyway, we had got to drinking, and I said, *'you buggers can carry on drinking, but if I'm flying the balloon in the morning, I'm going to bed.'*

'The next morning I woke up and they had all gone! Not only that, but the other bed in my room had gone. I was snoring so much that they all slept in the other room! They always reckon that the one who shares a room with me gets the short straw.' David chortled.
'I don't think I actually snore. David Smith said that I make snuffling noises like a hedgehog coming out of hibernation – amplified.'

'On that occasion, Ben Abruzzo was flying there-the chap who flew the Atlantic, I remember I beat him, and the one who came highest on the list had to buy a bottle of champagne. In actual fact, the order that we all took off was the order they finished, except Ben took off fourth, and I took off fifth, but I came fourth and Ben came fifth. It was a Hare and Hounds, and the wind was changing the whole time we were up there.

'I could see the Hare in front of me, but there were no landing places at all, the nearest park that was coming up was way over. I actually put the balloon into a tree and held it in there until my crew, arrived. I chucked them a line and they pulled

285

me down between a house and a garage. It was 4th July, Independence Day, and there were barbecues going on all around, and the crew were all hijacked to different barbecues. We were certainly made very welcome.

'But I always think with ballooning, if you win one competition, it is 5% skill and 95% luck, if you win two competitions, it is 10% skill, and 90% luck, and so on. The more competitions you win, the more skills you have.

'**18th August**, Julian Nott, the chap who was always trying to go the highest, asked me to take Leo Dickinson up, the famous photographer and parachutist, he wanted to parachute from the balloon, which he did, and I landed near Burghclere. On that occasion, I had a radio with me, and as I was coming down, I radioed Julian in the second balloon and said, *'Do NOT follow me in. I know the farmer here, but it is a no go area for balloons.'*
As we flew across this field of wheat, which was nearly ready for cutting, there was a grass track which went up between two fields of wheat, and I popped the basket down on the track, pulled the canopy off the crop onto the track.

'Kate was retrieving for me and she hadn't gone to see anyone to ask for permission. As she drove down the track to pick us up, I watched the farmer park his Land Rover across the track at the end blocking it, but didn't think anymore about it.
We carried on packing the balloon up and eventually the farmer strode up spouting steam. When he was close enough, I said, 'Good morning Andrew. Lovely morning.'
'Oh it's bloody you is it!'
'Yes' I said, 'I knew you wouldn't mind, we've not done any damage.'
'I can see that,' he said, *'Why can't the other buggers land balloons like that then?'*

286

'Andrew Davis is an old friend of mine, and is now secretary of the Country Landowners Association (CLA). We knew his parents who have been part of the farming community for years. Andrew writes the farming column in the Newbury Weekly News, and his Mother, Kit Davis, used to write for the Farmers Weekly. Andrew's parents really enjoy life, they are in their eighties now, but they go racing and do everything. Andrew Davis used to have the farm that Andrew Lloyd-Webber has got now, up at Watership Down. He gave up for the same reason I did, at about the same time. He had quite a good golden handshake, and so they bought this place at Highclere, and his wife, Victoria, does Physiotherapy. She is actually very good, I've been to her a couple of times. Victoria's brother is Henry Wilson up at Shefford Woodlands.

'Anyway, Andrew helped me pack it up and get it out, no problems really. But that is one of the advantages of knowing people and knowing what you are doing. I took him ballooning with me to Israel later.

'That September, we went back to Philadelphia again where we did Harrisburg and Allantown. Tethered in a car park, and tethered on top of a big store. During this trip, this Jewish lady took a shine to me, I could see that. She'd already killed one husband, died on the job! I think she was a nymphomaniac. She took us out to dinner that night, and as we sat down, she patted the seat next to her, and said, *'You'll sit here'* to me.
Another Dante member came in at that point, and I said, *'Let me pull up a chair for you.'* And he ended up next to her. He and I went to the loo later, and I said to him, 'It's your birthday isn't it?'
'What do you mean?'
'You're in the lucky seat boy! You'll do well tonight.'
'No no!

'Yes, you are the chosen one!'
We went back to the hotel, and just as we got there, he came up to me and whispered, *'I've just been told to go up to her room!'*
Next morning, ten o'clock, he came down, his eyes looked like piss holes in the snow.
'God' he said,*' I haven't slept all night!'*
We left as quickly as we could.

'Anyway, she organised the next balloon event for Dante, inviting us to Tampa. At the last moment I managed to take Jo with me. She met us at the airport and I said, 'Let me introduce my WIFE, Jo.' If looks could kill! She did not like that at all!

'That trip was just tethering on a piece of grass in front of a store for its' grand opening, no free flying. We did have a free day, so we all drove up to Disney World. We were looking around for a bit, and we came up to Space Mountain. *'What's this?'* asked Jo.
'Oh it's not too bad, come on, I've paid for you to go on, you've got to come on with me. We strapped ourselves in, and Jo said, *'What are all those people doing standing with bags at the side.'*
She found out later- she was white when we came out, but some people needed more help than that.

'At the end of January 1981 I remember taking off from Bradfords, I think Mike Drye was with me, and we were flying towards Shefford, trying to get to the Mill actually, and we could see this fog rolling in towards us. I knew the area pretty well, and we had to clear the village, we were at about 100 feet coming into land when the fog rolled in underneath us. It completely obliterated the ground. So we had to judge that one quite carefully, slightly difficult.

288

'We had to land through 50 feet of fog, but luckily I knew the field. But after we had landed, we couldn't see 20 feet in front of us! I had to go into the road to flag down the retrieve, they would never have found us. I have done three landings in fog, all by accident.

'The first one, back in 1973, I was doing a long distance to Wales with Mike Norton-Griffiths. It was soon after I had got my licence, and Mike said he wanted to do a long distance flight.
We seven bottles of gas aboard, and the wind was going to Wales, from Bradfords. He arrived with all the maps, the altimeter and everything. We borrowed two little walkie talkies from Gordon Passey as we didn't have airband radios in those days. We had a good start when Mike dropped the Altimeter in the basket, and it smashed against the side of a gas bottle. It was an antique pocket one, it never worked after that. We were flying along, North of the M4, heading for Swindon, and I could see this low cloud ahead.

'There's a lot of low cloud ahead', I said.
We were at about 4,000 or 5,000 feet then and I got out the radio to contact Richard.
'Richard, where are you?'
'On the M4 coming up to Swindon.'
'What is the cloud base?'
'I dunno Dad, we can only see twenty yards!'
'Son, that's cloud base!'
I said to Mike *'We've got to get down Mike, this looks like it stretches to Wales.'*
All of a sudden this plane, a Comet I think, came up out of the cloud! Terrifying! I got back on the radio to Richard. 'Richard, find a telephone and let RAF Lyneham know we are up here, quick!'
A few minutes later he came back on the radio that Lyneham

had already been notified by the plane.

'We came down and flew along the top of this fog. You could see the church steeples and the pylons sticking out, so you could gauge the height, but you couldn't see the ground! You didn't know what was down there.
I always prided myself on being able to fly a balloon fairly level, so we were skimming over the top of this fog. Mike suddenly said *I can hear a lot of traffic.'* We looked down and we were over the motorway, so at least we knew where we were. We landed eventually, it was alright, just South of the motorway, but so much for the long distance, we had only used about a bottle of gas.

'The funny thing is that about eight or ten years later, I was introduced to somebody who lived down in Bristol at a party. This guy said *'Oh you're a balloonist are you? Do you know, about eight years ago, I was driving down to Bristol and it was really thick fog, we couldn't see more than twenty yards or so, and there was this bloody balloon hanging only twenty feet up over the motorway!'*
I said 'Was it really? Good Heavens!'

'In May 1981, we went to South Africa, and we flew over the city of Johannesburg. Then we went to Vanderbijlpark for the second flight out there. This was for the South African Championships, organised by Terry Adams, but I only got two flights in South Africa. We flew out of the main ring at Pietermaritzburg at an Agricultural show, I think Celia was there. Good trip.

'The next month I went to Leninvaros in Hungary, to fly in a Hungarian home made balloon, type RSz-03, it was the third one they had built and the registration was HA-802. We flew from Ujtikos, which is right out in the sticks, and when we landed, they said, '*We'll have breakfast now*', and it was bread, wine and cheese.

Somebody wanted a training flight out there, and on the second flight, I took 'G-BEND' up, and came third in the competition they were holding. We took off from Gorbehaza and landed at Dankotanya and that was a two hour flight with three tanks in a Viva 56. Nice and cool.

'The competition was spot landings, and we were told where we had to go to, and given the maps. I would have done better but I ran out of fuel. I actually landed with every tank empty. I flew higher than we were supposed to go as well, I needed the height for the direction , but I got told off about that, I was at about 4000feet.

'While we were there, I got a flight in a Russian helicopter with Pete Bish. We were invited by the Head of the Agricultural Air Ministry to fly in his helicopter which was one of those with counter rotating rotors, and no tail rotor. We had a Hungarian pilot and he was cross eyed, I think he had been watching the rotor blades too much. We sat in a pod which was bolted behind the cabin. You could call it a passenger pod, or a fertiliser pod or a spray pod. The landing was like landing in a loose formation with a hundred nuts and bolts! Terrifying. I was really pleased to get out of it. Jo came with us on that trip too, and we stayed right out in the sticks in a modern concrete hotel.

'After James and Fiona got married, Jo and I decided we needed a holiday. I think it was Richard and Sarah who suggested a cruise. Anyway, we flew out to Toronto, Canada, stayed with Ruth and David Bunting for a bit, then took a flight down to New York and came back on the QE2. We got a taxi from the airport, and were taken to the Holiday Inn near the docks.

'It was that night at dinner that we met Sue and John Shonfeld who were also going on the QE2, and they have stayed friends ever since. We will always ask them to all our special occasions- they even drove all the way down from Manchester for our housewarming, then back again. Very nice couple. Anyway, the day after we met them, we boarded the QE2, and my first impression of it was that it was massive! Very, very impressive.'

'My first impression was that it was vast, absolutely vast.' remembers Jo. 'We left at about half past five, and sailing out with all the lights of the city, all the skyscrapers, it really was marvellous. I hate the word gobsmacked, but we were both gobsmacked. Really, really fantastic.

We were in a very lowly cabin, and so were the Schonfields, I think they had their children in with them. There are nurseries there, and the children used to go up to the nursery.

Of course we dressed for dinner, I had a kind of chiffon dress, almost see through for that first trip, and David wore white collar, he did have one you know.'

David continues,
'We have never tried any other cruise liner, we love it so much. She is a grand old lady, and the staff will do anything for you. We had a fabulous time, and vowed to do it again which we have done, many times now.

'Back home and ballooning again, another trip came up, this time to Bonn. We did two tethered flights there but it was so wet, it rained and rained. The British Ambassador's wife was there and I gave her a tethered flight. By that time it had started to rain so hard, that we all went under the balloon for shelter. But it was raining so much that water collected in the parachute and eventually, there was so much water, the weight pushed the parachute down, and all the water poured through, put the burner out and completely drenched us with

hot water, and the balloon collapsed in the water!
We had to wait for it to stop so we could blow the balloon up again and dry it out, it was the wettest I have ever known. Afterwards, she asked us to a party that evening, and it was one of the only times I hadn't taken a suit with me. I only had a sports jacket and trousers.
She said, 'Come in your overalls if you have nothing else, I want you to come to the party.'

'So we went to this party, and it was a proper Dinner Jacket, or Mess Kit job, for the minesweeper that had just come up the Rhine..
When we got there, they weren't going to let us in. Suddenly the Ambassador's wife saw us at the door, rushed across and greeted us and said to the butler, 'These are my friends, anything they want, they can have.'

'It was a super party, and we talked a lot to the Military Attaché. He had been out to see us tether that day in the rain, and we got on well with him. When the party started to flag he said, 'Why don't you all come on down to our club.'
Down under the British Embassy is this club. They have everything down there, just in case they were besieged, I think beer was about the equivalent of 8p a half pint!

'There was my son James, Ian Brereton, Dick Plume and myself, none of us known to be shy when it comes to drinking! So we had a fair few drinks down there, then they decided they would take us out and show us the night spots. I had had enough by then, and I asked them to write down the name of the hotel for a taxi driver and I'd pay him when we get there. I went at about half past twelve, I couldn't cope with any more, I was tired as I had been doing all the tethering.

'I think Dick packed it in at about half past two, three o'clock, and James and Ian got back at first light and found the Hotel locked. They were just arranging some deck loungers to go to sleep in the garden when the porter arrived to open up for the morning and let them in.

'I can remember taking the balloon to the airport when we came back, and James was completely zombie like, he'd only just got married too. We dropped him off at his Father-in-law's on the way home, where Fiona was, and left him to sort it out. James went on a lot of these trips because when he left University, I gave him a share in Dante.

'Then in July 1981, we went back to America, to Plymouth, Michigan, to celebrate something. This was the first time I had seen anybody fly on top of the balloon! I helped set it up. They had a big bit of board attached to the load ring, and a climbing harness, and a rope through the load ring, and he stood on top of the balloon as it went up.

'A year later in England, the crew of the Twilleys balloon tried it. I was there then and went across to see if they wanted any advice.
'What do you know about it?'
'Well I've actually seen it done.'
'But I thought we were the first.'
'You're not.'
'Ah.'
I only managed one tether and one free flight in Plymouth.

'I was very lucky, a couple of months later, a friend of mine gave me half an hour in the Goodyear airship with who ever I wanted to take. So I took Herbert Cottrell, who was a great aircraft enthusiast friend, and I used to give him rides in balloons now and again, he's dead now. Jo and I also took Jack Jessop- the British Airways Flights Director, his wife

294

and his mother.

'That was my second flight in the Goodyear Airship, I'd flown in her before from Greenham Common when we had actually flown over Bradfords and dipped down in the Balloon Field. In fact that time, I asked the American pilots back to Bradfords and gave them a flight in the balloon, but they didn't like that much, they would prefer something with an engine.

'Herbert Cottrell farmed up at Wash Common, in fact he married Mary Pratt, Ben Pratt's other sister, June Rabbitts and Mary Cottrell were twins. He was a very talented man, he was also a brilliant photographer. We used to go to Farnborough together, and he used to film everything. I remember one year we went, and Herbert couldn't get to film because we were too far back in the crowd, so he sat on my shoulders. He took loads of film, and I said that I would see it when he had developed it because I couldn't see anything, but he lost that film!

'I remember another occasion, I rang up and said, 'Herbert, I want £25 off you.'
'What for?'
'I've got you a ride in a Sunderland flying boat.'
'You haven't!'
'I have. I'll pick you up at nine o'clock.'
Jo made a picnic, Kate came with us, and we went down to Studland Bay where we had our picnic, and then met up with Pete Bish and the rest of them. We were ferried out to the Sunderland, then we flew all the way up the coast, over Southampton, out to Ryde and back again. That was the last flight she made because she holed one of her floats, and didn't do any more.
If I remember rightly, a Gipsy Moth came alongside, as did a replica of a Schneider Trophy. When we landed, people were

coming up, sitting in the cockpit and having a wonderful time, the plane was full of enthusiasts. It was a good day, and we stopped for a fine meal on the way home.

'Pete Bish had organised it, and about a fortnight later he said to me *'By the way, I charged you too much for that flight, when I worked it out, we had a full commitment on board, it only comes out at £23.50, so I've got £1.50 rebate for you and your mate.'*
So I rang up Herbert, 'Heh I've got £1.50 for you here.'
'What's that for?'
'I charged you too much for that flight.'
'Good Lord.' he said, *'The best day out in my life and now I get a rebate!'*

'The next Dante Group flight was in Anchorage in Alaska. A twelve hour flight in a 747 with an eleven hour time change. This was in July 1981, it was to celebrate Prince Charles's Wedding. To get there we flew over the Pole, and when we were up in the dome, our ears popped as the aeroplane depressurised at 33,000 feet! The engineer was in the loo, and he came rushing out, pulling his trousers up. The plane did an emergency descent to 12,000 feet and went back up after the crew sorted it out.

'I used to drink in those days, and there were only seven of us up there in the 747 dome, and we all had quite a few drinks, with a steward to ourselves. When we got to Anchorage I think we flowed out of the aeroplane. We arrived at three o'clock in the afternoon, their time, and we had taken off at two o'clock in the afternoon, our time, a twelve hour flight.

'We got through to the reception area, we were met by these American pilots, and they said, *'Come and fly with us in our balloon.'*

296

We half-heartedly agreed, went down to where the balloons were.

'You fly in that balloon.'

We were too weak to argue at that stage, I mean, it was two o'clock in the morning to us. The balloon was all ready to go when we arrived. So we got in and off we went. The pilot said after a minute, 'Ah, we are going the wrong way!'

'What do you mean, you are going the wrong way?' I said.

'There are no roads this way, we shall have to carry the balloons out!'

'You're joking!' I exclaimed.

'Well' he said 'helicopter retrieves are $500!'

'What do we do?'

'I'm glad you are on board actually, this is only my third flight!'

He hadn't even got a licence and I suddenly realised I was in charge!

He said, 'There is actually a logging road coming up.'

I had sobered up very quickly by then. The thought of a carry out, and being with a chap who hadn't got a licence had an amazing effect!

'Tell you what, you look for the road, and I'll fly the balloon.' I said.

'We flew on for about half an hour, I kept it low over the trees. Actually it was a wonderful flight, one of those flights I can remember very vividly. We were flying over these nice clear streams and you could see the salmon going up, and the dead salmon rolling down after they had spawned.

Suddenly he said' There's the road!'

It was about thirty yards ahead, I put the basket into the tree tops before I got to the road, and as the basket swung out, I ripped the top out and we dropped straight down onto the road, the trees pushed the balloon in as we went down, but they were only firs, no damage, and we landed dead centre on

297

the road.

'We pulled the balloon down onto the road, and packed it up. There was no trouble with the retrieve finding us as we were on the only road.
Ian Culley got down by the side of a road in his balloon, but Niall Duncan unfortunately couldn't find a road, and they landed when they ran out of fuel! He had to go and carry fuel cylinders in from the road so that they could fly to a more retrievable place. But he had to walk up this cold Alaskan stream because there was a moose and a young calf standing on the track.

'He actually arrived back at the hotel at about two o'clock in the morning - their time! He was wet through and stinking of bog, swearing never to come to Anchorage again.

'We had to do a tether there in a big football stadium. However, the Americans were firing a twenty one gun salute and Ian Culley was doing the tether, and the angle of their guns was straight at the balloon, and every time they fired, the balloon was affected.

'That night we went out for a meal. Now Dave Munson and Ian Culley were used to going to Anchorage, and knew all the places to go to, so they took us to the Alaskan Bush Company.
It wasn't until we got there that I realised what kind of bushes they were talking about! Everytime they put a new tune on, another girl came out and took all her clothes off!
For $10 they would come and do a table dance. The chap on the next table had had a bit to drink and tried to touch one of them and I've never seen a bloke knocked off his chair so fast in all my life! She floored him, Bang!
You can look but don't touch.

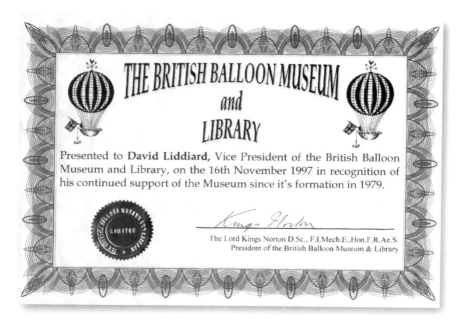

Certificate of the Vice Presidency of the British Balloon Museum and Library.

The British Balloon Museum and Library luncheon. 16th November 1997
(left to right back)   Noel Lewis, David Liddiard, Mike Allen,
(left to right front)   Lord Kings Norton, Lady Bellew, Alec Jenkinson.

David
Photograph taken during a world cruise on QE2. 1995

Formation flying, west of Moscow, 1991

Hayward Cross before (August 1990)

Hayward Cross after (August 1996)

'The next day we went up to see a glacier. That was really interesting. One of the disappointing things was that when we had fresh salmon sandwiches, they were so dry. There was so much salmon there, I was really looking forward to it, I thought it would be really nice, but they were dry.

On the way back, we stopped at one bar where there had been an earthquake. They had just left the whole pub at this amazing angle after the earthquake, and when they served you a drink, you couldn't put your glass on the bar because it was at such an angle it would slide off down the other end! It was a sawdust floor and an old log cabin type of thing.

'Then we stopped at another place called the Boar-Tide which was an upmarket sort of place for there. I think the original owner was supposed to have been Eskimo Nell.

'On that occasion the others really set me up. They said, 'We've bought you a tee-shirt, but you've got to take your shirt off for it.' Then they said that the owner was going to put it on for me.

I took my shirt off and she came up behind me. She leaned over the top of me, and you have never seen a pair of tits like it! The only time I've seen anything that big was on a cow!

I can't remember the sequence, but I know it went dark!

I was really set up, the buggers. They had all been up there before. They knew exactly what was going to happen, and I was gullible. I think I've still got the Tee shirt though. That was Anchorage.

'Then on August of that year it was back to Hanover again, they like us there. It was another Open Day, we did four inflations, and several tethered flights, it was very windy but worth doing, because the next year, the programme for the Open Day had the British Airways balloon on the front cover.

'Later in the same month we were off to Bremen. We were a bit short on that one, there was only Ian Culley and myself. It was a funny trip, we flew out, drove from the airport to Bremen, did a tethered flight. We were put up at a sort of boarding house, and flew home the next day. A very short trip!

'In January 1982, after the Icicle, Jo and I decided we would like to go to Gstaad. Hans Buker in Gstaad said that they would supply a bottom end of a balloon, if we brought the canopy. But when we went to put the balloon envelope on the top of the Subaru, it was too heavy for the roof rack, so we left it at home. We just drove out there, Jo, Kate. And myself. Hans Buker was arranging it, and when we got there, we said we were sorry we couldn't bring a balloon, but Hans said, *'It doesn't matter, you can fly my balloon.'*
So we had HB-BBE the Grand Palace balloon, which was 105,000 cubic ft. I did two flights there.

'The first flight, where I was flying people for Hans, we took off, went over the Alps into the next valley, down into the valley, and the winds then took us down the valley and round and back into Gstaad! That was about one and a half hour flight, the next day was a two hour flight, in the middle of the day. It was fantastic, we flew right up and over, down the valley towards Chateau-d'Oex where the winds then took us back up to Gstaad. Marvellous.

'The first day I landed two hundred yards from where I took off, and the second flight I was within a quarter of a mile. The trouble out there is that there a lot of wires, a hell of a lot of wires all across the valley. You fly along the top of the wires working out if you can get down in between them.

'I flew a few times in England for myself before the next

Dante trip which was in June 1982, and that was to Zambia.
We took the balloon to the Zambian Copperbelt Agricultural
Show, and we flew out of there a couple of times. Then we
took the balloon out to a farm, Frederiks Farm, belonging to a
farmer I'd met at the Agricultural Show.
He said, 'Come out to my farm, I'd like a flight.'
'Right.' I said, 'We'll come out tomorrow, and we'll take off
before it's light in the morning.'

'We drove out to his farm. His original house had been burned
down and they were all living in what used to be the squash
courts. Ian Culley, Chris Smith. and I went out there in the
dark, blew the balloon up with the headlights on, and we took
off and went up to about 2,000 feet. When we were up there,
we saw the sun rise, we then dropped a bit to 500 feet, and we
saw the sun rise again! The only trouble was when we went
down to 500 feet we were over chickens, I think the egg
production went down for a day or two!

'It was a good flight though, and that day, the farmer took me
to his friend who dealt in Malachite, I was choosing stuff for
presents, and at the end of it, I said 'How much?' and he told
me in whatever currency it was, 'Quatchas' or something, and
it worked out to about £75 at their current exchange rate. I
said, ' I don't have that much on me, do you take English
money?'
'Ooh yes' he said enthusiastically 'Let me see, oh that will be
£25.'
I got loads of stuff, eggs, elephant's beads and bits for
presents for only £25.

'Anyhow, that was Zambia. On the way back, I called to see
some friends, Edward Whedbourne's nephews, in Zimbabwe,
and we flew down to Harare, and stayed there for a couple of
days, visiting the Victoria Falls while I was there.

'Then in June, 1982 we went to Dulles Airport, Washington DC for it's twentieth Anniversary, and Jo came with me on that one. That was with the Concorde balloon. We did two tethered flights at Dulles for them, then a free flight and that was the last flight I did for more than two years.

'Just after the Dulles trip I had my second major car crash, where I wrote the vehicle off.
I was going back home to lunch, in my brand new car, well-seven months old, and I'd rung the vet to come and look at a cow. I was driving down from Ashmansworth, and just before I got to the main road, near the Yew Tree, the vet turned off the main road, and we stopped talking to each other, you know, through the window.
'Ooh,' I said. 'Seat belts are going to become compulsory very soon, I'd better try it on and see if it fits! '
I hadn't got my seat belt on, so I put it on.
We finished talking, and I drove off, and a mile and a half later, I wrote that vehicle off and a Jaguar.

'I hadn't worn the seatbelt before. I just put it on, and within a mile and a half, it saved my life!
What happened was that I saw this Jaguar coming towards me, and I recognised it as the same car that I had just bought for Jo. Exactly the same colour, same model, V12, same age, same prefix.

'I thought, 'That's like mine!' and then he drove across in front of me about sixty feet away! 47 feet was what they measured from my brake marks.

'I was probably doing about sixty miles an hour, my brakes started to go on at 47 feet, locked on at 35 feet, and I hit him right amidships, and as he went round, it was so hard that I

302

pushed him sideways and he came off his tubeless tyres! He ended up going down the road on his rims! My car spun and I was going down the road backwards. The front of my Subaru was half it's length and not where it should have been, it was only seven months old.'

'Lovely dark green one, 'remembered Jo. 'It was nice wasn't it?'

'I also had with me a two way radio, and that still worked, so I called up 'MAYDAY, MAYDAY, MAYDAY', on the firms radio, and the foreman's wife answered.

I said, 'Get the police, I've just had an accident. Some bugger nearly killed me.'

She came back on the radio after a couple of seconds and said, 'I've got the police on the way, do you need an ambulance?'

'No I'm alright.'

'Well the Police want to know if you need an Ambulance.'

'No I'm alright.'

The fitter came on the radio, and said, 'Do you want someone to come and get the car?'

'Yes,' I said., 'But I don't think it's driveable.'

Then someone came up to the car and opened the door and said, 'I think you ought to get out, there's lots of stuff running out of your car. Make sure the engine's off.'

So I switched the engine off.

I said, 'I can't move!'

She said, 'I think you should take your seatbelt off!'

Turned out she was a Doctor.

She helped me out, tried to make me lie down, but I got straight back up again.

She said, 'You ought to lie down.'

'No, I've got to get this car off the road.

With that, my Foreman and his wife arrived, my fitters arrived from Bradfords farm workshop, and the Police arrived.

'We marked the car's position on the road before moving the vehicle, and pulling it off down the road. The Police came with us down the side road, and a Policeman said, *'Now Sir, tell me what happened.'*

'Well,' I said, 'This gentleman I think misjudged my speed and pulled across in front of me and I am afraid I hit him.'

The Jaguar driver turned and shouted, *'It wasn't like that at all!'* he said. *'He hit me after I'd cleared the road! It was his fault.'*

I said, 'You what?! You've just nearly bloody well killed me, and now you're trying to blame me! Check the skids on the road, and where the dirt came off, I hit you right in the middle of my carriageway! I'm doing you for dangerous driving! I'm making it official!'

The Policeman said, *'Do you mean that Sir?'*

'Yes, I do.'

'Would you like to make a statement about it?'

'No, I don't think I do, I don't feel very well, I think I ought to go to hospital.'

I turned around to the Foreman, and said,

'Take me into Newbury Hospital.'

'They drove me to Newbury Hospital and as I walked into the main entrance, my legs collapsed. Luckily there were two Ambulance-men there, one with a wheelchair and one walking. I grabbed the radiator, and one of them grabbed me under the arms, and said, *'It's all right Mr Liddiard, we've got you.'*

The chap with the wheel chair swept me into it and took me to Casualty. They laid me down, and by that time Jo had arrived hadn't you?'

'Yes, Mike Hogan rang me.'

'The bush telegraph works marvellously in this area! Anyhow, the Doctor came and looked, and said to the Ambulance-men, *'This man had better go to Reading Hospital quick!'*

304

So they loaded me into the ambulance, Jo came up with me. I had 36 hours on a drip for shock! I still have tenderness where the seatbelt was.'

'I cannot touch him there at all.' Jo said, 'It really is peculiar.'

'That's right, if Jo puts an arm over me at night, I have to remove it, I cannot bear the weight of an arm on it. They X-rayed me, but they cannot find anything.'

'What they were worried about at the time was the spleen.' Jo added. 'He might have ruptured it.'

'I got £8,000 for that accident, that was all.

'I had whiplash injuries from it which have bothered me ever since, and I haven't been able to drink since. I've probably saved that much through not being able to drink, I'm allergic to alcohol now - I've got to thank God for small mercies! After that crash, I never felt right. I didn't touch a balloon for a few years

'You went to meetings though didn't you David?' Added Jo. 'There weren't many balloon trips then anyhow?'

'Well, I didn't even go flying in England. I think three years might be an exaggeration. Looking at this book.' David said flicking through his logbook. 'I flew on 27th June 1982, and I didn't fly again until 18th September 1984.'

'That was when I went to Toronto, but I didn't actually fly a balloon then. Not really, in actual fact, that was just one trip to Toronto to see some friends. Jo came with us, and General Motors paid for that one. When we got off the plane in Toronto, our friends met us, and took us to the most fabulous restaurant called 'Captain John's.''

Jo remembered the trip too,

'We had just had a long trip, and we were exhausted. But the last thing they wanted to hear about is jet lag, so we didn't mention it! We didn't get back until it was five o'clock in

England, I don't know what the time was there!'
'Yes, and it must have cost them a fortune. They also gave us a 'Cross' pen and pencil. I didn't use it so I gave it to Richard. I didn't realise how valuable they are.

Something went wrong with it so he sent it back and they sent him a new one, and then he had it stolen with his jacket, so the insurance company replaced it. I didn't really fly while we were in Toronto, though I did a short tether, that's all. I didn't really want to fly, we went with Pete Bish, Chris Smith and John Medlock.

'In actual fact, the time between flying in England and flying in England is 1982 to 1986! That was what the accident did. I think it was like having a very sharp knife, and running it over something and making it blunt, that's what I was like. I lost my edge.

'I lost the edge to life, I was very dull for a while. I didn't really do anything much in those three years did I Jo?'
'No.'
'I really took at least three years to get over that. I didn't want to do anything, see anyone, go anywhere.'
'Actually, I think apart from anything else, the trips had dried up, well there were not many.' Jo recalled.
'But I didn't fly in England either!'
'Yes that was odd.'
'It's fate again, I couldn't fly, so there weren't any trips.'
David roared with laughter at the thought that the British Airways trips had dried up because he couldn't fly.

'My first real flight in a balloon after the accident was 1985. The 15th June. This time I really did want to go flying, it was in Lodz in Poland. There was a pilot declared goal, and we landed within forty-five yards. I was P2 then and Pete was P1. We were staying in the Grand Hotel in Lodz, and someone came up and asked whether we wanted to change some money and we said, 'yes'.

We got it at about ten times the going rate, we had a hell of a good night that night, I think the crew drank the hotel dry of beer!

'Although I was a whisky drinker, I drank vodka, and I think I had nineteen vodkas that night. We had a wonderful meal in the restaurant, and on the way out of the restaurant, we were stopped by this woman who came up and started talking to us. Luckily we had a British Airways chap who was interpreting for us, and he turned round and said to me, *'This lady would like you to go back to her house for a party. It's her birthday. What is more, she would like you to sleep with her tonight!'*

Her husband was standing next to her. I declined the offer quite fast but she was not a bad looking bird.

'The next morning, Pete Bish, who was seeing to paying for everything said *'Do you know, last night cost us less than £4 each.!'*

It should have been about £30-£40 each really but we had exchanged money at such a good rate it was dirt cheap.

'Ironically, when we were coming back through Warsaw, there was absolutely nothing, nothing, to spend the money on. We had all this money, and we could find nothing! The shops were bare, there was nothing. In the duty free shop at the airport I bought a big bottle of Vodka. That was actually about all you could buy. I have never seen such a small duty free, it was more like a village shop!

'We had to show our passports about four or five times between getting there and getting on the plane. When we were sitting down in the plane waiting, two military chaps with Automatics, came through and counted us all to make sure that there were not too many of us.

'On 13th July, we went to Luxembourg and Phil Dunnington told me that I couldn't fly because my licence had expired. But I did have a flight in a Luxembourg balloon, the owner let me fly it. It was a nice flight, over the city and that big viaduct.

'Then at the end of August we went to Holland. I was the only one there who had anything like a licence, so Dick Plume had the first flight with me and checked me out, he didn't have a licence, but he checked me out anyway. We had also just had these 'cow burners' fitted.
'As we took off I said, 'Dick, I am just going to see if I still have the feel for it, I am going to do a fast descent and see if I can pull out. I'll do it over the lake so that the worst thing that can happen is that you'll get wet feet.'
So we did a fast descent, and we pulled out at about 3 feet.
We went across this lake at about 3feet, then across a field at about 3 feet. Then Dick said, *There's a motorway coming up!*
'Oh yeah,' I said, 'I'll change the lightbulbs on the way over.'

'It was a stupid thing to say, but we went over the motorway, and right by this lamp-post at the right height so that you could have leaned out and changed the bulb. The bloody motorway came to a standstill - both ways!
I landed the balloon down in the football field on the other side, changed the cylinders and messed around with burner, just in case anyone was watching. Then we took off again. We flew for a bit, landed, packed it up, and went back. The next day, the British Airways chap came up and said,
'Marvellous, look in the paper! Middle of the front page of the Daily paper has a big picture of you, 'British Airways Balloon makes Emergency Landing.'
They were so pleased.

'We did three flights there, the second one was when I had the chance to test the burner. We had just taken off, and as we came over this row of trees, there were a whole load of cows, and electric fences. So I turned the cow burner on just a little bit, and the cows didn't even move. The only one who got upset was the farmer running across the field behind us. We landed a bit further on, and the retrieve turned up and we packed it away, but those cow burners are magic, and so quiet.

'I saw this bumper sticker the other day. It said *'Wasn't it nice when Sex was Safe and Flying was Dangerous!'*

'Like when I started ballooning really, it was dangerous then, but there are so many safety features nowadays, modern pilots would think we were mad if we flew in the same conditions or with the same equipment today.
In the same vein, I am sure that if a young lady didn't get a pass made at her now and again, she would think there was something wrong with her. It's all court cases nowadays, I think they have taken it too far.'

Lord of the Manor.

'One day, my brother and I had been to SCATs, in Newbury, and he was in the vehicle behind me. We were in Shaw, driving over the bridge going over the A34, and there was a woman who had climbed over the parapet, over the main road. I pulled up, and John pulled up behind me.

'*Did you see that woman?*'

'Yes, it looks like she's going to jump, we'd better go and see what we can do.'

'*Bugger that,*' he said, put it in gear and drove off.

'Well, there was another woman walking up from the east side and she shouted to this woman, and started talking to her. I walked up from the other side quietly, which I can because I always wear spongy soled shoes. I got right behind her, and she never heard me coming. Just as I got up behind her, a Police car arrived, screeched to a halt, and a chap jumped out. The woman looked round, let go of the bridge and jumped!

'I managed to reach over and grabbed her arm and pulled it back so it was over the edge, and I was thinking 'I'll never be able to hold her!'

Luckily, she swung round, and the policeman was able to grab her by the other arm, and we pulled her back onto the bridge.

'So I was able to stop her committing suicide. If the fall hadn't killed her, the next car would have. Can you imagine some poor bugger driving under the bridge and having a woman splattered on his bonnet and windscreen!

Anyway, I stopped her.

'Ten days later, I was at a dinner party and I was asked to carve (Everyone always asks me to carve when I go to places!). So I went out into the kitchen to carve, and there was the hostess, and two of her friends helping get the food ready.

I told the story to them, like I've just told you, and the hostess said, *'Well well, she was just climbing over when I drove by, so I stopped at the next telephone box and rang the Police Station.'*

'Then one of her friends said that she had been working in the Doctor's surgery when they brought her in. What a coincidence, ten days later, and three out of the four people in that room were involved in the same incident!

'Funnily enough I was at the Rotary Club the other week, and I was talking to someone about the Samaritans. I said I would be no good as a Samaritan, but I had stopped someone committing suicide once, and I told the story.

One of our members said *'I think that was so-an-so.'*

I said 'It was a Police Sergeant's wife wasn't it?'

'That's right. She's alright now, they've moved away to so-an-so.'

He knew because he was an Inspector in the Police Force.'

'I remember in 1985 when we went to Africa, it was October, and we, the Dante Group, took the balloon to the Nairobi Agricultural Show. I had to do a couple of commentaries, when the others did the tethering. It is very difficult to do a commentary when you have to keep stopping whilst they translate it into Swahili!

'I wasn't quite sure if the crowds were more interested in the balloon, or in seeing three white men sweating away at three in the afternoon, when no self respecting black man would work because of the heat! On the fifth day, they came and said there would be no flying that day. So Celia, Ian Brereton, John Medlock and myself, got together and Ian said, *'Look, why don't we go down to Little Governors Camp in the Masai*

311

Mara Game Reserve and see Peter Langford. We can get a flight at 10.30.'

'So we chucked a few things in a bag, set off on this flight in a 1944 Dakota. Luckily we had radioed ahead to say we were coming because they chucked you out on a grass strip in the middle of nowhere and then take off again!

John Coleman came bouncing across in a Toyota, picked us up and took us back to the camp. On the way he said, *'Where are you sleeping tonight?'*

'On the floor of your bedroom if that's alright.'

He said, *'Ah, actually we are full up!'*

'As we approached the camp, there was another vehicle driving out and it pulled up alongside in a cloud of dust. John leaned out of the window and said, *'I've got some friends here from England and they've got nowhere to sleep.'*

This chap was the manager or something and he said, *'That's OK, I'm off to a wedding, they can use my place.'*

'So we had the manager's house for the night, which was very nice.

'It wasn't made of wood, it was stone and brick, very solid. The water was heated in fifty gallon oil drums outside, they used to build a wood fire underneath to heat the water, and pipe it through to the dwelling.

John Coleman took us out for a quick safari and I think we saw far more than most people would see on a full day. He said, *'I know where to take you.'*

He had been working out there with Peter Langford as a balloon pilot, taking groups of people for flights over the game reserve, and had a good knowledge of the area and the animals.

312

'We saw baboons, elephants, and a crocodile's nest with eggs on the bank of a river. There were some water buffalo too, but he said, *'We'll keep clear of them, they killed a bloke here last week! He got trampled to death whilst he was trying to take photographs of them!'*

'We had a very interesting tour, returning to the camp late afternoon. We joined the other people in the dining tent, and had a fantastic meal, really good. After dinner, we returned to our house and they sent two Masai warriors with spears to lead us. They repeatedly kept saying, *'left, left, left.'* We weren't quite sure why until we saw an elephant standing there, grazing on the tree! God, they're big close up, especially at night!

'The next morning, we went flying. We took off at 6.30am, (sunrise was 6.25am) and landed nearly an hour and a half later.
They had actually had a new balloon delivered a couple of days before and guess what, the guy who delivered it was Frank Barnes. It was really nice to see him again. The Kenyan Civil Aviation Authority had to give it their own ticket of airworthiness, the Colt one from England wasn't good enough for them. Apart from Frank, there was, Chris Kuto, the Kenyan CAA bloke, Celia, myself, Ian , John, Peter Langford, and a few African crew for ballast.

'Peter blew it up and off we went. After a bit, Peter said, *'You can fly it if you want. I'm fed up with flying.'*
'I'd love to.' I said, and I took over and flew the Colt 160A. First time I'd flown one that big! The registration was 5Y-BEH. It was incredible, we flew over birds nesting in the trees, and then I took it down below ground level! The river was at the bottom of a deep gully, and as I flew down it, I remember these hippos, we went over them at about ten feet.

313

'It was as low as we could go, and as we went over, they grunted at us and went under water. We went up again, and I finally landed it just before we crossed into Tanzania. It's evidently easy to get into Tanzania, but not so easy to get back. The other three balloons landed alongside us.

'We all walked away from the balloons and all these native chaps came and packed it all away. The gas bottles were taken out and laid on their side. Bits of plywood were put across other bottles to make a table, and we all sat around and had breakfast! Behind us were spears stuck in the ground to fend off any wild animals.

'Nobody is allowed to pick up a stick or a stone, it all has to be left exactly as it is, bones left for who ever eats the bones, it all has to be left so the balance is not disturbed within the reserve. 'Breakfast was good, Charles Heidsieck champagne, orange juice and coffee, with eggs, bacon, mushrooms, and sausages cooked on the burners. Very civilised.

'Peter Langford looked at his watch, and said we better move so that we could catch the plane back. He then took us back in the Toyota to the airstrip. That time of year the river was drying up, and from one bridge we could see fish eagles swooping down and coming out with great big fish in their talons, three of them. As we drove over the bridge, over the creek, we could see what was left of the river, a pool of writhing mud with all these fish which couldn't get away.'

Peter Langford dug out his logbooks to recall the flight for David. He said that every flight out there was a revelation, especially for pilots. They fly for about 40 minutes at tree top height which was about a 100 feet, over the riverene forest that grows along the banks of the Mara River, which meanders dramatically across the park, with many oxbows.

'We would frequently drop below the river banks to annoy the hippos and tease the crocodiles. After the final river crossing, we climb to about a thousand feet, for the view, and to position for landing. You can see the whole of the six hundred square miles of the reserve from up there and across the border, the Serengeti.

'Landings could be quite interesting for four months of the year, but at least we could fly. All game, regardless of size complied with the ANO and gave way. I did come across a stubborn Topi once, he didn't move until the envelope deflated above him.

Elephants, if peeved would chase us, and there was one slightly traumatic experience at breakfast when a lioness, part of a small pride resting about 300 yards away, suddenly got up and started walking straight towards us! As she got closer and closer, I was just suggesting to the passengers that they moved quietly back to the cars, when she lowered her head, and dragged off the remains of a gnu lying about 150 yards from us. She probably thought we had that hungry look.

'The most amusing memory was when we were at a 100 feet approaching a tree full of baboons. They all fled, but one, not looking where he was going, ran straight into a lion! As we flew past, the baboon was under the paw, I burned loud and long, this distracted the lion and the baboon wriggled free. The applause from the passengers was deafening!'

The morning of their return flight, David and the Dante Group drove straight from the breakfast site to the airstrip, boarded the plane and returned to Nairobi.

'When we landed, we drove from the airport direct to the showground to do a show straight away. Then we went out to a small school to do a tether, and the next morning, we had

315

to get up at three in the morning to go and fly at Lake Navasha, which is famous for all the flamingos, but there weren't any when we were there. We were with Frank Barnes, who knew where to fly, and Martin Mayer, the Military Attaché for the airport at Kenya. We flew for a bit, then we had to come down as Martin advised us we were approaching the ranch of whoever was the President of Kenya then - I can't remember his name. Frank flew with us in his little one man balloon. He lived out there then as a lecturer at the university. We certainly packed a lot into thirty hours.

'I'd known Frank since he was training. I remember that he was the first man I knew who flew completely on his own, I think I've mentioned that.

'15th February 1986 I took G-BHOT to Luxembourg. On the second flight, we ended up in Belgium, no trouble getting back, and the photo Pete took then, with all the snow on the ground was the one used by British Airways for G-BHOT's postcard.

'Then Pete Bish said that the Hungarians wanted to come and fly in England, but to enable them to come, they had to have an official invitation, could I sign it as the Vice President of the British Balloon & Airship Club. 'Of course I will.' I said.
I was made Vice President of the BBAC in about 1976, I know they gave me a silver salver which said 'Presented to David Liddiard by friends and members of the BBAC, in recognition of his contribution to the sport of hot-air ballooning.'
Jo left it on the table outside the Mill one day and it disappeared, we think the wind might have blown it in the river and it was swept away, we don't really know what happened. I was really sorry about that.

'Anyway, the Hungarians came over, and we gave them a barbecue, and Dante Group looked after them, and Laci, I think his name was, said *'You must come to our balloon meet in September.'* I said we'd love to, when was it. He told me the dates, and I said 'No sorry, the Newbury Show is on then. I can't!'

'You must come.' he said.

'I can't, I have to go to the show!'

'You must come even for just one day, you will come.'

'OK, but if I came for one day, I have missed the flight with the others, how can I get there?'

'We will send an aeroplane for you!'

Jo was invited as well, and so off we went on the Sunday after the Newbury Show, and flew into Budapest. As we taxied in, Jo looked out of the window and said *'Look, they've got a guard of honour, a band, loads of people, and a big car drawing up and everything, all for us!'*

'But it wasn't for us, the Queen of Belgium had just flown in. So we had to sit there on the plane while all that went on.

'Eventually they parked our plane, and before anyone could move, this chap came on and said, *'Mr Liddiard?'*

I said, 'Yes?'

'When you get off, the lady on the left is there to deal with you.'

Everyone was looking at us as we got off and got into a VIP car, and were whisked away. The woman said, *'If you give me your papers and passports, and luggage labels, I will deal with it all. '*

So we didn't have to do anything, we just went to the VIP Lounge and waited!

'After a while, a car took us to a little six seater Cessna. The others sat there with our luggage on their laps, and we started to taxi to take off. It was the longest taxi I have ever been on. It turned out that we had to taxi across the main airport to the

317

military airport, which is where we took off. It took about fifteen minutes!

'When we landed at Ocseny, a car met us and drove us to the Hotel. We were looked after superbly, they couldn't have done enough. It was good weather, and Pete Bish took an official from the Hungarian Aviation Authority for a flight.

'There was another trip to Luxembourg after that and then apart from the odd training flight, no more until April of 1987. This time we went to Boston in America. We had to do a five hour tether in Government Square outside the British Airways building. The only trouble with that one was that I was the only pilot, and that was a bloody long tether – time-wise that is, not height! I was attached to two concrete bollards, and the handrail of the underground or something. I took 310 or 370 people up on the tether in five hours, it was a hell of a lot of people.

'I took one person up, and he said.' *I've got a friend who used to fly balloons in England.'*
'Oh yeah.'
'Yes, he lives next door to me just up the street here.'
'What's his name?'
'Tim Stafford.'
I could not believe it! What a surprise! He went and got Tim, and later on, we went out with them for the evening. Small world isn't it?

'Home again, and then the next trip was back to Tempelhof again at the end of May.
'I had joined the Rotary Club by this time. Most people go on to the Rotary after the Round Table, but I never had time for the Round Table. I joined the Rotary after I had retired. You

318

see, you cannot take on these things unless you've got time to do them properly. Nothing half done is worth doing.

'I was the first Vice President when they started. In actual fact, I was invited to go along when they were trying to start the Hungerford Rotary Club, and the first meeting I went to there were fourteen people. John Pallett, who was from the Newbury Rotary, was trying to get it going and he said that they had been trying to get it going for at least six months, but unless we could get at least twenty, it was not worth doing. In the next five weeks, I had got eight new members I think. Strangely enough, I was the one voted in as Vice President that year.

'We were meeting at the Three Swans in Hungerford in those days. The first year of the Rotary was the year of the Hungerford Massacre. So with the Round Table, the people of Hungerford managed to raise a million pounds to help. Not bad eh?

'The Round Table could be bigger in Hungerford, but professional people today are too busy to give up their time to do other things. They are expected to work their full hours and longer. So we are suffering from the same thing. Rotary is more like Probus now, 'PROfessional retired BUSiness people'. I've given talks to them too. I give talks to them all, but I never take anything for it.

'I remember giving a talk to the Newbury Camera Club at Kintbury, and I nearly always talk about ballooning. That evening, first we had the meal, then the prizegiving, and then their thank you talk and a speech or two. By the time it came around to me giving a speech, it was eleven o'clock and they were all tiring. Luckily, I never plan it, I just talk, so I kept it light-hearted, and short, and afterwards, someone came up to

319

me and said, *'That was really interesting, you ought to write a book!'*
That was eleven at night, so I kept some people awake!

'Anyway, back to ballooning with the Dante Group.   In August, we went back to Massachusetts, to Plymouth this time, Chris Smith and I with our wives. There is a photo of the balloon somewhere, seen through the rigging of the Mayflower.   Then we went up to Edaville, and did a tether there where we were tied to two British Airways cars. After the cars had been dragged halfway down the car park, they realised it was a bit too windy!

'Afterwards, we went up to where they grow cranberries. Now cranberries are little flat bushes which grow low on the ground in a sort of boggy soil.   When it comes to picking them, they flood the ground, and then go across the ground with paddle wheels stirring up all the water, and the berries float off, and they scoop them all up. Where we were was a great big cranberry area, and they had a little railway that went around the edge to pick up all the cranberries. Really interesting that was.   They've doubled the railway up as a tourist attraction as well.   I think that where they used to scoop the berries up, they now suck them up with vacuum tanks like big slurry tanks.

'We met the archivist of the Plymouth Museum over there, and he lives in what is thought to be the oldest house in America. I said, 'Oh then it must nearly be as old as our house then!   Ours is mentioned in the Domesday Book.'   But he couldn't get his head around that.   They took us to see the house and it was all furnished and decorated like a museum.

'We arrived one day and they weren't expecting us and one of them was having a shower, but the shower was outside!

320

They didn't seem to mind though and asked us to stay to dinner, and we had a really nice meal.

'19th February 1988 was a special Press day. That was the flight of the first disabled basket, one where you can get a wheelchair into it as one of the sides comes down. It was a flight for Alec Jenkinson, and HTV and the BBC were there as well as a lot of press people. and we flew to Burbage from Marlborough. I was only a passenger then, being with Alec.

'A couple of weeks later, we went to Kuwait, one of the first balloons in Kuwait. Jo came with me on this one, John Calvert and Dick Plume. We were supposed to do two tethers outside the Regency Palace Hotel. One from 2.00-2.30pm and one from 4.30-5.00pm, which was for a children's tea-party! The first time so they could see it as they went into tea, and the second so they could see it when they came out.

'Now I have been around the world and stayed in many luxury hotels, but this one was superb. The chandelier was massive, you couldn't have got it in this room. There were two banqueting halls and they held 1,500 people each! We actually stayed at the hotel, and our rooms were fabulous. Obviously there was no alcohol, but I do remember that Dick Plume acquired a liking for Kiwi fruit. And over the three or four nights we were there, over £100 worth of Kiwi fruit juice was consumed by Mr Plume!

'The next Dante trip was to Camp Mowbray in Texas in June, an American army camp. When we got there, we took off in the evening, and after being given the briefing and the direction, they said, 'After you get about four miles down, do not go above 700 feet as you are under the approach to Austen airport!'

'I took Jo MacDonald, the British Airways representative as a passenger for the first hop, and then changed passengers. On the second hop, I said to my passenger, 'I am going to put it down in that car park.'

'You can't, there are too many wires.'

'America is full of wires, they are everywhere.' I said, 'I am aiming for that space in the middle of that car park, Square number 10 we are going to land on!'

'I came through the trees which slowed me up, and as I swung out from the trees, ripped out and put it down between two lampposts, right on the square I had aimed for. What I didn't know was that I had landed in the Police Station yard!

'Did you crash it, buddy?' they asked.

'No, I just landed.'

Anyway, we packed it up and left. The next day, briefing was at 7.30 in the morning, and it was mizzling with rain and blowing a gale.

'Well,' they said,' *As you know there will be no flying today, but we've got one hell of a lot of people turned up. If anyone can do a tether, we would sure appreciate it, especially those guys with a Cameron scoop to show us how bloody good they are.'*

That was a stupid thing to say to me!

We went out, tied one rope to bloody great army transporter, tied another to a big army truck positioned the other side, and down wind we put our vehicle, and I did a tether. It was so windy that when I looked up there was no balloon above me.

Eventually, the organiser came up to me and said, *'Gee, I appreciate what you are doing but the FAA are getting a bit worried, you'd better get her down now.'*

The Americans had actually tried to blow two balloons up and hadn't succeeded, but I showed them. I don't think that then, there was anyone who could tether better than I could. I proved it once or twice.

322

'The next night we had a chance to fly, and the direction had changed and we started to go across the Lake Austen or the Colorado River or whatever it was called. We got halfway across and the wind stopped! We started to go up the lake instead of across it.

'There were a lot of people water ski-ing, so we chucked a rope to some Italians in a boat and they started to tow us, the trouble was that if they went too fast it pulled the balloon into the water, and if we got too hot, it lifted the boat out! Eventually Dick Plume couldn't hold the rope and let go, and it was so tight that it shot down and tangled around their propeller, so they had to sort that out, luckily another boat came along and towed us into the shore.

'Then around 17th July 1988 we went to Boston to celebrate the 25th Anniversary of the Harvard 'Class of '63' and we stayed at the Charles Hotel, Jo was with me. We had all been invited out there to do these tethers, and there again, it was bloody windy but we did it, and they invited us to the barbecues. It was amazing, there were twelve lines of people queuing for twelve barbecues, with great big tables. The lunchtime one was chicken and the evening one was lobster. They had lorry loads of lobsters brought in. The lobsters were in crates with wire-mesh bottoms, and the barbecues had got big pans of boiling water on them and they just dunked the crates straight in them. I have never seen so much wasted lobster in all my life, or so much wasted food.'

Jo remembered this one well, '*I mean, they are difficult to eat anyway, but they were on paper plates with plastic cutlery, and you know, it was just too difficult for some people. I'll never forget that.*'

'No,' said David, 'It was an awful waste.'

'I did an awful lot of flying in England in 1988, we had given up farming, and I had the time then. I bought the airship then, G-BEPZ, and the first flight in that was in September that year, I think I've mentioned this one before though. My second airship.

'In October I flew it again, and we flew for two hours. We got it up and flew around, re-fuelled it, landed it at Ivor Gore's farm at Winding Wood, put on two more cylinders and flew down to Savernake and visited James.

'At the beginning of November, we did a two hour flight with eight landings and take-offs from the balloon field in the Airship, it was the British Balloon Museum & Library Inflation day. The day after, I flew Don Cameron in it, and he checked me out for an Airship Pilots licence. It was actually my birthday. That was when I found out that Don does not really like heights. I took it up to 1500 feet and he said, *'I think you are flying a bit too high, I think you should take it down.'*
'Right Don,' I said, 'you see that yellow marker, I am going to land the airship there. '

'That was pretty tricky actually because there were a lot of trees around then, but I did it, and he checked me out. I did my solo at the Icicle Meet in January. You have to do quite a lot when you fly solo, you need a lot of hands for throttles, rudders and such like. I flew it again in May but I think that might have been the last time I flew it. The trouble was, you needed a lot of crew for an airship, shame really.

'Dante trips were coming around once more, there was a quick trip to Tempelhof again in May, and in late May we went to Lithuania. They looked after us very well there. To get there, we had to fly in to Moscow, and then out again on Aeroflot.

You can forget that. Flying Aeroflot is more dangerous than flying four up with a Mark 1 burner I think! I mean, the plane's tyres were showing canvas through the rubber!

'Anyway, in Lithuania, we did nine flights, maximum height was 500 feet, minimum height was 60 feet, nice flying. Phil Dunnington was there, and Chris Smith. I think Phil checked me out on my annual CPL whilst we were there. We came down at one point, flying very low, about ten foot, and we came across these traffic lights at a crossroads.
'It's OK,' said Phil, 'They've turned green, you can go.'
It was fun. Everything belonged to the State, so there was no farmer problems. I'll never forget seeing Don Cameron riding shotgun on this army truck, which was driving straight through the middle of this field of crop. Although the pilots landed on tracks or on the edges of fields, our Army retrieves drove straight through the middle of everything, they didn't care!

'Actually, the only one to get into trouble was Phil Dunnington, and he had landed in a scrubby little patch covered in dandelions, he didn't like landing in crop, and it happened to be the only piece of land owned by the peasant who lived there, and she gave him hell for ruining her dandelion crop! We all felt really sorry for him.

'I did a very early flight in June. Steve Hall wanted a training flight, but I had to be somewhere at 9.00am, so I said yes I will give you a flight as long as you are here by four in the morning. He was, and we took off at 4.45am. Now I happened to know that Flying Pictures were doing some advertising tethers at Littlecote, so I said to him, 'I don't want to go this way, I want to go that way, climb and find the right winds,' and he did, and by playing with the heights as I told him, we got to Littlecote.

'If I had been flying, we could have landed in-between their baskets. But remember that Steve was under training, and he was a bit ground shy, and missed. I remember saying to him, 'For Goodness Sake, put both burners on, we're going to hit Littlecote House otherwise!

'We screamed up the side of the house about fifty feet away, burning hard, and as we passed one of the windows, a figure leaped out of bed and ran to the window, he was starkers - completely starkers! That was the only time I've ever seen anything through the windows of a house! Anyway, this figure with a beard watched us go up past his window missing the house, luckily for my insurance. Nine weeks later, I was introduced to him at the Newbury Show, Peter de Savary.

'I'm sorry if I woke you up the other morning.' I said.

'Oh yes, I remember,' said Peter, *'I woke up to hear this tremendous roaring noise, I thought the house was on fire, and I looked out of the window, and there were two people standing in a laundry basket about fifty feet away, level with my window! I then realised I had no clothes on!'*

'That's right', I said.

'In July 1989, I took Andrew Davis to Israel. It was not a Dante trip, we paid for it. The balloons went out cargo with El Al, and we flew out, and were billeted in a hotel right by the Dead Sea. It's a marvellous country, coming up to the Dead Sea in the dark with the sun rising over the top, fantastic, it really was.

'We used to fly from the Arad desert, Tel Arad desert. It was no special occasion, I think it was just the first Israeli balloon meet. There were a few places where you weren't supposed to fly, they would have a job to get you back. One guy did land in one, and they had a terrific job to get him out, the problem was also that they had had a bad landing, and one fellow had broken his ankle. It was a new balloon, they came from Reading I think, I forget who it was now.

'It was lovely flying out there, and on one occasion, I was in line for winning a prize. But I was flying a bit heavy, and talking to two Israelis in the basket with me, I lost concentration and hit the ground too soon, hard and bounced back up. I was at least a hundred yards from the target, no good at all. They said' *That's your mark now.'*
'Oh well, fair enough.' I said. So I flew up, and off at complete right angles to my previous tracking, right into the desert. I suddenly realised that there was only one road, and that was coming up and after it was pretty rough ground. So I landed on this track right next to a Bedouin encampment. A real Bedouin camp. They all came out to help, all the children and everyone.

'We were invited into their tent to have a drink with them, the retrieve crew was there, and our interpreter was there. We were given mint tea, all the men sitting, and all the women standing at the back. I'm not very good at sitting on floors, but I managed it. It was beautifully clean in there, and the tent was made of sacks stitched together, not animal skins anymore, sacks. The carpets were beautiful, and all the brass knick-knacks were beautifully shiny. It was all so clean. There were about eight couples with their children living there. Then our interpreter said, *'They have killed a sheep, and are cooking it for us as a special occasion.'*
'I don't really want to take their food, they have so little.' I said.
'They will be deeply offended and upset if you refuse.' he said.
So we all sat around and had barbecued sheep and Coke, and evidently what we didn't eat would be buried, it wouldn't keep until tomorrow.

'To go somewhere like that, and meet the real genuine Bedouin, not a tourist place, was fantastic. It really was one of the highlights of my trips abroad. That trip went down as something rather special because of that.

'Now in September we went to Vienna, back with the Dante Group. On this occasion, there was something wrong with the plane, and they were replacing it with a smaller one, and offering £150 to anyone who didn't mind waiting for a day. Of course all the students and backpackers were in there like a shot, but we needed to get out there. I asked the redcap if it was possible that we could have the jumpseats as we had to get there.

'So I sat behind the pilot, and the other crew member sat with the stewardesses. Ian Culley and his wife caught a later flight, but by the time we got to the hotel in Vienna, they had let our room.

'Come on,' I said, 'We've got to sleep somewhere!'

'Well the only room we've got left is the President's suite.'

'I'm not sharing a bed with him.' I said, talking about John Calvert. Anyway, we had the President's suite, and I had the biggest bed I have ever slept in, and John had a put-you-up in the adjoining room. It was an amazing suite, two bathrooms and everything.

'The next day we went to the Vienna racecourse. It was the equivalent to Ladies' Day at Ascot, and there were all these models there, everyone was dressed up, and lots of vintage cars Bentleys and the like. Our job was to tether the balloon for the British Airways sponsored race, and the British Embassy sponsored race, right by the racetrack, about a furlong from the winning post. We were supposed to tether on the left-hand side opposite the main stand as the horses would be coming up to the winning post.

'Are you sure about this?' I said, knowing how horses can be affected by balloon burners.

'Yes yes, it's all been agreed.'

So I did the tether, and I could see the horses start, and see them going all the way round, and as they were coming down the final straight, I gave a long burn, got the balloon really hot so that I didn't have to burn as they got close and went by me. We did two races like that and there was no bother, but I had been worried about spooking the horses. After that, we packed up the balloon and caught the plane home that night.

'The next month, we took the balloon to Portugal. 'We' being Pete Bish, Roger and Celia Kunert. But when we got off the plane the other end, we were met by British Airways who said, 'We don't want you.'

'Well we're here now.'

'Well, we don't want you, you should have been cancelled, you can go back again.'

Pete said,' Would it be alright, as we're here, to book a room, and go back tomorrow?'

'OK, as long as there is no expense to us.' they said.

'I had things to do at home, so I took the same aeroplane back and left the others there. I went all the way to Portugal, bought a bottle of Port and came home the same day.

'In November, we took the balloon back to Jamaica, and were booked into the Pegasus again. There was Dick Plume, Ian Brereton and John Baker, but I was the only one with a licence. The organisers said that they had permission for us to tether at the golf course at the British Airways sponsored golf match..

'Why can't we fly free?' I said.

'Oh no, they won't allow balloons to fly free in this part of Jamaica.' The organisers said, 'we can't get you permission to fly here, you can only do tethers.'

I said 'Don't be silly, I flew here 14 years ago.'

'Did you?' said the British Airways manager. 'Come on, let's go and see the Civil Aviation.'

So we went down to the Jamaican Civil Aviation.

I said, 'I'd like permission to fly free.'

They said, 'We have allowed balloons to fly up near Montego Bay but no one is allowed to fly free down here.'

I said 'I beg to differ, I flew free here 14 years ago!'

I showed them my logbook.

'Oh you took off right by Caymanas Airfieldt!'

'I've no intention of flying over 500 feet here because of the mountains, and if you have a Jumbo at that height here you're in trouble anyhow!'

'So you've done it before?'

He then gave me permission to go and fly free. When we came out, the British Airways Manager said, 'That's nice, you can fly around the golf course now.'

'It doesn't work like that you know.' I said.

'But I thought you could fly around the golf course!'

'No, we can fly from the golf course, but not round it.'

'So the next morning early, we got up and blew the balloon up on the first fairway. The golf tournament was on, and there was $26,000 first prize. Dick Plume and I flew down the first fairway and unfortunately left the golf course, so we went up to 450 feet, and the wind changed and we came back. We flew back across the eleventh, and as it was fairly slow, I decided to land and change passengers, so we landed on the twelfth fairway.

'There was this guy shaking his club at us from the twelfth tee, so I shouted 'Sorry' , changed passengers (Ian Brereton

David Liddiard Photographic Competition
Icicle Meet 1993

Photograph: Mark Pacan

David Liddiard Photographic Competition
Icicle Meet 1993

Photograph: Kevin Gafney

QE2 Norwegian Fjords. 1997

David and Jo, QE2. 1991

came with me then) and we took off, flew back and landed 20 yards from where we first took off on the second fairway, all in 60 minutes. Mind you, there was a slight attraction to landing at the take-off point, it was right outside the hospitality tent - and it was breakfast time!

This guy came in when we were there, and said *'Do you know what happened when my golf ball hit you? It melted and blistered!'*

I said,' I didn't feel a ball hit the basket!'

'No,' he said, *'I hit the balloon, and the ball went in and then bounced back out at me! '*

As there was a $26,000 prize riding on it he wasn't too happy. But he and his partner played another ball through to the end, and let the judges take a ruling on it. But I don't think he was far enough up to make any difference anyway. That night we took the balloon back and did some tethers by the Pegasus Hotel.

'The next morning, the wind had changed direction ,and John Baker and I took off from the first fairway. We touched down on the second, the eighteenth, the ninth, the eighth, the seventh, the seventeenth, second and then back to the first, to within 25 yards of the take-off point, in time for breakfast. That really was 'Round the golf course.' We were very, very, very lucky with the wind. We had a laugh there. A good trip.

'Then in December, I took the balloon to Bahrain, but I had no real crew with me that time. We went out on a night flight, arrived at five in the morning, had trouble getting the balloon out of customs. So I said 'Look, British Airways have arranged for it to come in.'

The guy said, *'I keep it here until British Airways have arranged it then.'*

'Fine.' I said, 'where are you going to put it.'

'Oh we keep it safe here.'

'Fine' I said, 'You're the best chap I have seen all day, the last thing I wanted to do was lug a balloon around at five in the morning.'

'So we left him looking rather sheepish by our balloon, and went off to our hotel, the Sheraton or the Intercontinental or somewhere and got a few hours sleep, returned later that morning and picked it up. British Airways took us to a dinner that night and a show, they were sponsoring a Brian Rix farce, good evening that was.

'The next day we did a tether for a children's party in a playground, and I thought that Bahrain would be hot and sunny, but it was cold wet and miserable, and the school playground was mud. We did our tether, packed it up ready for air-travel, took it to the airport about four thirty booked it in, went back to the hotel, had a shower and went back to the airport and caught a flight back home. Not a lot of sleep on that trip.

'Next year in May, we are in 1990 now, we went to Ryazan in Russia, I took Barry Side with me. This wasn't a British Airways one, this was one where I was paying to go. We had the army to look after us on this one, and we landed at Moscow, and went down to Ryazan by coach and all the balloons went out on a big articulated lorry like they had before. They had advised us to take small gifts, so I had loaded the basket up with things from the cash and carry. Some of the others thought it was strange that I took packets of pork scratchings, but there you are. Barry and I went off sightseeing whilst they tried to get the balloons out of customs.'

Dave Baker from the BT balloon remembered that the first balloon they took to pieces at the customs was David's, and because of all the gifts, and pork scratchings, the Head of the Customs decided that they were going to impound all the contents of the baskets. (he would have got a lot on the black market for all of it.).   Dave said that in the end all the pilots decided to call his bluff and tell him that although the balloons had come out as a favour to them for their celebrations, they were not going to pay, and if they insisted, then they would load the balloons back on the lorry and leave.   As this was being televised live, the guy had to stand down and let them through intact.

Dave remembered also that they were all being put up in this hotel on one side of a small square in the town. The balloon teams had all the rooms down two long corridors except one, and they discovered one morning, when the door of this other room was left slightly ajar, that the room was full of radio receivers, and they had bugged all the rooms. After that, each morning, everyone would wake up and shout 'Good morning to you chaps in Room XX'.

The first morning, they were woken really early by what they thought was an earthquake, the hotel was shaking, and the rumbling was really loud, however, when they looked out of the window, they discovered that tanks returning from Moscow from the May-Day celebrations, had made a detour around the little square to honour the balloonists! Unfortunately, the tanks were so big and heavy, that they completely destroyed the road surface in the square.   The balloons were supposed to tether in the main stadium, and it was very windy. Unfortunately, no vehicles were allowed onto the stadium ground, so the army gave each balloon about thirty soldiers, and they held the tether lines instead.

David remembers that they did quite a few free flights, with their army retrieves.

333

'One was really fast, and I had promised my retrieve that I would fly them, but I was worried about the speed. As it was, I happened to see an eroded gully coming up, no more than a 150 wide and 40 foot deep, and managed to touch down in it, a stand up landing, to change passengers. I was lucky, someone had a 150yard drag on landing, they were wide open plains, no shelter! Anyway, I took off again, the only one to do an intermediate that day, and had a reasonable landing, not a long drag, at the end. That was Russia.

'In August I went down to the Bristol Fiesta, and I learnt never to believe all that people tell you. I was asked to fly a disabled person in the disabled basket, and they were going to supply me with a 120,000 cubic foot envelope, this changed to a 90,000, and it was all laid out on the launch field and I never checked, and it turned out to be a 84,000 cubic foot balloon with 300 hours flying on it.

'There was me in the basket, the chap in the wheelchair, and two television people on board, and only two cylinders to do a short flight. I took off, and she flew like a brick, really heavy. The minute I had cleared the houses I landed in the first field I came to. Unfortunately on the approach was a timber-yard. Now it is alright hitting twelve oak trees when they are standing up, but hitting twelve lying down, and bouncing off them tends to take the forward speed out.

'Anyhow, we started off with one disabled person, and ended up with three! A wheelchair loose in a basket isn't very comfortable! Because it was flying like a brick, I was coming in five feet lower than I wanted to and there was nothing I could do. So that was my Fiesta.

'However, later that month we went to Zimbabwe. We flew from outside the Sheraton Hotel at ten to seven in the evening, it was my first flight in Zimbabwe. Anyway, we ended up flying in the wrong direction, and they got on the radio and told me to land as soon as possible as we were heading for the President's Palace, and anyone who drives past it at that time of night gets shot, let alone if they fly over it!

'OK, I'll land on the golf course.' I said.

'No, don't do that, it is all locked up, we won't be able to get you out.'

So I used my favourite trick of using trees to slow me up, so that I could land on the road. It was a very good landing actually, we swung off the trees and plonked it on the road.

The retrieve were there waiting, and I said 'that wasn't a bad landing was it?'

'No,' they said, 'but you didn't half shock those three blokes when you knocked them out of the tree!'

'What do you mean?'

'Well, when you hit that tree, there were three black men in there asleep, and you knocked them out!'

What happened was that some people who walked to work, had too far to walk back to their villages at night, so they built platforms in the trees and slept up trees close to their work. If they slept anywhere else, they would have been picked up as vagrants. We did a couple more flights there, and a tether at a party at the golf club.

'Then in October, we went to Albuquerque in America, the biggest balloon meet in the world I think it is now. I did about eight flights in G-BHOT, and then one flight in an American balloon with Ray Blair, an atomic scientist that I had met in England when he came over to Aldermaston. The rest of the crew went back without me as they had run out of holiday, and I brought the balloon back by myself.

'It was this year, 1990, that Sutton Estates wanted us to give up ballooning from Marsh Benham. Now I felt honour-bound

to find somewhere else as a site, otherwise it would have messed up everybody's ballooning. Gerald Ward had some land near me, outside Hungerford and I knew him. He is one of the world's real gentlemen, a very nice man. Anyway, he said, *'If there is anywhere on my farm that is right, you're welcome to it.'*
He told the manager to take me around and show me the farm and we chose Folly Dog Leg, and we've used it ever since. Although I don't do a lot of ballooning now, I still feel responsible you know. Stupid I suppose, but I do.

'In about October, the Newbury Weekly News rang me up. There were some titles, some 'Lordships of the Manor' coming up for sale, and they rang up and asked if I was intending to buy the title of Lord of the Manor of East Shefford. I hadn't really thought about it until then.
I thought that I might as well, and so we went up to the sale which just happened to be on my birthday.

'We got a train up to the sale which was being held in the Fanmakers Hall, one of the Guildhalls in the City of London. We found it, went and had some lunch, and then went and looked at the details. I was talking to the auctioneer, and I asked him what he thought it would fetch. He said there was a reserve on it, and I said 'Well I am willing to pay 'X', and as it is my birthday today, I feel lucky.'

'When it came up, I seemed to be bidding against only one other, and I won't say what I paid for it, but I got it for a thousand pounds less than I was going to pay. Being the Lord of the Manor means nothing, it entitles you to nothing, it is just bullshit. I have a crest, and in my passport, it says that the holder of this is also known as the Lord of East Shefford. It's only in there for a bit of a laugh, it doesn't get you anywhere.

336

'But I have always had an affinity to Shefford. Our family has always tried to help the village in one way or another.

'I had this on my passport when I went to fly in Solberg, in New Jersey, the next year. Now the British Airways manager in the States had rung me to organise this because she had met me over here or something. Anyway, she said she would meet us as New York, so we flew in to JFK, and she wasn't there. What she had actually said was Newark, not New York, so she was waiting for us at the wrong airport! It all got sorted out though and we flew at an airshow at an airfield in Somerset County, actually saw an old B-17 coming in to land.

'Anyway, in May '92, we went to Auckland, New Zealand for a balloon meet in Hamilton. We arrived there after a 22 hour flight, and had trouble getting the balloon into new Zealand as it had to go through the fumigator first as it had dirt on the basket. So although we got there mid morning, by the time we had got it fumigated and cleared, it was five in the evening. The local balloonists had laid on a barbecue for us which was fun.

'During the evening, they said' *Right, we are leaving here at five in the morning, and we are going to fly across Auckland Harbour. We have been waiting for four months for the wind to be in the right direction, and it will be right tomorrow morning.'*
So the next morning, we went up to a piece of land just south of Auckland, and we took off at 8.00am and flew across Auckland, the bridge, the harbour, across a big ammunition dump, over the creek and over the military airbase where they wouldn't let us land. The British Airways balloon was being flown by John Emery and Chris Smith, and I was in a New Zealand balloon. The pilot asked me if I wanted to take over, and I said yes.

'Let's see you do a splash and dash.' He said.
Well the first time, the water was over our ankles, and the second time he said *'You've missed!'*
'I don't think so, there's water coming off the bottom of the basket.'

'That was an amazing flight. I'll tell you what, I was amazed by the amount of deer there are there, and also the fencing. They actually farm deer there for the antlers which they grind up and sell to the Japanese as an aphrodisiac. Another thing was the extinct volcanoes, lots of craters, fascinating.

'After the Harbour flight, we went down to Hamilton for the show, and despite the wind, got a couple of flights in. We also went down to the hot springs to have a look.

'Anyway, we got back from that trip on the Tuesday, five days before our Ruby Wedding Anniversary party to which we had invited 150 guests. On the way back we stopped over in Singapore, and I bought two big boxes of orchids for about £14 a box, so for the party in the marquee, we had two huge displays of orchids, fantastic, they would have cost over £100 if I had bought them here. They were beautiful.'

'In May 1992 we went back to Solberg, landing at the right airport this time doing the same airshow. By next year I had almost dropped out of ballooning, but in March, I got a flight across the Valley of the Kings in Egypt.

'We had gone on holiday there, and before we had left, I had rung Kevin Meehan and asked him what the chances were for a flight. Anyway, it was fantastic, our pilot was Don Connors, the American, and it really was a very nice flight.

Incredible views from the balloon. They had got it right, champagne and the lot when you landed, it was all laid out. I enjoyed that one.

'I next flew in August. We had a trip to Norway, and on one day when we didn't have much to do, we drove over into Sweden with the balloon because, as you know, Pete Bish likes to get different countries in his logbook. I blew up the balloon, and tethered it, and then Pete had a short flight, and we packed up and drove back into Norway.

'Back in Norway, we had to do a tether in a showground, a sort of fairground, and the space they gave us was minimal. It was very windy, and after we managed to get it up, the wind veered right round, and one large gust blew the balloon into the side of a horse-box which had a large nail sticking out where the tailgate was held shut. The nail caught the envelope, and tore a ten foot hole right over the equator! We had some spare fabric, and I went over to the craft tent to see if there was anyone there who could help sew it up. The police introduced us to someone who said she could mend it. So we loaded the balloon up, drove it down to her workshop where she stitched it up for us. She was a rather large lady, and when she sat on the chair, there was no visible sign of support!

'Anyway, she mended it, and we were able to continue with our tethers and I think we did another three in Norway before we went home.

'I flew from the Newbury Show in September, and I was doing the commentary, and took the radio mike with me as I flew my own balloon out of the showground, and I also took the Chairman's wife. We were just leaving the ground, and I said, 'Come on Di, tell Geoffrey what you think of it so far.'

I gave Di the mike, and she said, *'Geoffrey, I'm really enjoying this.'*

I grabbed the mike and added, 'And she is enjoying the ballooning too!'

Of course it went out over the whole showground on all the speakers! Sometimes you regret saying things, and that time was one of them. The trouble is I've always been a bit of a wag, life's too short to be serious, I say.

'The next trip was in December to Calcutta, in India. We flew from the Victoria Park, Calcutta, which is absolutely enormous. Everywhere you looked there were games of cricket being played, some were played with teams in their whites, some were just in ordinary clothes, I have never seen so many cricket matches, and hardly anybody took any notice of the balloon, their cricket was far more important to them! We also flew from the Tollygunge Club.

It was in Calcutta that I asked Ian Brereton to go and tie a line to a tree, and he came back with a snake skin.

'Look what I've found.'

'It's still wet,' someone said, *'The skin has only just been shed! You were lucky, it was a King Cobra!'*

'My next trip abroad was in May to the San Duran Hotel in Mauritius. We did a tether there and then went out to the gymkhana club and I did two or three tethers there, an hour, two hours, and a half hour tether there. Mauritius was great, I paid for Jo to come, with Ian Brereton, Dave Munson , Niall Duncan and myself. The hotel was superb.

'In July 1994, I went back to Israel, to the Eyaton Valley where the big tank battle took place. Dave Smith, who was with me, flew the British Ambassador.

340

'The Newbury Show came round again, and this time I flew with Dave Partridge in the 'Pete the Pylon' balloon. Bloody good pilot he is too, superb. I think he is Managing Director of Virgin Airship & Balloon Company now.

'Then in October we went to Moscow, another private balloon meet, not a British Airways one. The Russian pilots wanted us to fly with them, I don't know the registration number of the balloons, I don't think they had any. Anyway, they tied three balloons together with load tapes, and hung flags on the load tapes, but they were tied so tight that the baskets were pulled in a bit towards each other.
The three Russian pilots took off, and they did 'picking leaves from trees', intermediate landings, and then they handed over to us, there were only three Brits over there, but the only trouble was, I was the only one who had a licence, so I was 'Pilot-in-Command' for three balloons! Formation flying! Amazing.

'In February the next year I went out to the Philippines, it was lovely flying out there. But on that occasion, I was flying for KLM, not British Airways, we put their banner on our blue and white balloon. Then we stopped on for a day or two, because British Airways wanted us to fly from a golf club. Anyway, we took off, and we flew over this small wood, and in this wood were what looked like blue playing cards stacked on their ends, lots and lots of them, all about four foot high. When we got closer, there was a fighting cock, tied to each blue cover - they were shelters. Cock fighting is a big thing in the Philippines.

'In May, we, the Dante Group, flew out to St Petersburg, and when we got there, we were asked not to fly above 500 feet, a pilot's dream! So first of all, Mike Drye flew from St Katherine's Palace, at Pushkin, then I flew the balloon from infront of St Isaacs Cathedral in the square, and flew up over the cathedral right over the river.

'I did a tether in front of the Winter Palace the next night, and the next day we did another flight. Mike did the first bit and then I took over after an intermediate. That was a good trip.

'After that, I went out to the Philippines in February, and then to Bahrain again.

'I'm giving up really now. I have had some fantastic flights, and amazing trips, but I think that after 26 years, I have had enough.

'I have to look after my back, my blood pressure is borderline, I am going to enjoy other things now. Enjoy my family, my life. There are things I am going to do, places to go. I ballooned in all the best years, I farmed during the best years, and know I am going to enjoy myself, but who knows what is round the corner?'

Finale.

'We have been lucky, we have used the QE2 for a lot of our holidays, we really love it. In fact, our breakfast waiter on our last trip, was one we knew from before, and he said that there were thirty eight different nationalities working on the QE2 now!

'Oh Mr Liddiard,' he said., 'I saw your name on the list, I thought it was you. How are you and your lovely lady wife?'

'Rather nice to be remembered.

'We often go for the value cruises, not many people think of going from New York in December, and you meet a nicer sort of person, not the glitzy ones. A lot of the people who don't like flying use it, especially if they are relocating from America. We met one couple with a big American four wheel drive, and a big people carrier, packed to the gunwales, there was just room for them to sit in them. Both vehicles were stacked solid with all their belongings. They were coming to London for a couple of years, and it was cheaper for them to bring two vehicles, and travel on the QE2, than to go any other way.

'You meet a lot of interesting people, and have a chat. There are parts of the ship we haven't visited yet she is so big. You can do your own thing and never meet others if you don't want to.

'I think it is the Americans who say that, 'This ship is for the well bred, the over fed and the nearly dead!'

And there are a few people who are like that on her. There was one couple I remember, and they must have been well into their nineties, but they were enjoying themselves, and the crew really know how to look after people like that.

'The crew are really good. I mean, if you don't want to come

343

out of your cabin to eat, you don't have to, they will bring it to you. If you're hungry, well that's your fault, there is so much food there, and you don't have to pay extra for it.

'The only thing you have to pay for is alcoholic drinks, drinks from the bar. You always had to have a collar and tie for dinner, always look smart and of course wear a dinner jacket for the formal occasions, but it is nice to dress for dinner, a sort of old fashioned elegance which you don't get on other cruises judging by the television programmes.

'We go for the elegance, and the air of opulence of the whole ship, she is a grand old lady, the last of her kind. My daughter calls her the Trans-Atlantic ferry when she is teasing us!

'She used to do the Atlantic in five days, but it is six now, people get an extra day, it is more comfortable, and they don't use so much fuel. Do you know they use one gallon every fifty feet! There is a wonderful trivia sheet which tells you it can take 1900 passengers, there are 1000 crew, that there are 9 engines, how much smoked salmon is consumed across the Atlantic, how much champagne etc. I like to have a light lunch, so we go to the cafeteria, and I usually have smoked salmon, crab, smoked New Zealand mussels, a couple of slices of brown bread and butter, delicious. You can just make your own salad up.

'The ship has a definite American slant to it, she is based in New York as you know, and all the prices are in US Dollars. Our last trip was New York to Los Angeles through the Panama Canal. Do you know, it cost $170,000 to take a boat through the canal? It is an amazing canal, enormous it really is, the size of the lock-gates is quite incredible.

'When we boarded, it must have been about our twelfth trip,

344

we were invited to the Captain's quarters for a cocktail party. Anyway, as we were going into the Captain's quarters, the Cruise Director who was welcoming us in, said to me, *'The Captain wants to see you to talk to you about ballooning.'*

So after a bit, the Captain came over to me and said, *'Ah, Mr Liddiard, it's nice to meet you. I think you knew my first wife. Karen Hunt.'*

'Oh yes I do.' I said, surprised.

'Now Karen had worked for Mike Allen, of Allen & Harris the Estate Agents. At that time, this Captain was an officer on a ship, and he used to bring books back from all over the world for Mike to put into the British Balloon Museum & Library. Mike Allen, was one of the founders of the British Balloon Museum and Library (BBM&L). as I was. Mike worked hard getting Charity status for the museum, and also to enable the museum to be called the 'British' Balloon Museum & Library. They now have a permanent display at Newbury District Museum, and also within the Shuttleworth Collection at Old Warden.

'Anyway, the Captain told me that when they were in the fjords of Norway on the QE2, he and his wife flew off the decks of the ship in a balloon. Isn't it a small world?

He is Captain Warwick, and his father had been the first captain of the QE2, and the last captain of the Queen Mary or the Queen Elizabeth, I forget which one.

I had tried some time ago to get permission to fly off the QE2, but now Captain Warwick is there....well, you never know do you? I know that they took off from the lower deck all those years ago, but they have a swimming pool there now, you would have to take off from the sports deck.

'We have been on the QE2 so many times now that we have a Gold Card, which entitles you to an upgrade, and the first $200

345

you spend, free.

'There is a superb physiotherapist on board, and I really had been suffering with my back for about three weeks before the last trip which was tethering the balloon outside the Intercontinental at Muscat, but one session with her and it was wonderful. She was only a slip of a thing, but she knew what she was doing. She rang up the steward and told him to put a board in my bed, and that made such a difference.

'I've actually given talks on ballooning there, you know a small afternoon slot. I've done it about four times now. They actually rang me up and asked if I would do it.
After one talk, someone came up to me and said, *'You know my son don't you?'*
'Who is your son?' I replied.
'John Cox, the round the world yachtsman.'
'Oh of course I do, he lives in Hungerford.'
His Mother was going round the world on a different sort of ship. John had taken part in the British Steel Challenge, organised by Chay Blythe. Then another couple came up and said, *'Don't you know John and Sue Burnell?'*
'Of course I do.'
'I was articled with Sue when I did my training.' This woman said.
It is such a small world isn't it?

'The couple we met on the last trip but one, Frank and Carol Forbes, when we said we were going on the last trip, decided to come too, which was rather nice. We shared a table, and when we docked, the four of us used to go on the tours but pay for our own cabs, we would negotiate, and get a far better deal than the others. He was a property developer, civil engineering and a self made man, so he didn't want to pay without negotiating, like me.

346

When we first met, and we said where we came from, he said *'Oh, that's near Welford, I built the Atom bomb bunkers up there, up at the bomb dump.'*

'When we stopped at Acapulco, we went to a hotel, a better one than the coaches went to, and it was a super place, built in the Inca style, fabulous hotel. Anyway, we were standing there photographing, and suddenly, *'Hello Frank, fancy seeing you here!'* and it was the captain of his Golf Club. As I said before, it really is a small world.

'Is it luck or fate? I don't know. I know I have been very lucky. Life is a terminal illness, when you're born, you've got to die, the best thing is, you don't know when or how , but fate plays a lot into it.

'I knew Donald Campbell, who used to make gyroplanes and gyrogliders at Membury, and Geoff Whatley who used to fly them.

'They went to Spain on a promotion job, and when they came to come home, just before they got on the plane, Campbell's wife said, *'I'm not getting on this plane, it's going to fly into a mountain. I can't get on. I've got a premonition it's going to fly into a mountain.'*
Whatley said, *'I don't care, I've GOT to get home, don't be stupid, I'm going home.'*
So he got on the plane and came home. Campbell and his wife stayed behind and got the next plane, the next day. Their plane, a Caravelle, flew into hills at Fernhurst, near Haslemere, Surrey, and they were both killed.

'When your number is up, it is up, and there is nothing you can do about it.'

Maybe Jo and David make more moments count than most. They have both experienced near fatal accidents, and life is very precious to both of them.

Every encounter with their children and Grandchildren is special, one more than might have been.

As David has said throughout 'I have been very lucky.'

Acknowledgements.

There are many people who have helped with anecdotes, proof reading and excellent photographs.

Dave Baker, anecdotes
Pete Bish, for the photographs, and for proof reading.
British Airways
Sue Burnell, legal advice
Joan Crawford, anecdotes
Cunard Lines, the QE2 photographers.
Richard d'Alton, for the cover design.
The Dante Group, for all their help
Tilly Fishlock, anecdotes
Mike Hogan, reading
Celia Kunert, anecdotes
Roger Kunert, anecdotes
Peter Langford, anecdotes
Fiona Liddiard, proof reading
James Parkin, proof reading
David Rabbitts, anecdotes
Reading Evening Post, photograph.
Llewellyn Robins, photograph
Kate Robinson, supplying family photographs.
Stella Sampson,
CS Snow(Uncle James) photographs.

Special thanks go to David and Jo Liddiard for all their Sundays, and their faith in me.

My main thanks are to my husband Richard, for his love and support.
Jennifer d'Alton.
July 1998.